# Shamanism, Racism, and
# Hip-Hop Culture

Black Religion / Womanist Thought / Social Justice
Series Editors Dwight N. Hopkins and Linda E. Thomas
Published by Palgrave Macmillan

# Shamanism, Racism, and Hip-Hop Culture

## Essays on White Supremacy and Black Subversion

*James W. Perkinson*

SHAMANISM, RACISM, AND HIP-HOP CULTURE
© James W. Perkinson, 2005.

First published in 2005 by
PALGRAVE MACMILLAN™
175 Fifth Avenue, New York, N.Y. 10010 and
Houndmills, Basingstoke, Hampshire, England RG21 6XS
Companies and representatives throughout the world.

PALGRAVE MACMILLAN is the global academic imprint of the Palgrave Macmillan division of St. Martin's Press, LLC and of Palgrave Macmillan Ltd. Macmillan® is a registered trademark in the United States, United Kingdom and other countries. Palgrave is a registered trademark in the European Union and other countries.

ISBN 1–4039–6786–5

A catalogue record for this book is available from the British Library.

Library of Congress Cataloging-in-Publication Data is available from the Library of Congress.

Design by Newgen Imaging Systems (P) Ltd., Chennai, India.

First edition: June 2005

10  9  8  7  6  5  4  3  2  1

Printed in the United States of America.

*Dedicated to the genius and incorrigibility of those who have resisted*

# Contents

# Series Editors' Preface

Following up on his groundbreaking first book, *White Theology: Outing Supremacy in Modernity*, Jim Perkinson continues to gift us with the novel (and usually hidden) self-examination of a white middle class, middle aged, American male. Perkinson begins with the uniqueness of his childhood socialization between African American constrained space and white American voluntary boundaries, including the borders and taboos of interracial dating. The vignette exposure of himself serves as metaphor for the larger narrative argument that anchors the entire book. The result is a series of cogent theoretical chapters on Witchcraft and Shamanism, markers of white and black beings, respectively in the United States. Moreover, Perkinson is an accomplished poet—as well as a community organizer and professor who has lived in inner city Detroit for a couple of decades. Consequently, the rhythm and rhyme of his writing show us how words on paper can actually talk to the reader and bring meaning to the ear as words in song mode. The theoretical academic approach couples with the popular poetic form because Witchcraft and Shamanism morph into disparate configurations. Here, Perkinson performs the act of conjuror. How? By betraying the silence over white male racial entitlement and siding with the black community's syncretistic creativity of survival and double living. Furthermore, Perkinson writes this book to act out conjuration on himself. In fact, as he asserts directly, part of the journey of producing this book is to turn the scalpel of knowledge discovery on himself—what he calls "self-exorcism."

For conjuror (magician?) Perkinson, the attendant question is: what are the cultural and spiritual underpinnings of modern white supremacy and black political (and spiritual) counter-resistance? Witchcraft is white supremacy in the United States, or, more exactly, it is what the structure, culture, and psyche of white America carry out in effect on black people in the same country. American identity is constituted by white entitlement and black disenfranchisement. At root, to be an American is to purchase ownership in the historical memory and current acceptance of white Christianity. For, Perkinson persuasively substantiates, white Christianity birthed and continues to suckle the Witch of white supremacy. Without Christianity, no white skin privileges. One could rapidly add, "no male perks," too. Racialized witchcraft defiles the black body by casting a curse or spell on ebony physiognomy. Othering people of African descent within U.S. borders, simultaneously, as if like magic, creates the identity of white people. Both groupings are part of a symbiotic ontology baked into a witches' brew. Ultimately, witchcraft harms black and white folk.

But blacks, in the conceptualization of Perkinson, aren't waiting for that "ultimately." They have crafted their own spiritual–psychic–material way of being in the world. African Americans transformed themselves into the practice of Shamanism—a reading back from the position of the bottom, a comprehensive and multilevel cavalry of resistance. The black Shamans offer the best outlet for Witchcraft. Shamanism calls Christianity back to its primordial or initial radicality of the founders of the religion. This is so because enslaved Africans/African Americans did and still do re-appropriate modalities of negative (white) Christian witchcraft and make these forms into a magical likeness of what Christianity was meant to be two thousand years ago. To indicate these concurrent activities of curse and counter-resistance, Perkinson presents two chapters on Hip-Hop.

Jim Perkinson's book represents one definite dimension of the black religion/womanist thought/social justice series—pioneering conceptual work and boundary pushing effort. The series will publish both authored and edited manuscripts that have depth, breadth, and theoretical edge, and will address both academic and nonspecialist audiences. It will produce works engaging any dimension of black religion or womanist thought as they pertain to social justice. Womanist thought is a new approach in the study of African American women's perspectives. The series will include a variety of African American religious expressions. By this we mean traditions such as Protestant and Catholic Christianity, Islam, Judaism, Humanism, African diasporic practices, religion and gender, religion and black gays/lesbians, ecological justice issues, African American religiosity and its relation to African religions, new black religious movements (e.g., Daddy Grace, Father Divine, or the Nation of Islam), or religious dimensions in African American "secular" experiences (such as the spiritual aspects of aesthetic efforts like the Harlem Renaissance and literary giants such as James Baldwin, or the religious fervor of the Black Consciousness movement, or the religion of compassion in the black women's club movement).

Dwight N. Hopkins, University of Chicago Divinity School
Linda E. Thomas, Lutheran School of Theology at Chicago

# Acknowledgments

This work represents the fruit of many years of quiet incubation and not so quiet cogitation and wrestling. In many ways it is merely a late and continuous effort to give expression to a depth first opened up in me at age four in my backyard before a huge sycamore tree as afternoon shadows lengthened and my young body first felt the premonition of loss. It was a sweet sadness that touched indefinably that day and has haunted ever since. Later adult years in the inner city of Detroit, when hot sun bubbled tar seams in the concrete and ribs cooking on steel drum stoves announced Labor Day respite from work, a different kind of sweetness, attended by a different kind of sadness, would crosscut my earlier experience. In either case, something of the ineffability of beauty, appearing side by side with its demise, has marked my memory and provoked an impossible quest to express ever since. Whatever of ancestry and unrequited struggle for justice, whatever muted voices of haints and saints and devils such irresolvable longing partakes, I owe it—them—my life and my creativity.

More prosaically, I wish to thank my parents, my many companions over the years of laboring in urban enclaves of poverty and university ghettos of literacy, my teachers on the street and in the classroom alike, my students who have challenged me to dig deeper, confess more profoundly, laugh more robustly, think more complexly. And especially, my wife Lily—both flower and storm—who has seen the abyss and known its song; my gratitude!

# Introduction

The character of this book is that of a collection of theoretical essays offering a creative rereading of the cultural and spiritual underpinnings of both modern white supremacy and black political resistance in terms of the construct of "shamanism." Its primary interest is that of effecting a kind of methodological inversion—a probe of "overworld" strategies of domination and of "underworld" tactics of survival—in terms of the very categories ("witchcraft," "sorcery," "shamanism") historically projected by European Colonizers to license their takeover of the world in the first place. As such, it ranges wide in assembling ideas and ideology and waxes wily in juxtaposing relationships and intimacies between things usually thought discrete. But the book's motive force is finally that of self-exorcism rather than merely objective documentation—a passionate attempt on the part of a white male activist/academic to rethink his own position (as indeed the entire racial presupposition of modernity) from beyond the pale of "normal" consideration. It begins, thus, with a confession of the importance of "location." In my case, this confession is really about the necessary efficacy of a *dis*-location—physically and culturally—as the very presupposition of my learning to think differently.

## Preliminary Epiphany

My first exposure to Detroit resulted in visceral repulsion. The year was 1973, I was twenty-two years old, and the occasion was a visit to a small activist Christian community on the near eastside that was living communally. The drive up Interstate-75 through the rust-belt fantasy-scape of Ford Motor Co.'s River Rouge plant, smokestacks ghosting the horizon with gray smog, burn-off pipes with orange top-knots of flame punctuating the skyline like a postmodern sign of Dante's Hell, did not exactly invite. Neither did the drive on Lafayette from downtown out through the remains of Black Bottom, where clapboard shards of houses and weed lots gestured forlornly in the early evening air of September. But, over the next fifteen years of settling into this Motown menagerie of decay as my place of living and working, I would find my suburban Cincinnati sensibility slowly purged and my vision intensified precisely through the daily encounter with such scenarios and with the creative conjure-work engaged in by the people forced to make industrial detritus and ghetto despair "home." More particularly over those years, I experienced a kind of "exorcism." I found the "whiteness" of my being sharply piqued, clearly exposed, gradually relativized, and painstakingly reconfigured in ongoing encounter with black capacity to transform hard concrete into beautiful rhythm in spite of real losses.

My eastside years coincided with the incubation of hip-hop and the birth of techno. In the early 1980s, the young men I was regularly meeting—and occasionally beating—on the basketball court, would blow, puff, and rhyme on break-time and before and after our hoop dream encounters. At the time, I scarcely recognized what was brewing on their lips—a Bronx scheme of sound, taking over a country and a world. Only after graduate school in Chicago and return to the same eastside Detroit neighborhood in 1996 would hip-hop begin to command my late attention as a significant "sign of the times" and an emerging international movement.

Likewise, Derrick May and company[1] would make it onto my cultural radar only in the late 1990s after I began to read my poetry in various spoken word venues around the city, and finally had a night where, after a particularly high-velocity offering, I was approached by a British-accented deal-maker who introduced himself as May's agent—and then introduced me to May himself, standing a few feet away, eager to thank me for the "word orgy." The encounter was ephemeral but indicative. At the time, electronica's capacity to "entrance" graffiti-tagged brick and abandoned factory site in sonic bombast and (rave-dance) "house" beat was just beginning to provoke appreciation in my otherwise jazz-attracted head.

Jazz itself was also a late affection, born of the drive I found within to give words free-play in a beat-poet mode after the long labors of dissertation discipline. I began reading my verse out loud for the first time in 1996, as the only means I had available to let the screams and keens of my inner city neighborhood career through my flesh as well as my consciousness. After fifteen years of living in the hot house of ghetto invention, and a further seven years of studying the phenomenon of Afro-diasporic innovation it was no longer enough merely to observe and love. My own body begged exercise in its need for exorcism. White supremacy's long crafting of European genes and American dreams into schemes of economic rapacity and political mendacity required active participation as well as new awareness. Growing up white in America had meant deep interpolation into the reigning ethnocentrism—despite all good intentions to the contrary of my parents and of a liberal education and serious Christian conversion as a young adult. Confrontation with the way supremacy "lived and moved and had its being" inside my own skin required years of immersion in an "other" way of being (in this case, the black ghetto), recurrent tears of regret and frustration, and a virtual career-choice to face rather than flee fears that were as old as modernity itself. It also meant willingness to experiment with a different way of "being me." The surprise of finding words walking across my tongue like a Mingus baseline, daring me to try to express them, or of feeling syncopations of inner sentiment—helpless before mere pen and paper—seeking a Coltrane-like velocity of articulation, awakened me to the genius of jazz and the wonder of beat. But the hour was old. Jazz too—though somehow a bone-truth for me—is a late love and dabble-ment.

Yet, all of this midlife eruption of musicality and poetics, borne of years of urban acclimation and later years of theoretical exploration, has become a motive-force of self-investigation. In this collection of essays, it serves as the underground source of the writing, the hot spring out of which my book-work bubbles. But it also leverages the leitmotif. That a white body could in some sense "channel" black creativity, could explore a current that is finally African-born in both style and intensity, signals the question the work explores.

The essays gathered here trace a slow search through a growing theoretical awareness. As I have gradually become conscious and articulate about my own formation as a white person, much of my self-reflection has emerged from a kind of mirror-discipline—a self-imposed requirement that I continually entertain new insight about old behavior as it is spoken and gestured back at me through various racialized others. This is a stance toward interracial and interethnic encounter that I have elsewhere styled as a process of "being signified upon."[2] The tone and timbre of encountered response—a certain supplement of humor, or anger, or silence, or unexpected warmth—is most telling.

In such moments, the possibility of gaining perspective on oneself is peak. Hidden transcripts may "wink out" from their otherwise carefully guarded subterfuge, subterranean meanings and evaluations break the surface of significance and offer brief glimpses of a counter-valence of events. This is murky terrain, opaque significance, body language often proliferating and complicating communication under the surface of the words. Its decipherment requires sustained attention and ruthless self-confrontation. There is no one meaning that can be assigned to such "off-timed"[3] expressions: the other person, could, after all, just be having a bad day (or a good one) that has nothing to do with oneself. But here, too, the "off-timing of otherness" lurks, the polyphony of suppressed voices and vitalities that dominant cultures and identities never allow full expression. Here, the eye of resistance suddenly, briefly, looks back. Foucault's writing has hipped an entire generation of white academics to a "micro-logics of power"—that is more commonly grasped only by those whose very survival depends upon such subtle resistances. The opportunity actually to entertain and learn from such resurgent signs and potencies is ever present but rarely embraced by those with power.

In this collection of essays, such a process of reflection is elaborated as methodology. The idea that identity must be learned lifelong and ever invented afresh in the crucible of contact is the underlying theme. The assertion that white identity is now as far-reaching in effect as the globe is wide, as longstanding as modernity, and as insufferable as cancer for most nonwhite peoples is the subtext. The initial inversion of analyses— the "thought experiment" that European race discourse is modernity's witchcraft practice—sets the bar for the other explorations of the book. Shamanism functions as a kind of overarching "trope" for questioning and comprehending black forms of resistance to the ever-renewed assaults of white supremacy that have worked hand in glove with capitalist grandiosity in taking over a planet. The playful and simultaneously serious construal of modern struggle as shamanic battle—white witchcraft contested by black root-craft (*voudou*, hoodoo, black church, spirituals, blues, jazz, hip-hop, civil rights activism, Nation of Islam separatism, etc.)—organizes the structure of the book. This introduction first sets out the history of the personal seduction such a (black) aesthetics has exercised on my own evolution as a white male academic and then outlines the rationale for the inclusion of the disparate considerations that make up the storyline of the work.

## Personal Odyssey

I first fell under the spell of black finesse in the domain of sport, while learning about marginalization in the experience of being (briefly) marginalized. A sudden love of basketball at age eight meant navigating the parochial school cadre of Catholic kids in my neighborhood and learning the game on their ground. The tutelage was hard: a public school youngster not yet fluid in dribble or fluent in court argot, I was made to undergo four years of initiation into the mechanics of court movement while simultaneously made the butt of both jokes and aggression. For a year, I could throw the ball in from out of bounds, but was punched if I shot. Muddy balls (the court was gravel) and muddy shoes were often "cleaned off" on my pants legs while I was held down by the older, bigger set. If we retired to the football field for a different kind of entertainment, I was only allowed to center the ball until that one moment per game when I was sent out for a pass and then gang-tackled—by both sides—and verbally pummeled with put-down while held in a headlock and roughed up. Summertime baseball was less physically abusive, but equally arduous emotionally. I remember especially being targeted for comment when my breasts for a time outstripped my shoulders in their rate of development. But my passion for all three games outstripped even the abuse.

Basketball, in particular, got into my blood. After three years, my skills commanded grudging respect; my psyche, however, huddled alone in despair and rage. While now allowed to contribute on the court, after any given game, parochial school friendship meant the crowd retired to someone's house for pop and talk while I was left out in the cold (often literally). The rage boiled over one day at age twelve. A six-foot sixteen year old went for a fake and I launched an accurate jumper over his flat-footed defense; as I came down, he sucker-punched me in the stomach. I crumpled into the gravel and got up volcanic. I had to jump just to swing at his chest. He flicked me back down into the gravel like some noisome fly. Two more attempts at hitting back sent me home bleeding from my hands scraping the gravel and crying in sheer frustration. My feeble attempts at defending myself did have the effect of elevating the respect level following that day. But I never cracked the group socially.

High-school hoops, however, offered a lot more inclusion. I attended a college prep school located in the inner city that drew its students from all over the metropolitan Cincinnati area. There I was part of a three-sided mix of backgrounds: the enrollment was a third WASP, a third Jewish, and a third African American. School basketball teams were usually a roughly similar mix. Socially, I found the going tough. Acne and awkwardness combined into a fearsome shyness that I did not begin to overcome until my twenties. But on the court, I found a niche that I scarcely knew how to name until much later.

I began to imitate moves and to work on skills that I observed all around me. I did not know enough even to recognize them as quintessentially "black" in style or urban in origin (even if rapidly taken up by whites such as myself). But I gained respect and won acclaim from dark voices commenting on moves as well as points. That I could split the lane against much larger opponents while shifting hands in midair was as important to how I was known on the court as the final stats on the scoreboard. I was not great—only a reserve team "star"—but within that second-rate domain, had a name and a recognized game. Without knowing what I was doing, I had internalized a certain kind of art in the process of pursuing sport. It was my first taste of the positive difference that race could make.

The negative difference I had learned earlier and harder. I had been barely ten when I had made the mistake of bringing a black friend to the neighborhood court for a game of horse and then afterward, been beaten up by the white kids who controlled the turf. That skin color as well as school companionship was bounded by invisible code I only discovered in the process of (inadvertently) breaking it. It was a mistake I made only once—in the neighborhood. But my very presence on the streets around the high school I attended—simply in trying to catch a bus home—also violated a certain code and brought down a kind of retribution. One late afternoon boarding the bus, I was popped in the jaw by an older black kid running by, without any provocation. The kid was not part of the student body of Walnut Hills High School, but I was on his street and in his business simply by being there. His gratuitous "hit" was both "an expression of and a protest against" (to borrow wantonly from Marx) a parsing of space by race in this country whose real meaning I would not even begin to grasp until almost twenty years later. At the time, it simply rearranged my high-school geography as "dangerous" in some way I could not fathom but only fear.

Later on (between my sophomore and junior years, in the summer of 1967), the lesson would be reinforced when I found myself naively visiting with a black classmate who had been a close friend since eighth grade on the playground of my former grade school (which had become all-black over the years) where she was a counselor. While standing near a swing-set talking, we suddenly found ourselves surrounded by seven or eight young black males, pointedly interrogating my presence there and closing in with their bodies. Sharon instantly started crying, grabbed my hand, and pulled me through the circle before it could close entirely, but not before I was socked in the head. Fortunate that nothing else happened, I was also fortunate that adults later on persuaded the leader of that little group to come and talk with me in Sharon's presence. I can not remember his precise words, but their import remains clairvoyant even to this day: I was a pretty boy, a blond trespasser not only on the physical terrain of their playground, but also on the sexual terrain of their relationships with women. Sharon and I would later date briefly, but ultimately settle for remaining (merely) friends. Gaining some modicum of understanding of the violent history and psychic complexity of romance entertained across the line of race in America would likewise require many more years of experience and sustained inquiry. This hard-won understanding of the fraught erotics of racial contact, coupled with recognition of the violent interlinkage of white racial privilege and black (and brown and red and yellow) struggle in this society, forms the baseline for the investigations pursued in what follows.

But it is also the case that these early positive and negative experiences of black–white encounter set up a spiritual itinerary for me that I continue to pursue to this day. After an undergraduate degree in Business Management from the University of Cincinnati, my newfound Christian commitments took me to Detroit to be part of a mixed race group of charismatics, translating the spirit-energies of a Pentecostal possession-experience into intensive experiments in communal living and urban organizing. The community involved married and single together, struggling on a poverty-level budget, black and white and Latino trying to reinvent family on a broader-than-nuclear basis. The organizing embraced administration of a school and daycare center and, after 1978, creation of a not-for-profit housing development corporation to buy out slumlords and work with neighborhood tenants to become owner-managers of their aging multiunit structures. My fifteen-plus years as a lay leader of the initiative, while working full time in healthcare labor relations, offered "education" unlike that found in the academy. By the time I got to graduate work—first at a nearby seminary followed by seven years at the University of Chicago—my values and passion had been profoundly shaped and deeply inculcated.

Chicago provided the forum for learning theory that would give bite and backup to the passion already burning in the bone. At the top of the agenda was giving articulation to the meaning of whiteness as both public political task and private personal exorcism. Outing supremacy in institution and psyche alike, and exploring remedy and alternative identity, has remained the vocational core of my teaching and living. The years have witnessed a morphing from Christian evangelical arrogance to interfaith practice with Hindu and Buddhist friends and ongoing study of Afro-diaspora traditions of countering domination with syncopation. Shamanism has slowly emerged on my academic horizon as a trope complimentary to prophecy: the latter rooted in Western traditions seeking to uproot evil by public challenge, the former ferreting out older styles of living in concert with energies human and other in an ecology of being that values shared rhythm above individual aggrandizement. In the work below, it is this older instinct to shape-shift and body-bend, to seek undoing of malaise by redoing of ways of moving and identifying, that commands my fascination.

Returning to near eastside Detroit in 1996 also turned me toward a new urban phenomenon previously unexplored in my activist days. Poetry quickly became as integral to surviving as breathing, and performance second only (by the slimmest of preferences) to the moment of the poem's conceiving. Here, in these two intertwined operations—giving birth to verse and then giving dramatic embodiment to what had been birthed—I confronted and learned to love an inner vortex of pain and pleasure that defied simple articulation. More specifically, my own history of struggle going back to my boyhood days found a certain easing in ecstatic utterance. The play was not innocent, but a borrowing that bordered on plunder—white man one more time turning to black soulcraft for healing. The turn has a long history in modern times and is itself indicative of the themes that exercise the writing below. My own excuse is that of stark choice: either a retreat back into the anomie and anemia of white middle-class ways of being and the supposed safety of suburban space or an acceptance of the need—as well as of the indebtedness—of being taught by those who know from long experience how to translate urban trauma into mini-triumphs of overcoming. The imposition I acknowledge here finds it only possible (and then only partial) redress in a commitment to honor continuously and publicly my tutors in living and to struggle lifelong for the overturning of the order of supremacy that attends white skin privilege and organizes so much of global concourse today.

## Theoretical Antiphony

The essays gathered in this volume represent my on-going struggle to understand and expurgate the social formation that I am part of in its most inchoate depths. The soundings of that "white" murk and miasma are largely experiments of "recusing"—modes of using theory to construct angles of vision and augurs of consequence that confess both "interest" and "conflict." They take their tact from the tactics of those who have been made "black" in modern social meanings and meanderings. The result is not a disciplined exploration of history or an exhaustive analysis of aesthetics, but something more like a theoretical "jam session," a juxtaposition of ideas and "sonic surmises" that seek to develop a poetics of perspectival "ahas," of surprising correlations from inverted gazes and tricky tongues. The goal is display of the "eye ball of objectivity" as it is comprehended and eluded by those subject to its constraints.

My immediate subject is the 500-year history of white Christian hegemony, which has so profoundly shaped American society, and of the arts of resistance brought to bear against such on the part of its most radically rejected "other." The basic theme is that American identity and history are profoundly informed by an ongoing interweaving of white entitlement and black disenfranchisement, together articulating the basic framework within which other ethnic groups negotiate their cultural differences and jockey for position in the social hierarchy of the country. The basic political conviction is that, historically, white supremacy is the child of Christian supremacy, and that contemporary American notions of its own global supremacy (that have emerged especially since World War II) are the offspring of both. The core argument is that European (and subsequent American) race discourse can be ironically understood as modernity's "witchcraft practice"—in fact, if not in name, leveraging and licensing an ongoing project of plunder that is effectively consuming (or in witchcraft terms, "eating") the substance of the rest of the globe. The essays contained herein therefore constitute a series of thought experiments, teasing out the insights and challenges such an overall understanding sets in motion.

The governing orientation is that of a shamanistic rereading of Euro-American Christianity and Western culture that seeks to probe and conjure the subterranean depths of the history they encode. The shamanic metaphor re-positions such a Christianity on the same ledger as indigenous religious practices, asking about meaning not in the modality of theological hyperbole or scientific category but practical effect. It calls to the foreground that which is hidden as the subject of a hard-fought labor of decipherment and exposure. Unlike the modality of ideology critique that could be cited as its modernist cousin, it refuses to reify indigenous practice in a conceptuality of difference (i.e., "they" are superstitious and "we" know better).[4] Rather, it reads back at domination from the position of the subordinate, using the very terms created by the former to construct subordination in the first place.

The purpose of such a reading is to unmask hidden presuppositions of superiority (much like a reagent in chemistry that causes particular elements to fall back out of solution), to probe the degree to which European Christianity, in its role as the ground and progenitor of Western secularity, has become so wedded to modern white supremacy that it has effectively lost the ability even to remember its beginnings as a messianic movement of liberated slaves and struggling peasants. Within this compass, my argument is that there is no overcoming of incipient or explicit forms of white supremacy until and unless their predecessor form of Christian supremacy is "outed" and called back into genuine dialogical give and take with other religions and value systems, absent the long-standing spiritual imperialism that has ghosted and co-opted Christian practice since at least Constantine. Attempting to reimagine Christianity itself from within the orientation and cosmology of an indigenous practice like shamanism (rather than the usual missiological operation that tries to do the inverse), is one way of bringing out the radicality of the demand for mutual hermeneusis, for reciprocal translation and exchange, that today's situation of violent global struggle urgently demands.

An initial chapter (chapter 1) sketches out the continuing presence of "whiteness" as an organizing trope of identity that is simultaneously vacuous in biological and anthropological fact but virulent in historical and practical effect, and articulates a call to white identified people to raise political issue with such an easy ascription and "buy off" of dissent or creative effort. The essay offered stirs the waters and observes the ripples. Under the surface of American invocations of generic sameness and formal equality ("I don't see race!"), white presumption continues to work its magic of privilege and pride for the fair-skinned and to hide its consequence of pain and *pathos* for those proscribed as "dark." The aim is orientation to the present before beginning some of the archaeological and genealogical work that subsequent chapters tackle.

Chapter 2 establishes the paradigm for the book. In this manner of reading history, early modern European evaluations of indigenous religious practices (around the globe) as "superstitious sorcery" find their quintessence in the Enlightenment characterization of Africa as the very "continent of sorcery," the "heart of darkness," the open maw of the black witch *writ large* in tropical modality. Blackness is traced as the emerging emblem of such a projection, leveraging theological payoff back inside European self-understanding. The kickback is that European subjectivity is thereby underscored as *the* (enlightened) form of selfhood par excellence, transcending primitive magic in the direction of scientific self-identification and taxonomic delineation of the "world out there" in a great hierarchical chain of being. But the characterization can be read the other way around as well. To the degree that witchcraft practice, on the ground in indigenous cultures, is grasped as the mobilization of a curse to destroy the flesh and plunder the substance of other human beings, European-based notions of white supremacy can themselves be re-imagined as the most militant mode of witch-practice ever unleashed on the planet, articulating color as a code of curse on dark skin, enslaving the African body and pillaging its land and labor.

Early modern Europe, in this frame, emerges as a theological projection of anti-witchery that itself becomes witchery on a grand scale. European forms of colonization and their neoliberal American successors beg analysis as the most ruthless realization of sorcery in history, a clandestine and complex "whitening" of the practices of plunder that ends up effectively hiding those practices most of all from the practitioners themselves. The witch can no longer recognize itself in the mirror of witchery. On the other hand, blackness, in this reading, can be traced as a category of imposed curse that has been regularly reappropriated by the communities it has colonized and made a source of political critique, cultural pride, and spiritual innovation. Such a reappropriation is construed, in chapter 3, as functionally a modality of counter-shamanism, working healing out of the very toxin broadcast to license the plundering (of "darkened" peoples) in the first place. Here, the historical means of shamanic practice (diagnosis of dis-ease, spirit-travel to other times and places to recover lost energies and vitalities, and mastery of oppressive forces/spirits) are correlated with African American religious sensibility and cultural creativity (black preaching, antiphonal singing, political organizing) to argue that visionary clarity and rhythmic therapy have been singularly unique gifts that the black community embodies in the midst of modern travesty.

Chapter 4 specifies the collective shamanism examined in chapter 3 as quintessentially a capacity to innovate in a temporal mode. Time and timing emerge, in Afro-diaspora rituals of re-creation and resistance, as surreptitious repositories of liberty and license—a fecund infinity of possibility, hidden precisely in capitalism's uniformities of clock and calendar, harboring all manner of outlaw motions and ribald auditions—that allow a community under constraint to create its own definition and rites of recognition. Work with syncopated time signatures—in slave spirituals and black preaching, in antiphonal shouts and gospel trance, in jazz improvisation and hip-hop rhythm, in sartorial play with the body and gestural takeover of street corners—articulates a partial antidote to annihilation and mediates an alternative vision of human being desired even by the dominant culture.

In the line-up of this genealogy of temporal prodigality, hip-hop culture is examined, in chapters 5 and 6, as merely the latest of cultural–spiritual forms of "doing judo" on aggression from without. The strategies of such inversions of oppression are markedly homeo-pathic and shamanistic, countering demonization by inviting the demon "inside" the body, there to be wrestled ritually and made (or not) to yield an antidote. (Richard Wright's *Native Son*, the Black Power Movement's public revalorization of blackness in the 1960s, and [the rap group] Public Enemy's posturing of itself *as* public enemy are variations on this theme.) The effects of such practices—both within and beyond the oppressed community—are paradigmatic, a "return of the repressed" back into the psyche and society of oppression (indeed, today, back into the suburb) in the form of a Dread and a Delirium that is finally religious in import. The work required—no matter the naïveté of the lyrics[5] or the cynicism of the economics—is mythic. And the stakes of refusal are catastrophic, a continued (unconscious and habitual) mis-identification of the Western tradition with superiority and success . . . and a continued denial of the violence that has been regularly brought to bear to insure as much over the entire course of modernity.

Within such a framework, hip-hop polyphony will be read, in chapter 5, as the latest probe in a long history of "sonic interroga-tions" of American society, an "insurrection of subjugated sexualities," in the words of Jon Michael Spencer, that unmasks white Christianity as largely a failed middle-class prophylactic against its own violent underpinnings. White skin is read as a structure of denial of the mortality that American society so harshly seeks to eliminate from its everyday awareness by means of gated community antiseptics and ghetto "quarantines." Hip-hop percussion is analyzed as a resurgent appearance of the fact of death back inside the gate—a shamanistic grenade of sound that continues to encode something of the repressed history of the country even when its consumers have little clue about that repression. Chapter 6 situates hip-hop in an even longer line of consideration, going back to cave drawings of the Paleolithic era in

Europe and South Africa, where the "drive to shamanize" human experience (the search for alternative consciousness), led to vision work etched on rock walls, inducing trance, initiating novice shamans into the recognition that the entire cosmos reverberates with energy, multiplicity, and perhaps even "mentality" of a sort—an intuition that the new physics is giving curious substance to in its explorations of quantum mechanics and string theory.[6] Here, hip-hop style and rhyme work appear as another riff on the theme of making hard circumstance yield astonishing remonstrance: in this case, ghetto concrete is tagged with visual entreaty, dark skin made to dance with virtual sublimity, staccato words peppered with ribald desires. Racial constraint is relativized in rhythmic cacophony.

The final section rounds out the serendipity of associations. The chapter on liturgy (chapter 7) pulls the investigation pursued in this writing into relationship with advertising and economics to argue that late capitalism has functioned as a great huge rite of passage without determinable deliverance—a journey into an imagined infinity of accumulation that volatilizes its own meaning. Indigenous rites of passage are solicited as a historical counterpoint, testifying to a different kind of social liturgy in a very different political order that effectively de-programmed the "child-body" of initiates and reconstructed its social inscription as "adult" through ritual experiences of multiplicity. The result arguably was a kind of "sensate wisdom"—a "somatic certainty" that more than one world exists and thus that any given world of habitation and habituation is itself relative and arbitrary. Indigenous plurality in this sense commands attention for its recognition of the importance of rhythm in the education of human "being." Liturgy is constitutive of humanity; market liturgy (in the modality of rendering everything a commodity), the great shaper of modern identity. Work to extricate consciousness and politics from this overarching "sacramentality" of the market requires savvy counter-liturgy, labor within the labyrinth of ritual repetition aimed at breaking open the (commercial and racial) stereotypes and breaking down the passivity of mere consumption as a lifestyle. Hip-hop emerges here as new liturgical possibility.

Chapter 8 revisits the question of contemporary constructions of whiteness that began the book by means of a tenacious probe of the way urban space is effectively made the container and arbiter of race (even as the commercial has become the great container and arbiter of "class" as chapter 7 intimated). White male middle-class embodiment is profiled as the dominant form of "possession" in American culture, in an evocation that riffs on the beating of Rodney King as the archetypal moment of reproducing racialized perception. The task here is one of correlating the different technologies of political control (police surveillance in the city and security monitoring in the gated community) with the "production" of racialized bodies habituated to their assigned spaces of living and acting. White male "posture," in this view, reigns supreme as the normative mode of being that silently exercises its power to possess both bodies and spaces through a whole chain of institutional disciplines and discourses that effectively police geography as well as mentality. Once again the argument is that contending with such—conscientizing white people and organizing effective resistance—involves willingness to experiment not just with a different way of thinking, but also with an altered sense of physical bearing, a different form of embodiment. The classic mode of engaging such a demand is shamanism; one contemporary means of exploring such, despite all of its enervations and buy-offs, is hip-hop culture. Unless and until white males in particular come to grips with their own "incarceration" inside the white body, supremacy will continue to wield batons and fire bullets and drop bombs to ensure its continuance.

# I

# White Supremacy, African Sorcery, and Euro-Christianity

This section constructs the phenomenon of white supremacy as the historical offspring of Christian supremacy in Europe's colonial encounters with indigenous cultures around the globe, and traces its abiding influence on Western society in general and Euro-American identity in particular. Methodologically it proposes a rereading of European racialization discourses from the spaces of indigenous religions and subject peoples dismissed and repressed by Euro-colonists as non-Christian, superstitious, and sorcerous. In particular, the rubric of witchcraft is taken up in connection with early European evaluations of Africa and played back into the ongoing theological projection that gave rise to an imagination of "blackness" as an evident curse. The payoff of such a projection—the fiction of "whiteness"—is traced historically and constructively as a surreptitious enculturation of supremacy that continues to inflect and infect social practice and Christian praxis even when explicitly disavowed.

The opening essay (chapter 1) "Beyond Occasional Whiteness," was published in 1997, as a first attempt to summarize the research I had been doing for my dissertation, which became the book *White Theology: Outing Supremacy in Modernity*. It offers a phenomenological characterization of white identity as a continuing historical effect of the racialized practices that have constituted America since its colonial beginnings. In part, the essay is self-confessional, articulating a challenge to other white-identified persons to take up the task of disavowing covert supremacies by tracing genealogy and combating passivity.

Whiteness emerges historically as a buy-off of various immigrant European identities, a ticket to admission into the fiction of white superiority even as such immigrant groups were forcibly integrated into the exploitative industrial order of the new nation. Yet, whiteness remains a political choice, capable of being repudiated and struggled against even as its privileges and powers are confessed and traced. The essay sets the general tone for the rest of the writings, which wax more explicit and polemic in sharpening perception and mobilizing strategy for a lifetime of counter-hegemonic struggle.

The second essay (chapter 2) was first given as a paper for a conference on "Race and the Humanities" held in November of 2001. Originally entitled, "Between Unconsciously White and Mythically Black: European Race Discourse as Modern Witchcraft Practice," the thought experiment it enacts establishes the framework for the book in seeking to respond to the demand of historian of religions, Charles Long, for a hermeneutics of reciprocity between the West and "the rest." The tack taken is to rethink European colonial encounter with its others in the terms used to differentiate Euro-Christianity from indigenous religiosity in the first place. Early modern European characterizations of native religious practices—especially in Africa— as sorcery are inverted back on Euro-practices themselves. What began as a theological demonization—the delineation of a hidden project of violence, in which one coterie of indigenous practitioners mobilizes curses and poisons to attack the flesh and consume the substance of others in the community—ends up as an apt characterization of the real life effects of European race discourse itself. It emerges as a practice that constructs dark skin as an evident curse, at the same time creating and affixing "blackness" onto various peoples of color as the irrefutable emblem of recalcitrance toward God, reinterpreted by the likes of a Hegel as the appropriate designation of an entire continent. Africa becomes, in European perception and practice, the home of the cannibalistic tooth, both demanding and legitimizing enslavement as "salvation" (from such witchcraft). The result, however, is the erection of the largest economy of witchcraft yet witnessed on this planet of voracious appetites and rapacious eyes. Race discourse shows up as the ultimate project of consigning a designated collectivity to the maw of a consuming other. "Whiteness," in this compass, is a "witch-pact," operative even up to the present moment of transnational traffic in the souls and substance of cultures metabolized by the West.

# I

# Beyond Occasional Whiteness

*All peoples can fall into Whiteness under the appropriate circumstances…*

—*Charles Mills (*The Racial Contract, *128)*

America at the end of the 20th century witnessed a new revelation of an old apparition that demands unremitting theoretical vigilance. Euphemistically, it could be called "white surprise"—the surprise that race remains a live issue in America and racial violence recurs. It is a surprise that comes to us in unwanted irony, harsh with epiphany. In 1995 alone, for instance surprise that black people generally (though not, it must be noted and understood, "unanimously") responded with joy to the O. J. Simpson acquittal, while white people generally (with a similar caveat) were depressed and angered. Surprise that Louis Farrakan could be a major player in the mobilization of a million black men of various religious persuasions to descend on Washington, DC in an auburn hour of activism one fall. Surprise that southern churches were burning again, leaving ash piles that were largely black. Surprise, really, because it was no surprise at all that a Ted Koppel late-spring interview with white people from Wisconsin (or was it Willamette, or Wilcox, or Walla Walla?) in a segment of Nightline entitled "America in Black and White" revealed a people decidedly "*not* pre-occupied with race or the question of their own whiteness." Race was something in the past, a problem still found here and there, in the outback of Idaho or in the imagination of the academy. Or in the ceaseless self-justifications of the ghetto. But not in real life. Not in that late hour of the third century of republican experiment. Not at the threshold of the millennium, on the brink of a future already overtaxed with other, more immediate, concerns. But there it was (is). Surprise! White! An un-endangered species! Or could it be?

In one sense, "surprise" is the very opposite of my topic here. Whiteness in America is perhaps the least surprising thing around. Indeed, that is its very nature, its social character. It is taken for granted. Only other things—blackness, Asianness, salsa, dreadlocks, sushi, dreamcatchers—are "other" and thus capable of provoking surprise. Whiteness just is. Familiar. There. Home. American. "Us" (for those of us with the requisite pallor to escape remark). Not surprising at all. Not self-conscious at all. Until "we" are jolted into awareness by a jubilant brown face unable for a moment to contain its joy over an October announcement of acquittal.

In the recast words of Karl Marx, taken in a direction he might not have approved, white surprise could be said to be "full of metaphysical subtleties, theological niceties" (Marx, 1967, 71). Strange creature that it is, it births its head only after its body is in full view. A verdict is announced and before the mask can be found and placed, surprise finds and names its subject. A "we" is discovered in a sudden reflex of feeling, a pronoun after the fact. Whiteness is, indeed, at some level, a fact of feeling. But it is also so much more. And yet at the same time, nothing. Whiteness is everywhere in America and yet is nothing at all. Like its euphemism, the American Dream here at the end of "American" capitalism, it is oneiric in its fleetingness. Doomed to disappear. Immigration, contraception, and aging to the fore, postindustrial America is also on its way to becoming "post-white." Or is it?

## The Choice to Be White

In a recent popular rag in Chicago, the central political question got asked in all of its loaded simplicity, its seeming innocence. Why be white? As if it were a choice. Peter Leki opined that it was and that it amounted to simply, and only, a choice *for* privilege. Whiteness, in his mind, is a location on a scale of gradation, mapping pathways to power for those willing and able to pay the price. Its payoff can be actual, illusory, or merely only hoped for, like a promise on the horizon. But its place is an advantage one chooses to assume.

Like the author of *How the Irish Became White*, Leki argues that, historically, white identification represents the ascendant pole of a quintessential American hierarchy (Ignatiev, 1; Leki, 12–17). It first emerged as the homogeneous identity offered to newly arrived European immigrants in lieu of their own peculiar peculiarities. It functioned in this new world as a substitute category that allowed time and terrain to do their work on old identities. Under its rubric, citizenship was predicated, land appropriated, and superiority imagined. Over against the myth of white sameness, African slaves and aboriginal "savages" anchored a fantasy of "colored" difference and a fiction of natural inferiority. In a nutshell, whiteness theologized a tactic of legitimation, while a continent was subdued and an economy secured. The God of light was its supposed author (Bastide, 281; Manning, 319). Red and black skin its civilizing burden. Order its task of imposition. Neither biologically based nor culturally constituted, white identity sustained—and sustains—a politics of empire. But it remains a choice.

Why be white?—it is not a habitual question among us, indeed, for most, not even a question. But for all that, it *is* askable. And for Leki, insistent. "You don't have to be white," he emphasizes. James Baldwin offers a bit more precision: "White is a state of mind. It's even a moral choice (Baldwin, 1985, 666)." What is the morality of being white? Here we edge toward the undoing of racialization as a historic form of "American" salvation. I want to suggest that whatever else it might be, American whiteness constitutes not only a moral choice, but also a theological predicament. Whatever one's religion or disbelief, "Why be white?" is finally a question not just of identity, but of ultimacy. A matter of faith, of destiny as well as ancestry.

### Whiteness and Ancestral Inheritance

Ancestry is a good place to begin. Is the genealogy of America white? Is any of our heritage, is my own family tree or yours, pure pink whiteness? It is the implicit dream of purity that whiteness solicits and solemnizes. Historically, in American law, more than 1/32 of "black blood" in one's veins meant one was actually only 3/5 of a person in one's country.[1] Racial identity and national character balanced on the edge of a fraction! But Americans never were good at fractions. Such slippery little devils, damnable slips of integers, of whole bodies, against one another, producing confusion, engendering partiality! A nefarious slide of significance from almost whole to almost half—by the sheer magic of legislative fiat, speaking for a blind lady, holding a scale, not so good at fractions. While in the Caribbean, 1/32 might define not blackness, but whiteness! (Carter, 79).

The comparison bears comment. Apparently, the "fifth generation"—the blood-calculus in terms of "32nds"—has something metaphysically compelling about it. But who had it right as to whether we were talking about black or white? In either place alone—"a pint of blood, a pound of destiny." But considering the United States and Jamaica, together—a whole boatload of confusion! Think. Hypothetically, in sailing from Miami to Kingston (or the other way round), one could cross a line, someplace out in the Caribbean, where, for a split second, the body straddling an invisible divide, would have been both black and white. The ultimate creolization! A genuinely Afro-Euro "utopia" in the form of an invisible threshold. That may be the real truth about the Bermuda triangle. Those who supposedly disappeared really only got ontologically confused when they unwittingly crossed the threshold. They are alive and well, just not recognizable, because they no longer know whether they are black or white.

What is in an ancestor? Who knows whose line is pure and pure what? The bloodline and the storyline, the genes and the jokes, the DNA and the dances, the codes and the cultures are all hopelessly intertwined before ever we get back to the fifth generation. A veritable thicket of verisimilitude—borrowing here, stealing there, copies of copies everywhere, nookie on the side, consent upfront, business dealing and backroom wheeling inseparable from the physical transaction of fluid. Ancestral meaning- and love-making are an indecipherable mix—a cacophonous symphony played by a brood, composed by a buffoon, directed by a laughing beggar, with notes and note-players coming and going like cottonwood puffs on a late afternoon breeze in July. Who are you really? And whose? Where does the germ line *not* extend after a couple of generations?

Ironically, it is Farrakan's chosen brood that has perhaps most amusingly captured the truth of the absurdity (or is it the other way around?). In a fantastic vision bearing a strange veracity, the Black Muslim "myth of origins" posits whiteness as a scientific experiment gone awry. Some 6,000 years ago, Yacob, a mad black experimenter, tampered with the pure African line and produced an albino offshoot. By accident, in the unexplainable fickleness common to most cosmogonic tales of world rupture and reversal, this mutant white gene gained power and was destined to rule until the mid-1980s. After that point, the original black race would regain ascendancy and resume its global reign. In genesis, though, there was only "black." Like the claims of the more scientific-minded gene-tracers of today, the Yacob myth has us all beginning in the great Guinea originally. My mother, as everyone else's, was African. And whiteness—the mirage in the mirror of an originally black Narcissus—was a mad mistake, appearing as the miasma dream of the melanin-ically challenged.

At all events, it is historically accurate to say that whiteness as a category is a late invention. It is indeed a mythic substance, a wish made willful. With a short memory. In matters of race, of struggling against racism, the task for white people is at least that of "thickening" white skin, restoring a sense of history and complexity, materiality and perplexity, to its present-day taken-for-grantedness. It is at least a matter of tracing back white ancestry to its moment of "passing," when someone in the family shifted categories by mere fiat, became "white" because it was possible to choose to do so. That moment is in fact present in the bloodline of *every* white person.

Why hobble our present and damn our future by truncating our past? We are all "post-black" people, recovering "passers," struggling to find the handle of the closet door, even if we think we might abhor the darkness the light will magnify. "The light will set you free," the book testifies. *What* it will set free—in this case—is color. The truth about us is mixture. Whiteness is a creole cover-up. As the Yacob myth says—a pseudostep in history, an aberration. Given the intransigence of time and tyranny—at least the tyranny of the times we are caught in presently in this country—I must indeed confess that I am "proximately" white, with all the implications that carries for guilt and responsibility. But ultimately, my reality is colored. Historically, mythically, my "fall" (as in Genesis) was "into" whiteness. Gift of the conquest and the colony. But my postcolonial destiny is multichromatic.

Genealogically, for instance, I am some combination of Dutch–Irish–English–German and who-knows-what-else (unfortunately, some affiliations may remain submerged in the "passing" phenomenon and can only be claimed as a present "absence") and from-where-else.[2] Historically, I am the beneficiary of European, Aboriginal, African, and Asian travail and overcoming, labor and longing, innovation and remembering. Socially, I am Midwestern urban middle class, cross-cut by inner city (fifteen years in Detroit's low income, near eastside) and blue collar affinities. In religious formation, I come out as a disaffected Presbyterian, Pentecostal, sometime Episcopalian, Roman Catholic–educated, ashram-instructed, traditional-religion fascinated "something." And culturally, I am the product of a mixed WASP, Jewish, African American grade- and high-school, and three heterogeneous neighborhoods (lower middle class in transition in Cincinnati, so-called underclass black in Detroit, and integrated, middle class, university in Chicago). Do I really have more in common with George Washington than with Martin King? With seventeenth-century Puritan Pilgrims than with contemporary Mexican migrants? I am already genetically and culturally what I soon must become existentially and consciously: *meti, mestizo, mulatto,* multi-*com-madre*-d. It is a simple matter of choice—of owning my history and preparing my future.

Thus, merely white no longer!—by choice. Not simply choice. Not a simple choice. But a simple *matter* of choice. A choice for a certain kind of materiality, and the materiality of a certain kind of choosing. Whiteness is finally something we who "are" white choose to be, because to choose otherwise would be costly. But not to choose otherwise, I would argue, is even more costly. And here lies the rub. What is at stake humanly, morally, yes, even finally theologically and eschatologically, in the choice "to be," or "not to be," white? Why would anyone choose to eschew privilege?

The answer is not easily formulated. It goes by monikers like "to grow up" (thus Baldwin), to develop personal integrity, to deepen human solidarity, to recover roots, to forge a destiny. The words sound ideal, pious even, like nice bourgeois platitudes or Sunday morning in somebody's pew. But the issue is material like Madonna's girl. It cuts across all the registers of identity. The question of whiteness has to do with our deepest intimations of interiority, our most prosaic everyday encounters, our most exacting political commitments. It is intimate, interpersonal, organizational. Ultimately, it is a question of our relative "wholeness"—our "salvation."

## Whiteness and Bodily Performance

At the level of interiority, the choice against white identity is a choice to recover the "whole" body. Historically, white identification has frequently meant psychosomatic alienation, an option for Apollonian control at the expense of Dionysian ecstasy. To the degree rationality and propriety have been racialized as white, expressive intimacy and performative dexterity have been sacrificed as black. The result is a kind of white gestural illiteracy, a "choked" orality, a stilted physicality. *White men can't jump,* the movie marquee blinks. But they can learn to play. And to dance and sing and walk and talk with grace. The "white-possessed body" (read "the white patriarchal body") can be exorcised, relieved of its paralysis, returned to its pain, restored to its expressive potentialities. But in the process, whiteness itself, as a recognizable category of awkwardness and affliction, will become less than clear.

For instance, in a Chicago appearance in the winter of 1996, the Asian American singer Yoko Ono gave a performance that amazed her

*Chicago Tribune* critic. His entire write-up could be glossed simply as "astonishment."

> [A]t the outset, the audience seemed protective of the diminutive 62 year old. One was struck by how young and vibrant she looked, but also how soft and fragile. What a delusion. All notions of this woman's frailty were quickly extinguished when Ono launched into "Turned the Corner." At song's end, the singer finds herself staring into the abyss. "Where there used to be a smile/Now I see a stranger." And she doubled over as her voice grasped for meaning where there is none. In its place came a ululation of anguish, the first of what would be many tiny exorcisms. Ono often built musical monuments both hushed and harrowing around a single word or phrase: "I'm dying," "Will I," "Kurushi," which translates roughly as "tormented" or "pained." Her voice worked a startling range of essentially wordless emotions, from a suffocated hush to a feline roar. After one volley had ended, Ono smiled and said, "I didn't promise you a rose garden, right?". . . As Ono sang, "My tears are now rivers, my flesh earth," a baby's cry from the audience added surreal accompaniment . . . the slow rhythm became heavier . . . muted volume higher, until Ono's invocation of "Rising, rising, rising," soared like a hymn. (Kot, 5)

An interesting ode to Ono, but the real question here is, whence our critic's amazement? From what presupposition arose his presumption? A supposition about Asian aloofness or female delicacy or aged vulnerability? Possibly. But given the history of the country and the language of his description, the more likely undercurrent is racial: our critic friend anticipated a "white" performance, but he experienced its actuality as "black." And he was thus surprised, on a number of levels at once. If so, in the process, he only revealed himself captive to a stereotypically "American" expectation and experience.

All stereotypes aside, however, it is at least arguable that Ono's evident "overcoming" in fact owes no small debt to her medium. Beneficiary and victim at once of a tradition of white rock music tracing its multiple roots back to black jazz and blues, she has indeed performed a continuous exorcism. What has been exorcised is not her personal pain alone, nor only the anguish of postwar Japan, but indeed any lingering immigrant temptation to embrace American whiteness as the style of redemption. Performatively, Ono has rather become an unlikely place of polyphony, a stormfront of white and black and Asian energy promising lightning, delivering rain.

In the most intimate reaches of the body, the choice against identifying white can indeed be a choice for expressive freedom and cathartic healing. As one native tribe puts it: Do we dare to live in a "long body," excavating soul by rooting our voice in the belly, auguring ancestry by offering living bones for ancient invocations? Do we dare to refuse the tight commodification of our communications, the suburban sequestering of our sensibilities? Or do we consent to a prepackaged incarnation kept safely within the social pale by the tiny disciplines of "common sense" about where we can go and who we can be with and what we can be like and how we can present ourselves when we get there? Whether we grow in wisdom or atrophy in boredom, develop spiritual dignity or sink into psychic flab, become socially fluid and culturally complex or stiffen into a generic mono-being—our significance is at stake in our comportment. Do we settle for a huddled existence in the flesh? Or, do we explore the full range of the fact that our soul is a body?

## Whiteness and Interpersonal Witness

The choice away from white normally also has everyday ramifications. At the level of interpersonal relations, it is a question, especially, of our use of language. Identity is narrative and metaphor at once, the nexus of words by which we project ourselves into the world and from which we retrieve our "eventful formation." We are living history, walking syntax, talking tropes. When "white speak" offers its seductions, do we play or pay? Leki once again offers helpful hints. He speaks of the tiny "messages of toxic hate" regularly sent out by white aspirants in each other's company (Leki, 16). They appear as gestures of joining seeking reciprocation—the ethnic jokes, the furtive use of the "n_____" word, all the little "feelers for racist camaraderie." When rejoined, they occasion "insider's delight," a small fest of "sure glad we aren't them." A blue collar neighbor talks of "those n___s." A middle class relative remonstrates against "welfare queens." Friends describe their experience walking into the "wrong" bar, laughing nervously because in the dim lighting, they couldn't see if anyone was there. A moment of choice.

Leki has a friend who regularly interrupts such attempts at inclusion. She says that she's part of whatever group is being put down. "My mother is Jewish." "Did you know I have an African American grandfather?" "My aunt is from Arabia." Reportedly, the results are quite telling and usually without rancor. Vastly more effective than hypothetical arguments over racism and welfare, these deliberate tearings of the little spider webs of white identity provoke instant response. Apologies and corrections abound. An observable "schism open[s] up in the person who has just let loose some racist flatulence" (Leki, 16). Whatever the supposed facts of genetic ancestry, the represented ancestry strikes truth "in kind." Myth meets myth, at the level of its genuine import. We *are* all related, in ways native cultures remember so elegantly: brother to the buffalo, sister to the sun, "family" stretching out the length of the food chain. And across the human race. The connotations of our kin words are at least as true as their denotations. The intervention is not disingenuous.

But such a step is minute. The payoff, however, is immediate and exorcistic. A sharp tang of adventure and freedom, of having reauthored one's own affiliation, and broken the thrall of a demon. But not only for oneself. In the same way that the presence of a woman instantly alters a dialogue between men, or the arrival of an African American revises Anglo interaction, so European-looking individuals can occasion instant change in the world of whiteness by how they identify in the moment they enter the speech community. Skin privilege is also skin opportunity. A moment that can further wind the coils of hate (and ultimately all such hate is self-hate) is always also a threshold moment. It presents the possibility of release, of a leap into new reaches of being. What remains impossible in such a moment, however, is removal from the crucible of choice. Such is the burden of privilege. Inevitably, each episode, each subtle temptation to enter into the presumption of whiteness is a crossroad. There is no begging off the responsibility. There is only capitulation. Or creation. The rituals of whiteness, indeed, require ritual combat.

### Whiteness and Political Resistance

There remains yet another moment of white refusal, a risky third move and motive that has to do with political organization. Leki recounts the story of another friend, an Irish factory worker, who was laid off, along with numerous others, in a recent downsizing. The pink-slipped included an African American higher up the seniority list. Before leaving the plant, however, the "white" friend was reoffered work, on the sly, in violation of the seniority system. Rather than simply accept the privilege, Leki recounts, the junior laborer found his senior coworker and together the two confronted the foreman. The "mistake" was rectified; the African American was given the job, the less senior shown to the door of unemployment. Leki generalizes: as a communist and trade unionist, his friend had a worldview and a community that enabled his moral courage and supported him in his material vulnerability. His union culture expected no less of him; his family understood.

Identity, we must then confess, is also a matter of community—and thus, alternative identity a matter of alternative community. Our sense of self is local. It requires reciprocity and feeds upon familiarity and support. But in our postmodern, postindustrial context, the supports are thin, the familiarity fleeting, the locus, all too often, generic and empty. Whence, in such a context, the communal resources for an alternative construction of the self? In a culture of conformity and market mentality, where contact is so often confined to mere similarity, and interaction to advantage seeking, whence genuinely supportive "common interest"? In the face of the commodity form and the cult of consumption, whence an experience of mutuality strong enough to risk more than merely symbolic resistance? The materiality of whiteness also requires material combat. But amidst the mega-structures of global capitalism, the mini-gestures of the resistant individual stand impotent. What is needed is a mediating structure between the individual and the system. Local community and alternative culture are musts. The economy of supremacy can only be effectively countered if the risks of noncompliance can be shared.

And here, we begin to touch upon a peculiar social difference in the ways whiteness and blackness are collectively experienced in America. White identification can never give access to a positive experience of culture and community. Its historical project has ever been (only) negative: a quintessential "not that," "not black." It offers its organizing difference only in the presence of the excluded. Behind the front lines of race, however, the idealized "white community" quickly dissolves into the real machinations of the overclass[3] against everyone else (even if the ideology is actually "one against all," like lotto). Fortresslike suburbs, enclosed communities of affluence, rim cities ringed with political mandates and policed margins provide little of the cultural substance capable of sustaining communal identity. Narcissistic consumption and competitive production do not combine into durable forms of social integration or cultural competence. The ethos secured remains rather corporative than communal, its affiliations transnational rather than local. White-collar whiteness tends to resolve itself into the anomic individual[4] and the opportunistic company.

At the blue collar end of things, the edge of white identity remains more fraught, more vitalized in what it excludes. It, too, is finally only negatively constituted as "not black." But that negation is complexly mediated. Materially, the relationship between white working-class identity and black culture is complex and symbiotic. Historically, European immigrants and African American workers have been locked into forms of competitive struggle that translated into reciprocal influence as well as rejection, cross-fertilization as well as fighting. In their forms of self-consciousness, however, immigrant workers have opted again and again to identify themselves as exclusively "white." Blackness has served as the foil for a gradual political amalgamation of divergent immigrant cultures.

The historical process is now patent, affecting even non-Europeans. For a time, newly arrived groups sustain communal traditions and ethnic locations. Cities across the country have indeed witnessed the temporary viability of Irish areas, Italian enclaves, German gardens, French quarters, China towns. But within a generation or two, assimilation alchemizes difference into indifference. Upward mobility segregates the achievers from the wannabes, and class prerogative cauterizes conscience and consciousness alike.

At the bottom end, however, racism continues to grant the vacuous, but vicious, reward of white pride. Lower income and unemployed African Americans in nearby neighborhoods become the anchors of alienation, the worst case scenario that can never happen to "oneself." But once again, any communal sense thus concretized remains negative and thin. Whiteness, here, cannot recognize itself in the mirror, offers no substantive content other than violence, has no ethical imperative other than hierarchy. From top to bottom, white identity thus remains culturally empty and communally void.

Black identity, on the other hand, shows a different face and formation. It retains cultural substance in its suchness, offers communal memory in its practice. While its formal significance is no less contingent than the whiteness that opposes it, its material genealogy is rooted in necessity. Black identification began with the chain locked around Bantu or Congo or Dahomian legs. It admitted no self-reflection. It granted no self-knowledge. It fixed one at the bottom of a hierarchy, materialized one's body as property, localized one's place on the plantation, socialized one's person as subhuman, economized one's labor as mandatory and unrelieved, politicized one's will as "subject," legalized one's flesh as violable. Blackness was the color of African experience of the American reality. America was simply impenetrably "there": an irresistible, immovable, unintelligible, opaque hardness of existence. In the words of Charles Long, it was a "lithic" reality (Long, 1986, 178, 197).

Something *against* which the self had to struggle constantly simply "to be" and in relationship to which it had to embrace allies wherever they could be found.

Which is to say, African American history witnesses to a story of creativity and communality alongside of its account of damnable exploitation. African Americans could not *not* forge a cultural competence out of the blackness they found themselves saddled with. Survival dictated using the master's tools against the master's purposes—taking what was inescapably imposed and translating it to advantage. White suppositions about black sameness became the veil, the "hidden recess in plain view" under whose cover Yoruba and Fon and Hausa and Angola individuals could take refuge and work out tactics.

Here, the white stereotype worked paradoxically. Its constraint also operated as a cover, relaxing surveillance, curtailing oversight. Within its "dark dumbness," a community was indeed born, birthing simultaneously the possibility of alternative identities, subversive "second selves," unbowed by the slavemaster's whip. For oppressed slaves, blackness harbored the possibility of a creative duplicity. The suffering of various forms of violence for the crime of carrying high levels of melanin in one's skin supplied a "commonness" of experience enabling *creative differences* of response. The community of pain indeed gave rise to a commonality of code that granted an alternative sense of belonging and acted like an affirmative chorus for individual innovation.

In the "Invisible Institution," for instance—in slave prayer meetings conducted in the "hush arbor" or out in the fields away from the master's ears—ritual redress of the agony indeed engendered a cultural congress of ecstasy. But this shared structure of feeling also opened space for a remarkable range of individual improvisation and experimentation. Identity was nurtured by familiarity, difference by the sameness it could presuppose and inflect. Terror was overcome not in heroic denial, but in a collective tempering and rearticulation of its intensity (Long, 1986, 166–170). For the individual, the expressive community represented both a mirror of the pain and a mimetic staging of its overcoming. Here, anguish was being transfigured into eloquence, demonic incursion into *daemonic* vitality, through communal acts of individual articulation. A way could be made precisely out of the no way that "blackness" seemed to represent. Despite the irreducible tragedy and inexcusable trauma.

In sum, where white identity constellates its meanings only in a negative outline, black identity yields a positive content. In their religious communities and their aesthetic activities, African Americans have continuously crafted the negative imposition into positive constructions. Blackness has become, in historical struggle, a category of creative virtuosity sustained in a culture of ruminating mimesis.[5]

For those willing to entertain a choice away from the passivity of white identity, black communality and creativity thus stand as signs. Communal potency and cultural positivity are the results of a tradition of overcoming. They are not forms of booty carried off by conquering someone else or magically conjured by putting another down. They result from effort, shared struggle, commitment to survive and to create in the face—the very maw—of the devil. Community is a gift, but one given at the place of spiritual combat, where external oppression is met with internal resolve and humanizing resistance. Culture is grace, but its beauty is forged in a sustained effort to overcome chaos with meaning. Culture-creating community cannot be bought in commodity form. It can only be accreted in a history of faithfulness. It feeds on the memory of violence resisted and despair overcome. It grows in the vision of something better and the labor to begin to realize that vision now. And for "white" Americans, it remains a possibility only in a resolved step away from the birthright signified by their whiteness.

## (Post-)White Integrity

Perhaps the major motivation to eschew white privilege is to become eligible for community and available for culture. But here lies the irony of our history. What for African Americans has been imposed as a necessity for physical survival, "recovering whites" must enter as a necessity for spiritual survival. In theological terms, there is no salvation for white people as "white." There can be no realization of wholeness while occupying the position of oppressive privilege.

Once again, here, there is a burden of choice. Solidarity in a concrete context of struggle must be chosen—and chosen again and again—as the crucible of one's deliverance from a living death to a dying life. The necessary contexts abound—in the ongoing struggles against racism (citizens groups working against continued redlining in insurance and banking industries, tutoring programs for inner city youth, advocacy efforts for migrant workers, etc.), sexism (shelters for battered women and abused children, support groups for single mothers, legal initiatives to deal with sexual harassment as well as domestic violence, etc.), classism (homeless shelters, unions, living wage initiatives, etc.), homophobia (advocacy for gay and lesbian rights, support groups for AIDS sufferers, etc.), and eco-genocide (various environ-mental groups, community organizations fighting "fly dumping" in the inner city, etc.). The political causes and spirited collaborations needing support are manifold.

The key, however, is genuine community and long-term encultura-tion. It is easy for individualist Americans to become dilettantist activists or shopping-mall spiritualists—samplers of the multicultural surface rather than committed combatants for a sustainable future. But the real work requires rootage; the effective move outside privilege and into potency demands durability.

Human community may well hang in the balance. It is time to rethink our identity as regional.[6] The profound questions of race may finally be resolved only at the level of our relationship to the land, where cultural difference finds its deepest rationale in differences of landscape and ecology. Traditional cultures and peoples have loved the peculiarities of environment, encoding its requirements in their adaptations, its life forms in their myths, its sensations in their own sensibility and arts and cooking. But they also embraced its hardnesses as pedagogy, as the teaching of life itself. It is perhaps high time to exorcize "hardness" as the character that culture assumes when it is violently imposed by one people on another, and let it once again become the spiritual gift of an existence lived in concert with an ecological "place." There is an abiding surprise of spirit when mutu-al respect becomes the ultimate watchword between life and life. A never-ending surprise that is at once clean and hard and vitalizing. Communal identity and cultural vitality are indeed the surprising products of a hard encounter. But unfortunately, tellingly, white surprise is not.

# 2

# Modernity's Witchcraft Practice

*The "sorcery of whites" haunts me and my relationships.*

—Cécé Kolié ("Jesus as Healer?" 146)

Beyond necessary personal confession and committed political action, confrontation and transformation of white "race-work" requires serious theoretical interrogation of the ways and wiles of whiteness. In 1983, African American Historian of Religions Charles Long reiterated his long-standing challenge to the Western academy to understand the entire postcolonial situation as an intercultural encounter demanding not so much scientific elucidation as "serious human conversation" (Long, 1983, 102). Where scientific categorization has historically tended to "fix" meaning (African cultures are "undeveloped," native peoples are "primitive," etc.) rather than explore it, human conversation opens up the possibility of mutual *hermeneusis* and the prospect of (re-)discovery of oneself in the eyes and words of one's other. Long's challenge finds its root concern in his insistence that colonial contact resulted in modes of experience that were qualitatively different on different sides of the colonial divide and gave rise to modes of meaning-making commensurate with those differences of experience. While the West has been quick to scrutinize, categorize, and analyze its various subjects of conquest, it has been considerably less sanguine about learning of itself from the representations and figurations of those others. What would happen if the gaze and its "knowing" were reversed?

Long's argument is incisive. Aboriginal cultures the world over were made to "undergo the West" in such an intensity and extent of "metabolic violence" that the result was terror at the level of metaphysics

(Long, 1986, 9, 110, 181). The overwhelming and irresistible epiphany of Western commercial and cultural interests on indigenous practices did not only shatter native bodies in the wars and rapine of conquest, but also ruptured the entire cosmogram of native forms of intelligence in the drive to civilize (Long, 1986, 177). For the colonized, the experience was irremediably "religious" (Long, 1983, 102). Where the Western Christian "myth of origins" was maintained intact and even hyper-fetishistically "confirmed" in the experience of contact, in virtue of the ruthlessness of Western domination, indigenous myths of origin were utterly shattered (Long, 1986, 193, 170).

For Long, this experience of overwhelming violence, of a depth of dismemberment that cuts not only into bone but brain, exploding not only the body but the birth-memory, which cannot even be "sited" in the mode of meaning-making of local culture, is experienced in those cultures as the kind of rupture that founds a "myth of origin" in the first place (Long, 1986, 123–125). That is to say, indigenous culture was pushed, by contact, all the way back into its *primordium*, had its full universe exploded, had to renegotiate its entire existence—and did so in the only mode capable of comprehending a cosmos: myth. Unlike for the West, for the rest, the experience was irreducibly "religious" (Long, 1986, 165). It required dealing with contingency and terror on a cosmic scale. The result was Native American "Ghost Dance," African millenarian prophetism, Caribbean *vodun*, Jamaican Rastafari, black church in the United States, and cargo cult in the South Pacific (Long, 1986, 166–167).

Long's project has been to try to take seriously the conditions of the postcolony in a manner that does not elide the depths and delirium of the rupture that modernity has meant across the globe. Simply to advert to Western scientific/humanitarian discourse to attempt even to perceive such—much less explain it—is already to miss the meaning for presuming the superiority. Long will not have it. He insists on a conversation that entertains the possibility that cargo cult idiom or Rasta ritual may well be more accurate to the real human meanings of contact than the dis-passions of objectified "othering" that constitute Western academic disciplines beholden to the Enlightenment. At the very least, he insists on reciprocal *interpretation* (Long, 1983, 102).

The writing that follows here is an attempt, in light of that demand, to think of race in terms of indigenous ritual. At the very least, it is an effort to relativize the Western scientific paradigm and the universalizing humanities discourses that have nestled close in to that paradigm. It is not an attempt to repudiate such an *episteme*, but rather—to borrow a jazz term—to "swing" it, to put it into antiphonal and improvisational circulation (West, 1989, 93, 1991, 136, 144). The essay constitutes a thought experiment, not pretending to pull capitalist practice and humanist *apologia* fully into indigenous forms of discourse (as V. Y. Mudimbe has well argued, there is no such thing as pure pre-contact "tradition" left), but rather attempting "bricolage" under their influence (Mudimbe, x–xi, 4–5).

In the process, I am under no illusions that I am making any great dent in the power of imperial rhetoric, any great deconstructive foray into the canopy of hegemony, but simply want to offer a small gesture, flea-like, on the back of the body politic, trying to bite what I can before getting crushed or sprayed into impotence. Long, at one point— invoking fellow religious studies scholar Mircea Eliade's morphological analysis of indigenous religious forms—differentiates the sun-loving rationalisms of the sky gods from the oppositional "lithic consciousness" of the stone-dwelling chthonic deities (Long, 1995, 5, 1986, 178, 197). As a long-time resident and activist in a low-income "ghetto" neighborhood on Detroit's near eastside, I simply serve notice I am on the side of the stones.

More specifically, this essay seeks to probe the historical emergence of white supremacist practice as a kind of modernist embodiment of "witchcraft discourse," which discovers its "witch-enemy" precisely in the moment of attempting to eliminate discourse about such from social intercourse. Race, racialization, and racism are comprehended as integral to the constitution of the humanities in the European academy, which established itself, in part, as a repudiation not only of religious superstition at home but also magic and sorcery in the colonies (Eze, 1997a, 1–8; Gilroy, 1993, 56, 60). The analysis invokes the historical metaphor of the "great chain of being" by which European colonialism and imperialism organized its others into a manageable taxonomy to argue that something like that ontological grammar remains at work in contemporary social organization, has as its intention the stealing and consumption of the substance of others in a now global enterprise of capitalist appropriation and accumulation, and masks its own avaricious and rapacious potency under the naturalizing function of a cultural "common sense" that until recently could claim authoritative backing by way of philosophy and the social sciences (Eze, 1997a, 5; Gramsci, 330; Haymes, 4, 21–22; Mills, 16, 32–35). In such an enterprise, witchcraft, I am arguing, can be "good to think with" as a mode of communicative action, signifying with a kind of "boomerang effect" in the intercultural space of rupture between the West and the rest.

## African Witchcraft and European Statecraft

The first part of the argument I formalize under the double-delineation of "craftwork" to highlight the active prosecution of world-construction engaged in both by *indigenous village cultures* in Africa and the *globalizing nation-states* of modern Europe. Fundamental to my understanding is the perception of modernity as having, in some sense, begun with the commercial enterprise of 1492, quickly finding its peculiarities of "production for exchange" ramified in the colonial competitions emerging between nation-states following the break-up of religious Europe in the Reformation, and gradually organizing its class priorities in monopolistic enterprises pursuing their economic hegemony in successive regimes of political imperialism and slave trading (Dussel, 9–14).

Within the archives of these emergent European nationalisms are records of the attempts of various colonial administrations to manage their respective encounters with certain indigenous practices collectively delineated, by way of supposed homology with European experience, as "witchcraft." That such a homology organizes non-gender-specific native practices into a gendered European category is not incidental to its power. But these "official" struggles disclose a fundamental paradox: a domain of indigenous practice is comprehended in post-Enlightenment European discourses as largely superstitious and fictional, but simultaneously occasions legislative sanction and punitive surveillance (Bongmba, 49; Fields, 74, 79–83, 89–90, 273–277). "Witchcraft" reproduces its wiliness in the very moment of its suppression.

Witchcraft emerges in colonial perspective and practice as a structuring device that mediates meanings of European order and indigenous disorder. This sleight-of-hand potency as an accusation that creates the very thing it projects is not dissimilar to its power at the level of local village life. In indigenous practice, the charge that someone is a "witch," or has acted as such, often serves as a retroactive explanation for disease, death, or a difference of fortune (Bongmba, 20, 26–29). It functions both to open and to delineate a field of conflict inside extended family relations, which then witnesses accusation and counteraccusation in a context of crisis (Bongmba, 38). Ironically, colonial policies seeking to suppress native practices demarcated as "witchcraft," in effect, accomplish the same kind of differentiation and explanation. The very charge of "witchcraft practice" can itself be understood as a form of witchcraft. In this colonial permutation however, the crisis it marks and mediates is one of political administration, not interpersonal fortune.

### Wimbum Tfu-ery

But the slipperiness gets very slick indeed in thinking this way. Academic study of indigenous practice pursued under the rubric of witchcraft is far too broad and much too debated a subject to do justice to in a single essay. For the purposes of the assay proposed here, I will root reflection among considerations of only one study of local practices and discourses delineated as witchcraft. Elias Kifon Bongmba's *African Witchcraft and Otherness: A Philosophical and Theological Critique of Intersubjective Relations* offers a self-reflective probe of such practices among the Wimbum people of contemporary Cameroon under the indigenous rubric of *tfu*. Bongmba is careful in his study, and that care will have to suffice, for now, for the particular spin I want to introduce into the academic discussion. Far from universalizing his examinations of witchcraft, Bongmba tracks *tfu* in its specifically local spatial context (the Northwest Province), across a recognized time of historical change (the intensified local effects of globalization and urbanization in the latter half of the twentieth century), and in relationship to his own personal predilection for postmodern perspectives on ethnographic initiatives. My own use of Bongmba's insights obviously will take him out of context.

Like Long, Bongmba is committed to hearing, not dismissing, the call of "the other"—even if its craft is "occult." His project, nonetheless, is avowedly critical: a reading of practices native to his own place, under the impress of the ethics of Emmanuel Levinas. My own is obviously the inverse—witchcraft "read back" toward ethics. Both of us, however, take seriously the prospect of meaning-making in multiple modalities and the circumscription of the mode in local code. (Indeed, part of the charge to be leveled at Enlightenment-based academics and their contemporary offspring is a profoundly interested occultation of their own local benefits and effects—the metabolism of "exotic" cultures and "other" myths not only for the sake of Western "new-age" solace but also for academic profit in selling "knowledges" and imperialist advantage in gathering "intelligence." The adventitious Western claim of universalism for its own regimes of truth is simply one more gesture of domination. But this is not a new criticism.) Bongmba seeks to take seriously—rather than dismiss off-handedly or totalize morally—the idiom of witchcraft practice, while still evaluating critically its negative manifestations and pursuits (xxii). I seek rather to site Western discourse inside such a craft and ask which is really "witch"? But first we need a bit more (Geertzian) "thickness."

## Tfu Yibi

Bongmba's project seeks to challenge the overshadowing power of *tfu* discourse to account for experiences of violation within the moral space of interpersonal relations (20). What he aims for is "not fantastic tales of witchcraft per se, nor the drama of hunting down witches and cleansing the community of them," but rather display of the way "specific problems [are] perceived among Wimbum when charges and accusations are made by one person against another" (Bongmba, 20). It is a question of indigenous articulations of "who is causing another to be ill," and how that "other" perceives it (Bongmba, 20). In the process, Bongmba distinguishes three local terms for practices that could be comprehended as witchcraft-like interventions into the social and/or natural orders in clarifying his choice to focus on *tfu*. The latter is the most comprehensive historical term that invokes local meanings of practices pursued "under cover of night," partaking of intimations of "darkness" and "secrecy," which usually carry a tonality of malevolence and demand healing remedies or protective medicines (Bongmba, 24).

In further delineating the practice, though, the terrain gets tricky. For Bongmba, *tfu*, on the ground, seems to designate a form of both knowledge and ability that is secret, non-hereditary, and capable of being "intentionally deployed for the benefit of the practitioner, possibly at the expense of the victim" (25–26). It is not involuntary, although a person who has *tfu* can supposedly "open the eyes" of those who heretofore have not had it by giving the latter the human flesh (of a sacrificed relative of the former) to eat disguised as some other kind of meat (Bongmba, 26–27). The result is a chain of indebtedness that requires a payback in kind of sacrificed human flesh that is then (reputedly) consumed by a gathering of *tfu* practitioners (Bongmba, 27). The degree to which the belief in such a "*tfu* cannibalism" represents a metaphorical account of illness and social stress "eating people alive" (rather than actual physical consumption) is an open question, but Bongmba refuses to entirely dismiss the phenomenon as metaphor (Bongmba, 28–29). He simply confesses that—like anyone else uninitiated into the destructive domain of *tfu yibi*—he cannot know of a knowledge that, by definition, he does not have (29).

More recently, the advent of capitalist relations in the local Wimbum economy has rendered *tfu* talk potent in deciphering a new horizon of aggression (Bongmba, 82–83). The metabolizing of the village in a metropolitan aggrandizement that is finally global in scope is grasped in local knowledge as a new modality of "eating and being eaten." Wimbum have negotiated their own interpolation in world markets and metropolitan politics in a logical extension of *tfu* metaphorics. The traditional notions of "local family" *tfu* practice have been supplemented by terms that designate a nationalizing of witchcraft patterns (Bongmba, 37). *Nyongo* and *kupe* witchcraft imply activities to create zombies who, rather than being killed and eaten, are supposedly "entranced" into a form of ongoing slave labor (Bongmba, 37). The emphasis here is on explaining acquisitions of wealth. These new terms push *tfu* out of its consanguineous orbit, adumbrating uses of the power to gain riches that can preempt blood relationship in favor of a money nexus (Bongmba, 38, 78). In the process, the space of *tfu* is expanded beyond the family, and, at the same time, the practice is narrowed to a single transaction between otherwise unrelated "individuals" (Bongmba, 38). Either a gift or a loan, it is believed, is sufficient to render one unwittingly vulnerable to "sacrifice" (Bongmba, 38). Structurally, this expansion of *tfu* suspicion is intimately linked to the emergence of urban elites who "have inserted themselves into the exploitative capitalist relations by pursuing an extravagant lifestyle" (Bongmba, 39).

And even the academic enterprise becomes fodder for the mill of accusation. Bongmba himself sets the stage for our own deliberations-to-come when he has the good graces to recount a playful challenge to his construction of *tfu* by fellow African scholar Emmanuel Eze (Bongmba, 53). Eze acknowledges the maze of perplexity entertained in the scholarly attempt to "read" *tfu*, and then asks whether Bongmba does not himself "have *tfu*," since he has argued that "only those who have the power know the power" and he (Bongmba) has, in fact, been able to make that form of knowledge convincingly clear (i.e., "known") in his writing (Bongmba, 53). Either that, Eze agues, or Bongmba should perhaps dispel the mystery once and for all and assert that no such knowledge really exists, that it is all a ruse of power, holding generations in thrall to various configurations of domination and dissembling (Bongmba, 53). A third possibility—that *tfu* practitioners may perhaps be the promulgators of powers and knowledge that they do not know they have—is also laid on the table (Bongmba, 53). Bongmba is uncompromising in asserting that he does not have *tfu*, but equally that he cannot just "write it off" as ruse (53). He is also adamant that such powers are intentionally prosecuted in practice and are not just lying there "dormant . . . waiting for the researcher to awaken [them]" (53). But the great unaddressed possibility in Bongmba's response is the degree to which "academic study" itself may not be comprehended, from the side of indigenous practice, as effectively a form of *tfu* practice operating through a researcher like him, even though it remains for the researcher to acknowledge its arousing by the indigenous community (Bongmba, 53).

Maybe Bongmba—and scholars in general—do unwittingly practice *tfu* in a form that is prodigiously effective precisely in its relative imperceptibility. Whether such a construction would be useful at all in a general sense, my own project here does seek to specify that, at least in the case of explicitly "racializing" knowledges, as well as in the more implicitly "normalizing" social practices of whiteness, *tfu*-like effects have taken place in the ongoing histories of Western contacts and exchanges with indigenous cultures, as I shall outline below.

## *Tfu Kupe*

To recapitulate, the "*tfu* effects" mentioned at the end of the last section, characterizing the history of contact, are primarily those of finding one's self and substance "being consumed" by an invisible "project" that resists analysis. The diminishment is brought to the forefront of consciousness and query by a discourse field that identifies occult powers serving an asymmetrical economy. In a mystery, advantaged power players, perceived as using insider information, are brought under local suspicion as the "secret agents" of intractable illnesses and early demises. While public charges may succeed in mobilizing local communal sanctions against such suspects, the charges can also backfire and occasion a continuous round of charge and counter-charge, intensifying suspicion and investing the entire economy of interaction with misgiving and accusatory ire.

The ambiguity of such a field of knowledge/power shows up when one asks how *tfu*-practitioners might understand their own *tfu*-actions. Apparently, the power is at times actively prosecuted to bring about deleterious effects, and confessions of such are offered by the practitioners. But what exactly is the motive force of such action? In village culture, presumably, the prize is power/knowledge itself: having recourse—or at least being perceived as having recourse—to an occult domain of force that rewards with a certain pleasure in consuming (figurative, if not real) "flesh-of-the-other." What is "accumulated" is perhaps both social status and interior confidence— a kind of self-awareness of potency and mobility in a context of ceaseless calculations of power and consequences. The "capital" accumulated would be a certain "fear" that protects against incursions-in-kind. While this line of reflection does not purport to decide the issue of the reality of *tfu*, it does at least position its potency in the realm of perception. In a culture of *tfu* suspicion and belief, the possibility is open to ongoing manipulation and brokerage.

And, of course, once the village is metabolized in the metropolitan circuits of globalizing capital, it is not surprising in the least that *tfu* is imagined behind a new kind of accumulation. Not only bad fortune is comprehended in the explanatory scheme, but also good "fortune." Wealth accumulation is probatively imagined as the outcome of a similar mobilization of unseen powers, leveraged, in one way or another, by "sacrifice" of human flesh somewhere along the line (only now in a "zombified" form of living death). Whether expressing mis-fortune or meta-fortune, the condition to be explained is a perceived break in the texture of mundane mutuality and reciprocity.

*Tfu* is, thus, simultaneously the perception and predication of a particular kind of *difference making*, its coding and questioning as the knowledge of a threat and the threat of a knowledge, which works at the depth level where cultural symbolics and psychic investments intertwine and define a world. It bifurcates the world into an in-group of *tfu* practitioners, who are understood to sacrifice the "flesh" of outsiders to the group members, and *tfu* discoursers, who, not having access to the power/knowledge of the practitioners, talk about its possible employment and presumed effects. The former are understood more in terms of covert use of a power than of overt discourse about a morality; the latter have as their only protection (unless they secure patronage of, or themselves employ, a practitioner), the mobilization of talk about that power as a moral question.

At core, *tfu* discourse would then seem to designate a domain of secretive and differentiating power that is fundamentally preoccupied with consumption, with "eating and being eaten." To what degree the "physical consumption of actual human flesh" is in view, as compared with a more metaphorical figuration for different kinds of material deterioration like illness, stress, mental incapacity, and finally death, on the one hand, or material aggrandizement at the expense of others elsewhere, on the other, remains an open question that is beyond my concern here. I am concerned with the "imagination of consumption" in the social field of *tfu* practice as a metaphorical perception of a real metabolism of the material conditions and psychic vitalities of life, which has power to teach beyond itself.

Enter into the discussion Frantz Fanon, Martiniquean colonial subject seeking education in the French state capital, writing of his experience on the streets of mid-century Paris, where he is accosted by the cry of a mere boy, shivering in fear of this sudden apparition of darkness, puncturing his bright safe world with untold epiphany, throwing himself into his mother's arms with the shout "Look Mama . . . a Negro . . . Look . . . a Negro . . . Mama, the [Negro]'s going to eat me up" (Fanon, 1967, 114).

## Mythic Blackness and Unconscious Whiteness

When Europe began its conquest and colonization of the rest of the globe in 1492, the colonial theater ultimately became the site of struggles for economic hegemony on the part of emerging European powers. Resource flows from the colonies were critical in underwriting intra-European conflict, and increasingly became the focus of the ongoing competition in the international slave trade and the control of colonial lands that solidified into separate European identities (Dussel, 11–14). To what degree, however, the practical "crafting" of the modern state can also be understood as dialectically "colored" by the craftwork of the colonized remains an open question (Herskovits, 8; Murphy, 1988, 115). The historical process was inevitably complex, and the way of describing it just ventured, only a gross caricature. But it does set the stage for the question of import here.

European power, in effect, "ate" African substance in the slave trade (as well as "native" substance in the colonial structures set up throughout the Americas, Asia, and the Pacific). Whatever the discourse, the fact of the effect is clear. A "witchery" of heretofore unimaginable potency ravaged African and aboriginal cultures. The necessary reflexive consideration that must be probed in turn is the degree to which a fear of "being eaten in kind" is then constitutive of the modern identities that emerge out of that process.

Fanon's account centuries later is revealing. The great truism of modern white supremacy in America is the white male fear that black males will attract and intermarry with white females and produce, in the words of the Grand Wizards of KKK infamy, "a bastardized mongrol race!" (Spencer, 165–171). Of course, who really produced illegitimate mixed-blood offspring is the telling question of the history of so-called misogyny. But that is still a white male fear that remains "outside" the white male body. It is a fear about status and competition in connection with sexuality that arguably has structured gender relationships and erotics in the white community—not to mention almost everything else in our social order—at quite profound psychosocial levels in this country. The little boy in Fanon's account, however, fears "being eaten."

It is not my purpose to offer psychoanalytic speculations on the origins of such a fantasy but to read it metaphorically and politically. In *The Isis Papers*, for instance, Frances Cress Welsing homes in on what she calls "the white supremacy system" as the organizing construct necessary to fathom the deep purpose underneath much of the machinations and mesmorize-ations of the global order in both its local and translocal sweep. This purpose, according to her, is finally the forestalling of "white genetic annihilation" (Cress Welsing, ii). Combating the global system of oppression and the exploitation of people of color, which is that system's necessary condition of possibility, entails, she says, unlocking the "secret of the colors" (Cress Welsing, viii). It is a secret largely inaccessible to our more usual "high frequency" order of everyday awareness, as being too profoundly encoded into our subconscious (Cress Welsing, xii). It must be engaged on the lower frequency level of the symbol (Cress Welsing, xii).

Grafting my own take onto her approach, I would similarly intersplice genetics and symbolics. Genetically, white disappearance would obviously be disappearance *back into* the registers of melanin that "whiteness" mutated out of in the first place (given our best understanding, to date, of the evolutionary trajectory of *homo sapiens sapiens* as having originated in Africa). That is to say, it would be disappearance back into "color." Symbolically, I would suggest, the deep fear is then that of "being eaten" by perceived difference. But the attempt to forestall such by mobilizing a *practice* of white supremacy masked in a *discourse* of black racialization is indeed a riddle and a secret—an attempt to combat fear that constructs the very "difference" it fears in the first place. I would suggest that one productive way of reading such a tactic is to consider it as a kind of preemptive "first strike"—on the part of a profoundly prodigal witchcraft—aiming the accusation of "blackness" at people of color in order to lock them up inside a discourse of charge and countercharge that fractures unity and bleeds energy in endless calculations of which "which" is the real witch.

All the while, of course, the ultimate witch stands devouring and invisible, shrouded in the enigma of an invisible white light. But here again, in tracking the development and power of such a tactic, history is helpful.

## White Supremacy

The last 500 years of modern geopolitical aggression and transnational economic domination by which Europe transplanted itself around the globe and took over, is more clearly organized in its basic life-world patterns and power privileges by the racial category of white/non-white than by any other observable category of demarcation (Mills, 138). Modernity *is* the advent of white supremacy as a global system of hegemony. My contention is simply that "whiteness" is also the great category of bewitchment that both masks and mobilizes the basic circuits of consumption, which are that system's raison d'être.

In developing a "genealogy" of this claim regarding whiteness, we can imagine the construct as a linkage of Foucauldian erudite and naïve knowledges (Foucault, 1980, 82–83). The erudite knowledge will be supplied by Hegel, subject to criticism. The naïve knowledge is this indigenous African reading of trauma and early death as "unnatural," caused by an enemy. The two combined form my overall attempt to "know" racialization as a form of witchcraft.

The claim runs something like this: White supremacy is the basic structuring practice of the modern world system in terms of which extraction, appropriation, production, and consumption of resources are differentially organized. The race discourse mobilized by that practice has gone through continuous "development" that can be periodized historically (Pagden, 1–2). It was first worked out as a theological discourse effecting a sharp divide of spiritual discernment between presumed "Christianity" and perceived infidelity and sorcery in the early period of conquest and colonization (Omi and Winant, 61–62). It was reworked into a metaphysical discourse on geography and biology in the Enlightenment, and further shifted into anthropological discourse regarding cultural difference in the twentieth century (Mills, 17, 25–27, 46; Omi and Winant, 63–64; Pagden, 1–2; West, 1982, 47, 51). In the United States in particular, in the 1960s, this discourse was contested in the identity politics of black power activism, challenging the "assimilation designs" of the Chicago School "ethnicity paradigm" with a demand for pluralism and autonomy, and despite its subsequent dismemberment in the "reform and co-opt" tactics of the state, was emulated by other groups concerned to preserve other forms of identity from being "metabolized" by whiteness (Omi and Winant, 104–106, 108–109). I understand my own effort here as also contestatory in attempting to mobilize indigenous categories to unmask race discourse as perhaps most suggestively "known," if not accurately analyzed, not as theology, ontology, or anthropology, but as itself the quintessential witchery of modernity.

The genealogy of the claim finds its root in an observation made by Cress Welsing. In outlining her theory that white genetic survival is the core motivation of the white supremacy system, she finds signs of a white fear of annihilation by black potency continuously exhibited in the symbolic productions of Western society—most notably in connection with the Christian rite of communion (Cress Welsing, xiii–xv). This rite is built on eating the body and drinking the blood of a Jesus whose originally dark features have only been lightened over two millennia in a gradual process of repressing the raw form of the terror of what I would call "eating and divinizing the scapegoat." This complex ritual alchemy transposing the "horrific" into the "heroic"— the dream of a dark divinity compelled to offer its flesh to the teeth of believers in the light—will serve as a kind of template for our own analysis. Obviously, such an interpretation of the opaque depths of Christian symbolics, imagining a layer of deep liturgical "forgetting," is heuristic and provisional—a positing of denial in the very act of probing it.

### Supremacist Theory

Hegel's work on Africa in his *Lectures on the Philosophy of World History* provides the "classically" modern perception of the so-called Dark Continent as through and through the land of the cannibal (in what follows, as excerpted by Eze). Review of the "principal moments within the African spirit" for Hegel, as with any other review of spirit, requires grasping the religion. It is through and through a religion of sorcery, he says, of arrogating to oneself a "power over nature," which leads directly into the belief that death is never simply a matter of natural causes but of the will of an enemy using such sorcery to kill (Eze, 1997a, 129–130). It occasions a resort to sorcery in kind, a battle of magics (Eze, 1997a, 130). Its mode is "frenzy" and "delirium," convulsive efforts of a "dreadful enthusiasm," which, should they fail in successfully manipulating nature itself or the natural object set up as empowered fetish, will then occasion wholesale sacrifice of onlookers by the sorcerers, whose bodies are then devoured and blood drunk "by their fellows" (Eze, 1997a, 131). Dead ancestors are likewise conjured for assistance in power mongering and indeed, in the "most fearful" moment of abomination, says Hegel, will possess their priestly *serviteurs* and command "human sacrifice" (Eze, 1997a, 132). The sum of such, for him, is "the superstition of witchcraft, whose terrible rule once prevailed in Europe too" (Eze, 1997a, 132). It issues in a political order of tyranny—the fetishizing of a power of contempt for all that is human, the licensing of cannibalism, the normalizing of the devouring of the human body as simply flesh "like all other [animal] flesh" (Eze, 1997a, 134). But then Hegel waxes unwittingly revealing in his subsequent analysis, saying more than he undoubtedly intended.

Such cannibalistic offerings of human flesh are not primarily for the sake of food, says Hegel, but "for festivals" (Eze, 1997a, 134). After being tortured and beheaded, for instance, the body parts of many hundreds of sacrificed prisoners "are returned to those who took them prisoner so that they may distribute the parts" (Eze, 1997a, 134). Hegel does not tell us why. He only says, "[i]n some places, it is true, human flesh has even been seen on sale in the markets" (Eze, 1997a, 134). But in any case, "[a]t the death of a rich man, hundreds [of such prisoners] may well be slaughtered and devoured" and "as a rule the victor consumes the heart of his enemy" and "at magical ceremonies . . . the sorcerer will [kill] . . . and divide [a] body among the crowd" (Eze, 1997a, 134).

And then, without any pause, Hegel immediately links *this practice* with a *rationale for slavery*. "Since human beings are valued so cheaply," he says, "it is easily explained why *slavery* is the basic relationship in Africa" (Eze, 1997a, 134; emphasis Hegel). Basic for whom? He continues: "[t]he only significant relationship between the Negroes and the Europeans has been—and still is—that of slavery" (Eze, 1997a, 134). But Hegel is underscoring African, not European, motivation: "[t]he Negroes see nothing improper about it, and the English, although they have done most to abolish slavery and the slave trade, are treated as enemies by the Negroes themselves" (Eze, 1997a, 134). Or rather, we might have to say, Hegel is working toward a simultaneous apology for European involvement: "[f]or one of the main ambitions of the kings is to sell their captured enemies or even their own subjects, and, to this extent at least, slavery has awakened *more humanity* among the Negroes" (Eze, 1997a, 134; emphasis added). "More humanity" as compared with what? Presumably with the aforementioned sacrifice and ritual devouring, or marketing, of prisoners' flesh.

Hegel will continue with a justification for the project of a slavery that, although "unjust in and of itself," nevertheless is a necessary part of the process of human movement from the "state of nature" to the "higher ethical existence" in the rational cultures exemplified by European states (Eze, 1997a, 135). Slavery, in this compass, is "a moment of transition" in the development of the Idea toward the historical achievement of a "substantial ethical life of a rational state" in which slavery then ceases to exist (Eze, 1997a, 135). Africa as a whole, for Hegel, remains enmeshed in the "natural spirit" on the far side of the threshold of history: the necessary dialectical move of the African spirit is from "witchcraft" through "slavery" toward ethical rationality (Eze, 1997a, 142).

For my purposes in this essay, there are two important reflections that offer themselves in such thinking. Africa is, in the Enlightenment imagination embodied by Hegel, the land of the open mouth, the cavernous orifice of darkness. For this quintessential modern, who stands at the apex of modernity, African cannibalism is not a peripheral manifestation but a central characteristic. According to Hegel, before captured African prisoners began to be traded to European slavers, they faced the prospect of being eaten. Compared to the local Cameroonian practice we examined above, in which *tfu*-practice was originally limited to family conflicts, Hegel's account presents a somewhat more encompassing practice. He appears to be talking about "enemies" captured from beyond the clan or village. Yet, the *denouement* is the same. Flesh is ritualistically consumed.

For Hegel, the advent of the slave trade in such a situation constitutes an improvement of conditions on the ground. And what's more, witchcraft practice becomes the rationale for enslavement. "Since human beings are valued so cheaply," he says, slavery is "easily explained" (Eze, 1997a, 134). But *mutatis mutandis* then, I would argue that the linkage between witchcraft and slavery might just as readily be understood in inverse relationship. Slavery itself might just as easily be explained as "witchcraft in a more rigorous mode." It does not at all escape the "fest of flesh" it supposedly remedies. It is perhaps more accurately conceived as a cult-in-kind, actively acceding to the communion-in-carrion, now traded in living form, for an appetite exponentially expanded. For Hegel, we might say, "Africa *is* witchcraft." The mouth is open and ravenous and unrestrained. But his remedy is simply a slower tooth and a more ruthless use, a metabolism consuming brain as well as brawn.

Of course, Hegel reads his remediation teleologically. The Great Chain of Being is tipped over on its side and given both historical dynamism and moral import. Spirit wends its way in one ultimate direction only. The culture of the witch is destined, somewhere, to cross the crevasse, face its opposition with mouth closed and eyes alight to the universal truth of reason, seeking escape from the chain. Slavery will deliver spirit from the maw of nature.

But it is not at all clear that Hegel's *telos* exists. What is clear in history is that European rapacity has eaten African substance unremittingly. As noted above, in recent years, Cameroonian culture has articulated a new wrinkle in the practice of *tfu*: witchery leveraging wealth through "the *zombi*." Flesh is devoured in modern mode, not so much in the immediacy of death, but in slow motion, through labor. *Tfu* sacrifice is no longer limited to blood relations, but the necessary linkage between witch and victim can be effected through money alone; it merely requires that the latter wittingly or unwittingly accept the "gift" of the former. Here, indigenous knowledge grasps better the real human meaning of the wage-nexus than most Western economic theory. Wealth is accumulated through *eating* the work of others.

Hegel's philosophy differentiates itself from the supposed foolery of African witchery in the predication of an absolute divide. Modern metaphysics in Enlightenment mode thinks itself entirely removed from, and innocent of, modernity's metabolics. But the mask has its mouth open. A third world country is falling out in the form of a well-gnawed bone. The European charge of African witchery itself hides the deepest practice of witchery yet witnessed in history. Metaphysics misrepresents the mouth that consumes. It is rather the preceding historical "moment"—to continue to use Hegel's peculiar matrix here—of more overt "theological battle" that, I would argue, more clearly demarcates the character of the competition. Hegel perhaps represents modern witchcraft's greatest sophistry—that nonetheless remains instructive and brilliant precisely for its analytical density. But his erudition is given a reverse charge of potency when it is hooked to the supposedly naïve knowledge of an African question about power: not "what" is wrong with me, but "who"? Who is behind the demise? In this sense, witchcraft discourse reverses the "fetishism of commodities" that Marx so elaborately mapped out in *Kapital*.

African diagnosis applied to European practice asks of modernity: Why do Africans die early and often (of war, of wanton violence, of AIDS, of disease, of starvation, etc.) whereas (relatively speaking) Europeans die late and slowly? It expects an answer that is rooted in a subjective intention. African witchcraft culture suspects early illness and death to be the work of an enemy, not the mysterious outcome of an arbitrarily discriminating "nature." European belief fetishizes subjectivity as an "object," explains social condition as individual choice, reads the "slow death" of impoverished unemployment and the "living death" of wage slavery as the victim's own failure to compete. To grasp this wild efflorescence of the impulse to fetishize, it is necessary to go back behind the Enlightenment's reputed disenchantments to the depth-work accomplished in European ritual activity.

## Supremacist Liturgy

The first moment of sustained encounter between European commerce and African culture was profoundly liturgical. From the beginning of the competitive project of conquest and colonization, the wholesale expropriation and plundering of non-European cultures had to be underwritten in a manner that secured both its presumed *legitimacy* inside the still broadly shared intra-European Christian worldview and its projected *superiority* inside the cultures of the colonized. Christian theological categories, of course, supplied the initial construct, in which the primary question was one of salvation: are these newfound "creatures" capable of embracing the faith and thus of proving themselves "human," like Europeans are human? (Omi and Winant, 61–64 White, 160–164). Or are they merely "human-appearing," but in theological truth only beasts of burden intended by the Creator for European use? (Dussel, 54–55). The debate raged in rhetoric all around Europe but was never in serious doubt on the ground in the colonies or in the slave trade.

Indeed the *Requerimiento* read out loud to Amerindian populations in a language they couldn't understand, demanding that they instantly embrace Christ and submit to the kings of Spain or Portugal, or suffer the consequences of a Just War that would be thereby unleashed against them, actually "effected" a liturgical consignment of all *indigenes* to subhuman status, while legitimizing, in the European legal order, conquest of their land (Mills, 22; Wessels, 60). And in the slave trade along the coasts of Africa, such a legal ruse was not even necessary. The rituals of exchange, incarceration, and transport were themselves "proof" of the "appropriateness" of the (enslaved) condition (much as a "bent back" was proof for Aristotle, in his day, that a slave was such "by nature"). Theological assessment quickly invested itself in epidermal appearances both light and dark. Christian supremacy gave birth to white supremacy. Indigenous religious practice, in both the Americas and Africa, was frequently "divined" as a demonically inspired "black art."

The race discourse that emerges from such a charge of witchcraft, however, gets entangled in its own taunt. African practice and appearance emerge historically as the test case of European liturgy: they present Europe with its most "disturbing" negotiation of difference and consequently bear the most radical forms of theological condemnation. But the "blackness" that is conjured in all the various rituals of differentiation and denigration does not simply stay put on its object. Or at least that is my argument. Reading the theological charge of sorcery from within the idiom of projection itself yields an interesting comparison.

For instance, traditional African witchcraft discourse is a mode of accusation about misfortune caused to an other by a supposed witch. Early modern European race discourse, on the other hand, can be understood as a mode of accusation about misfortune "caused" to oneself by resisting God (Bastide, 272). The dark hues of African skin were fairly quickly interpolated in European theological schemas as a "sign"—on the surface of the body—of a heart unwilling immediately to convert to Christ upon hearing the gospel (Bastide, 281). Swarthy appearance signified a "black" heart. "Blackness" as a term, in Spanish or Portuguese (or later Dutch, French, English, etc.), may or may not have been explicitly used in any given instance, but its symbolic implications were made to stick like hot tar. Those implications partook deeply of a theological discourse on the demonic. The initial evaluation of dark skin associated it with an illicit domain of spirits whose character was presumed to be dangerous and aggressive (Bastide, 281).

In comparison with something like contemporary *tfu* discourse, however, early race discourse works by surreption. Rather than leveling a charge of de facto aggression toward another, it operates its accusation by way of a two-fold implication: the imputation of a *threat* of aggression toward another (i.e., the fear that African witchcraft would be turned upon European colonizers) and the imputation of a *fact* of aggression toward oneself (the culpability implied in resisting God, signified in the darkness that has taken over the bodily surface). Along these same lines, witchcraft discourse explicitly imagines (and witch "confessions" sometimes confirm) the use of a poison, charm, spell, and the like that effects the erosion and disease that finally kills. It implies the mobilization of a materialized form of curse that itself "causes" the cursedness to happen. Interestingly, early

European race discourse can similarly be imagined as the mobilization of a curse—in this case, one that in fact *does* become explicitly formalized as just that, in the "Curse of Ham" mythology that European Christianity predicated as the theological explanation for the "darkness" of African skin. But this was a curse with a difference. The predication of implied blackness, in effect, materialized its spell not in an exterior object that eroded well-being but in an *objectification of skin* as a *cursed object*. The discourse itself accomplishes the spell/curse it names so that the flesh can be "eaten" with impunity.

The complex of attraction/fear such a theological predication "knots up together" is a multilayered tangle. It can be teased out as (1) a European perception of "Africans eating each other," (2) a European fear of "Europeans being eaten by their African other," which (3) coagulate together into the European imagination of "blackness as witchcraft" that becomes the rationale for "European consumption of African substance" (in slave and wage labor and plundering of African resources). The effect of such a predication is to lock Africans up in a domain of "blackness eating itself" that displaces awareness of the real history of consumption the projection underwrites and carries out in the first place. It is even tempting to say that, in this complex projection of witchcraft, whiteness bewitches itself, mislabeling Western metabolism of Africa as "saving and civilizing," while mythologizing Africans under the cover of a blackness that both hides and effects the "project of devouring" that is the real meaning of whiteness. In this compass, European liturgy and African sorcery constitute a difference not in religious kind but in degree of rapacity. The first frontier of historical encounter between Europe and Africa is a theater of occult combat, a labor of competing witchcrafts, organized by a virulent new discourse of malaise. The "supremacy" of white over black that is made to emerge from the encounter is finally one of appetite.

But the ritual combat thus apostrophized is complexly contradictory. Cress Welding's comment on Christian communion cited above becomes interesting to think with in this regard. It is possible to imagine European eucharistic celebration in the late Middle Ages as effecting a bivalent symbolic structure. The immediately available sign is that of white European Christian eating the saving flesh of a savior whose features have been Europeanized. But underneath that surface level is an "other" meaning-structure, which after 1492 begins to signify with a new, unrecognized potency. The memory of Jesus as Middle Eastern Jew—likely swarthy-featured and dark-haired—and the stories of his childhood exile to and education in Egypt (while Herod waged infanticide in Palestine proper) would have still been alive in the culture—both in gospel narrations and in iconographic representations. The symbolic structure of such a late medieval eucharistic celebration, however, would have been immediate consciousness of "light-skinned communicant consuming light-skinned Christ." But only partially erased underneath that surface significance is the elided idea of "white believer eating dark body." This double feature of the central ritual of late medieval Europe is a veritable pedagogy in the requirements of the modern slave trade. It both augurs and hides its own witchery inside its symbology of interaction with the divine.

But another layer of this symbolic conflation of racialization and consumption becomes evident from a post-Enlightenment vantage point. As we have already been investigating, in later moments of modernity, European perceptions of Africa identified it as the continent of the cannibal. The fear found echoed in the boy on the Parisian street reacting to Frantz Fanon's presence simply came clean with its most primal expression. It was a fear of *being* eaten. European contact with African populations, throughout the modern era, consistently demonstrates terror of miscegenation and mongrolization, as indicated above. Fear of being devoured by blackness is a primary coordinate of the modern European psyche, even if—*especially* if—repressed under a more "civilized" veneer of awareness.

Combined, then, these two symbolic structures present a veritable Gordian knot. The theological moment in the history of European relations with Africa would have partaken of both medieval liturgical "forgetting" and this repressed European imaginary arising from the slave trade. The immediate consciousness of a "drive to save and civilize" riding on top of a deeper ambivalence about "who is really eating whom" would give emblematic representation to the alchemic working of Euro-Christian liturgy during the early phase of contact and enslavement. The fear is an inchoate one of being eaten by blackness. The deep-text of the "eucharistic sacrifice"—underneath the tamer version of white believer eating the "whitened" flesh of a hero-savior—is actually "white believer eating black saving body." The actual social process is European consumption of African substance in slavery.

The fundamental ambivalence emerging in the act of consuming the other is interiorized and hidden. "Eating the other" has as its almost inevitable reflex effect the terror of "being eaten *by* the other." The complex is perhaps better understood in witchcraft terms than in "rational" debate about racial characteristics. Early modern European Christian sacramentality can be characterized as a form of witch-combat, hiding its voraciousness under the banner of "whitened" skin, sublimating its own witchery as an act of civility, bewitching the witch itself. "Blackness" is complexly ramified as the theological symbol of witchery incarnate, the open maw of unrestrained cannibalism. While in the "forgetting" of deep repression, whiteness is made to incarnate a merely delicate taste for the refined wafer of salvation.

Over time, after the break-up of Catholic Europe in the Refor-mation and the resulting bloodbath of the Thirty Years War, Reason is made the watchword of practice in European self-understanding. What began as a theological "discernment" of African spirituality as sorcery, is buried in Enlightenment categories of Being, taxonomized in the ever-flexing "Great Chain," even as real chains reinforce the ontology in a ruthless sociology. White theological supremacy, we might say, successfully fetishized "blackness" as a negative power of "possession" and placed it "in" the African body like a magic "spirit-chain," rendering it vulnerable and available for sacrifice to the new suppos-edly "scientific" project of global commerce. Here blackness emerges as a cipher working a mysterious density of significance: as philosophical taxonomy, it explains European supremacy in empirical terms; as theo-logical symbology, it is hidden as the inchoate "felt terror" of witchery.

Whiteness, on the other hand, is increasingly a category of distance and deception, a veritable incarnation of denial, consciousness without a body, eating the body of its chosen witch, while "witching" its own eating "out of mind." It is a mindless eating, understanding itself as a bodiless mind. In the political economy of the modern slave trade and its continuation as the globalizing system of white supremacist capital, its body is the "blackness" it metabolizes as its own white flesh.

## Race Discourse as White Witchcraft

What Mills calls, as a critique of modern social contract theory, "the Racial Contract," I am underscoring, out of its historical emer-gence, as a white witch-pact. It creates an in-group of flesh consumers, who share a secretive power/knowledge designated, gradually over time and occasionally in experience (when the necessity to specify the contrast irritatingly presents itself), as "whiteness." It is, in fact, on its own terms, a form of "theological blackness" or witchery, rewritten as ontology and anthropology. But this pact operates with peculiarity. In the dissimulation of modern white supremacy, it is racial *discourse* itself that is the witchcraft *practice*. That is not quite the same as saying race discourse is witchcraft "discourse." Race discourse organizes a material object (dark skin) as a spiritual curse/spell/erosion. Compared to indigenous forms of witchcraft practice still extant in Africa, it represents a shift from a nonverbal manipulation of an object for the sake of "sacrificing" and securing the flesh of an other, to a *verbal* manipulation effecting the same result. Of course, as discussed above in Bongmba's work, we do not know if or how actual flesh is consumed in indigenous practice, but only that such may become an accusation/explanation when people die. With white supremacist practice, however, we do know that the flesh *is* consumed (in slave and wage labor), and we know *how it is secured* (by military force, institutional discrimination, cultural normalization, etc.).

While I agree fully with Mills when he argues that we must recognize the historical propensity of the Racial Contract to rewrite itself to accommodate new needs for its white-identified signatories, and thus must understand that its real payoff is the securing of whiteness over-against non-whiteness, I am *also* arguing that we do not fully appreciate race discourse if we let its bottomline category of "blackness" disappear in the more general and encompassing term "non-white." It is only with respect to Africa that the deep character of racialization as witchery comes clear. It is not merely a matter of whiteness securing its plunder by way of a "firebreak" predicated between itself and non-whites, but the chain of associations put in operation through the category/meaning "blackness." Its first valence was theological and dense with demonic significance. That such numinosity gets hidden in the Enlightenment "turn to reason" does not mean its visceral evocation disappears. A simple glance, for instance, at KKK lynchings reveals the degree to which the entire domain of race, even in the twentieth century, remains a mythic idiom demanding ritual prosecution. It was never enough "merely" (!) to destroy the black body; its imagined threat was dealt with in terms of the "blood-sacrament" of castration. The "felt need" was profoundly fetishistic.

Whiteness, under the veneer of its "heavenly" pallor, is a great grinding witch-tooth, sucking blood and tearing flesh without apology. It is interesting that in post-contact Africa, the means for detecting and "outing" witches is by way of catching them in a mirror. I would argue, witchcraft itself is the mirror in which whiteness must be caught.

It is also possible to periodize the metaphor historically. Where indigenous practice of witchcraft is understood to involve the consumption of "dead" flesh, the slavery of early modernity (1) opens a new "after-death" prospect: the *zombi* state, the living cannibalization of commercial capital, flesh not so much as food-for-thought but as gold-for-trade. In the industrial phase, (2) whiteness shifts its modality of consumption to that of the machine: flesh as "dead labor" in Marx's phrase, the *zombi* rendered bionic, the massive and mysterious transubstantiation of laboring flesh into grinding metal. In so-called late capitalism, (3) the move is to the modality of information, the postmodern magic of transmogrifying flesh into digit. But, at heart, the consumption continues to metabolize real muscle.

In sum, modern commerce mobilizes a white death-grin to hide its traffic in "blackened" substance. What is talked about indigenously in the idiom of ritual is routinized and "rationalized" in modern practice—first by way of the shackle, then in the form of gear-boxes and axles, and, finally, in postindustrial sophistication, as a mere pixel. The mouth opens ever wider while the packaging and storage of the flesh-to-be-feasted is ever narrowed. In African witchcraft, human health is devoured as an object of ritual. In modern race-craft, human substance is delineated as an object of discourse. Physical masticulation is supposedly overcome in metaphysical matriculation. What has really happened is merely patent: an economy of flesh has been made the flesh of the economy.

## Excursus

The depths revealed/concealed in the palimpsest-like operation of the eucharistic sacrament (as a kind of "*Ur*-text" of Christian practice) are adumbrated in the work of Historian of Religions Charles Long. Long's labor to expose the difference between Western and indigenous apprehensions of divinity in the colonial encounter around the globe makes use of Rudolph Otto's experientially oriented phrase for ultimate reality, the *mysterium tremendum et fascinosum*. Otto's concern in the first part of the twentieth century was to try to escape theologically loaded language in doing comparative work on religious traditions around the globe. Otto theorized that cultures across the globe bear witness to an "ultimate mysteriousness" operating in human life that seems to be apprehended in a double experience. It is sometimes alluring and attractive, and other times terrifying and repulsive, and the mystery "irrupts" in such a way that neither experience can entirely be resolved into the other. For Otto, this double formulation captured the essence of Christian as well as non-Christian experience.

But Otto's mantra all to the good, it is arguable that in medieval European liturgy, the second element of this apprehension was gradually repressed. The older premonition of God as not only the great Wooer of Hearts (much less as the great Reason in the Sky later imagined by the Enlightenment), but as also inscrutable and terrifying *Tremendum*, dying in a grotesque execution ritual, had been buried under the surface of the liturgy. For instance, early Christian art shied away from depiction of the Crucifixion—perhaps not only because of apologetics (a desire to appeal to educated Roman elites), but also because the "scene of torture" got too close to a more archaic and disturbing intuition: "Sometimes, God seems simply to devour!" (This latter perception could be said to be the basic meaning of the scripture text memorializing Jesus' final scream from the cross: "my God, my God, why have you forsaken me!?" [Mk. 15. 33–39].) In the practice of a Christianity that was still outlawed and persecuted prior to Constantine, the eucharistic symbolics would perhaps have mediated something closer to the ambivalence Otto notes in terms of (1) a subtext of God as the Great Precipitous Horror that Devours, overlaid with (2) the open text of God as the Great Hero Who is Willing to be Devoured.

### The God Who is Devoured in Jesus (The God Who Devours Jesus)

But by the time Europe emerges, in the high Middle Ages, out of its own "dark night" of threatened extinction at the hands of a highly organized and sophisticated Islam, the text has swallowed the subtext. The ritualized structure of medieval Christian consciousness has "transubstantiated" the threat of the *Tremendum* into the Fascination of the sacramental "body and blood." There is no extant imagery for God grasped as "devourer" that is iconically figured or ritually remembered in the Christian tradition of the scholastics or the reformers. Unlike say, Hinduism's mother figure, Kali, mainstream Roman and later Protestant representations of God present One who is unambiguously "good."

Undoubtedly some of the repression involved in this process of "iconographic domestication" finds its motive force in the recodification of anti-imperial resistance as imperial conformity and the gradual incorporation of a prophetic movement of slaves and peasants into a ruling class hegemony. The ferocious God of Moses and Ezekiel, of John and Jesus, had to be reformulated as the very image of Roman aristocracy. The Backer of Revolting Laborers, the Angry Author of

Exilic Upheaval, the Chopper of the Tree of Genealogy, the Closed-mouth Father Watching the Son "Fry" on Cosmic Prime Time was "transfigured" into the soft crumbling bread of bowing believers, the paper-thin host of a blessed adoration. The ideological eclipse of terror and its epiphanies of resistance was a fait accompli by the time modernity began "showing" in the womb of Europe.

That bloody birth finds its augury in premodern Spain. Castilian Christian triumph over the Muslim "menace" in the 700-year-long *Reconquista* of Spain gave rise to a ferocity of selective forgetting. After "eating" its way through Moorish culture and cult, Spanish Christian identity emerges as a modality of occultation. The ambivalent and inarticulate *pathos* that Columbus and crew carry West is rife with passion remembered and unremembered. It is ripe for the ritual grotesqueries of the slavery it will underwrite. Analysis of such by way of Otto introduces an interesting caveat into the canon of European colonization. A certain "seductive" longing masks a practice of "terrible" severity.

But it is Long who most compellingly conjures the consequence. Long takes up Otto's aphorism and breaks open its binarism on the hard rock of colonial violence to underscore a radical difference of experience between Europe and its others (Long, 1986, 123, 137–139).

Western culture, in this perspective, lives its mythology of itself in the mode of *fascination*—a relentless quest of curiosity violently crossing and crisscrossing the surface of the globe in search of conquerable and exploitable space, an equally relentless (and profoundly interrelated) resolve to reengineer nature into ever-more fascinating surfaces of consumption. (It is interesting in this regard to think not only of Kant's eighteenth-century metaphysical assertion that we can only ever "know" the phenomenal exteriority of things, not their noumenal essences, but also indeed, today as well, the shift in economics to the marketing of the mere sign of an object—the Nike swoosh or the Hilfiger insignia—as its "real" value.) (Long, 1986, 142).

The rest of the globe, in the process of "undergoing" Westernization—of being violently remade "in the image of" Europe *for* Europe—has been made to experience its utter contingency under the sign of a swiftly descending and completely overwhelming *Terribleness* (Long, 1986, 139, 196–197). It is this latter experience—the unpredictable and inscrutable advent of a depth of disaster that entirely ruptures native categories of local cosmology—that Long comprehends as *Tremendum* (Long, 1986, 142). Reality experienced as Terror, as Indecipherable Nightmare, as the Mystery that Shatters—pushes indigenous cultures into a labor of "knowing" that is unlike anything the West has had to fathom. Native practice ends up having to negotiate—not empirically, but mythically—the cosmos itself as now a form of irresistible violence, a kind of All-Consuming Maw (Long, 1986, 167, 170). In the Christian category of "God" that said populations are increasingly forced to embrace, Divinity must be combated and conciliated as Devouring Opacity.

Long is clear—like Otto—that sudden epiphanies of radical and incomprehensible "terror" (a sudden uncanny sense of "coming apart," a fear of insanity, a "dread" of dismemberment, etc.) are not peculiar to oppressed populations. He notes that modern Western literature regularly circumambulates disturbing "returns" of the contents of repression (Long, 1986, 160, 169). But it is his argument that such experiences *are* peculiarly *figured* in Western expression—they are comprehended as patently "individual" and are dealt with either psychotherapeutically or turned into acclaimed aesthetic productions of "mad" genius (Long, 1986, 165, 169, 170). In modernized societies, the intuition of dissolution is no longer ritualized and worked through in a communal theatrics (Long, 1986, 164). Neither is it given expressive shape in a manner that implicates the real history of violence that it references (Long, 1986, 161).

In Longian terms, then, the entire postcolonial global situation could perhaps be said to reflect a profoundly occulted structure:

for the West : reality is *Fascinosum* : Divinity as What Is Devoured
(for the Rest) (reality is *Tremendum*) (Divinity as Devouring)

The way such a construct signifies on race is ribald. Or perhaps, better said, the way race articulates (and articulates with) such an organization of experience is prodigal. The cross-coding represents a veritable Gordian knot of implication and confusion. The postcolonial complex is thick with delirium. Whiteness is a fantasy-scape; blackness is deep night. White is fascinated with devouring. Black is a gnawed bone of terror. Whiteness is the unconsciously cannibalistic predilection to eat "God"; blackness is the posttraumatic stress syndrome of being eaten by "God." Which "which" is really witch?

# II

# Black Creativity, Shamanic Remedy, and Afro-Polyphony

This section examines the way Afro-diasporic communities, in general, and African American communities, in particular, have taken up the very terms of their own demonization and, in effect, "shamanized" them into modalities of vitality. The work done has generally involved wit and wile elaborated in the "cracks" of the system of domination. Where racialization is largely a discourse of the eye, resistance by blacks has had recourse to tactics of the tongue and echoes of the ear, working rhythm into alternative economies of identity and community.

The opening essay of this section (chapter 3) was first delivered at the 1999 American Academy of Religions Annual Conference for the Mysticism Group and subsequently aired as well at the 1999 Parliament of the World's Religions in Capetown, South Africa. It represented an attempt to take seriously W. E. B. Du Bois's hint, in his famous double-consciousness formulation in *The Souls of Black Folk*, that "second sight" was not only racial affliction but also shamanic gift, in African American experience of the hardness of white American cultural domination. The Afro-folk expression of someone having been "born with a veil or caul" (and thus supposedly endowed with shamanic "insight") is hypostasized by Du Bois in *Souls* as emblematic of the entire condition of being made "black" in America, and is explored in this essay as a counter-therapy to white ocular "incarceration" of the dark body. After surveying and summarizing scholarly writing on shamanism in general, slave conversion narratives are reconstructed as memorializing a shamanistic (and "African") appropriation of Christianity every bit as much as eulogizing a Christian metabolism of slave spirituality. Black preaching, in particular, as well as black tactics of negotiating slavery and racism, in general, are exhibited as a collective force of shamanistic "therapy," forging black skin into a spiritized "cloak" of subterfuge and survival. In so characterizing African American creativity against the grain of racialization and repression, however, the final move will acknowledge that the dismemberment piece of shamanistic experience, in the case of this community, is no trope, but an ongoing condition that has not yet been remedied.

The second essay on Afro-diaspora technologies of sound (chapter 4) was first delivered as a companion piece to the second chapter of this book (on white witchcraft) at the Race and Humanities Conference hosted by the University of Wisconsin in 2001. While it is really the essay on shamanism just described above that mirrors the argument of white supremacy as Euro-sorcery (by reframing black resistance to that aggression as a kind of counter-sorcery or shamanism), the turn to sonic insurgence tracked in this essay marks the distinctively Afro-American modality of resistance that is now remaking Western society in the "image" of its own beat (in a two-centuries long take-over of Western musical tastes by an African aesthetic of polyphony). This essay roots itself in the insight of Charles Long that European colonization was experienced by those colonized as quintessentially religious in that it visited upon them an experience of rupture that cut back all the way to their myth of origin. Not merely the body was violated (by war, disease, forced labor, rape, etc.), but the entire indigenous cosmos was irreparably rent and all the explanatory categories of the native cosmology shattered. Survival of such an experience has demanded—and occasioned—creativity at the level of mythic re-creation. I argue that, in the Afro-diaspora world, this has frequently involved what I call "syncopated tricksterism," a displacement and relativization of the structures of racial domination by way of unanticipated mobilizations of time and timing, precisely at the place of "rupture." The result has been a peculiar kind of initiation, the historical engenderment of a "people of the break," capable of regularly opening out forms of Afro-tranced *kairos* inside Anglo-capitalist *chronos*.

# 3

# The Gift/Curse of "Second Sight"

*Our struggle is the by-product of a deeper calculated systemic condition endemic to American domestic political apathy and a social denial which has poisoned the American psyche since the atomic devastation of Hiroshima and Nagasaki. Ours is not, nor has it ever been, a nation-specific discourse. Our struggle affects the entire planet and everyone on it. And I must see through to this. And so I have grown yet another eye, a primal orb density which provides me constant dual sight.*

—*Wanda Coleman* (Primal Orb Density, 209)

In his 1903 publication called *The Souls of Black Folk*, W. E. B. Du Bois articulates the pain of enduring racial oppression in terms of the affliction of "double-consciousness" that he also describes as the experience of "being born with a veil and gifted with second sight in this American world" (Du Bois, 1961, 16). This latter description ("born with a veil," "gifted with second sight") is itself a veiled reference to being born with a "caul" (or gauzy film covering the eyes) in African American culture—sign of a peculiar shamanistic ability to see beyond the ordinary (Bambara, 310). Much as chapter 2 read European race discourse as a modality of modern witchcraft practice, this chapter will read this famous Du Boisian formula as a poignantly "African" reformulation of the peculiarities of American racialization and its "discontents" as a (modern or even postmodern) mode of shamanic struggle. If shamanism can be theorized as (among other things) a trope pointing to certain kinds of transgressive practices, the negotiation of situations of social contradiction and psychological trauma, in which techniques of ecstasy are solicited to force affliction to yield healing and vitality, then African American transformations of the experience of being made black in

America may be productively examined as a form of shamanic combat. In pursuing such a thesis, however, it is imperative to emphasize that no attempt to make oppression productive should ever be allowed to enervate struggles to eliminate the fact of oppression itself. Indeed, creative appropriation of the conditions of their own suffering exercised by the dominated or exploited is always a sign of warning to those benefiting from such domination/exploitation. What the content of that warning might be is the subject of what follows.

## Shamanism in the Sight of the Academy

Academic attempts to formulate shamanism as a subject of study have found their classic text in Mircea Eliade's articulation of shamanism as an "archaic technique of ecstasy," outlined in his book by that subtitle. For Eliade, shamanism is indicative of a primordial "situation of the human being in the cosmos," borne witness to by the dreams, hallucinations, and images of ascent (or descent) found the world over (Eliade, xiv). It is not a mere historical ideology of oriental origins but rather a phenomenon of the "boundary-line situations" of the species. It demands deciphering from a history of religions perspective, willing to ferret out the "deep meaning" of a "religious phenomenon" whose content is not exhausted in its historical realizations (Eliade, xv). It is part of the lifetime argument of Eliade with modernity that the dialectic of the sacred exhibits archetypal forces in hierophantic appearances that offer structural equivalences to each other across thousands of years of time and miles of space (Eliade, xvii). For him, the manifestation of the sacred in stone or tree is not less mysterious or more ahistorical than its appearance in a god. Indeed, any form, any history, is partial and limited, subject to degradation or inflation, succession or reversal (Eliade, xix). Shamanism, within such a broader argument, is a recurrent phenomenon on the religious horizon of the world, extant in combination with various other elements of particular traditions and cultures but visible as a primal ideology and technology of ecstasy (Eliade, 6).

Eliade delineates and explores the elements constitutive of shamanism in terms of an initiation (and subsequent practice) involving dismemberment of the candidate's body, followed by renewal of the internal organs and viscera, insertion of magical substances into the candidate's body, revelation of religious or shamanic secrets, ascent to the sky and dialogue with the gods or spirits, descent to the underworld to bring back the patient's soul or to escort the dead, evocation and incarnation of ("possession by") the "spirits" in order to undertake the ecstatic journey, magic flight, mastery over fire, consort with animal familiars, and so forth (Eliade, 6, 34, 89, 314, 376). In contradistinction to the priestly role, shamanism, for Eliade, emphasizes the capacity for ecstasy, and contrary to sorcery's antisocial employments, it concentrates on positive social activities (although the lines here are not always clear) (Eliade, 298–299). Altogether, shamanism focuses its energies on a three-fold task of diagnosis, travel, and mastery (of spirits) (Eliade, 243). Travel is generally for the sake of healing—traversing the world axis vertically in ascending a cosmic mountain or tree or in descending through an aperture to the realm of the dead, or moving horizontally across the world sea to a blessed isle or cursed land, to win revelation of a cause or release of a soul (Eliade, 355).

The travel motif itself gives evidence of a commonly found cosmic structure. Myth across the globe remembers (and renders briefly accessible again) a paradisal time "when communication between heaven and earth was possible" (Eliade, 133). All of humanity knew regular contact with the gods, but "in consequence of a certain event or ritual fault, the communication was broken off"; now, only the shamanic figure is able to reestablish the connection through flight or by climbing or moving through an otherwise inaccessible door (Eliade, 133, 265, 480). Whereas in the (imagined) beginning, such universal access was simply part of life, now, the heavenly realm is widely available only through death (Eliade, 480). Shamans, thus, are figures empowered to enjoy death at will (by coming out of the form of the body and flying, usually as birds) (Eliade, 479). They alone "know the mystery of the break-through in plane"—moving between the three levels of sky, earth and underworld by navigating the central axis structuring the universe through their techniques of passage (Eliade, 259).

In connection with the above, Eliade offers that the "trance body" of the shaman, in a sense, homologizes or recapitulates the world-body (Eliade, 408). The bridge previously connecting earth and heaven without obstacle is now reconstructed only via initiation rituals and even then remains fraught with danger, thick with confusion, haunted by demonic guardian figures or monstrous animals seeking to devour whoever would seek to cross over (Eliade, 483). Passage is now possible only "in spirit," by way of actual death or the virtual death of ecstatic trance. Only those who face the peril—whether "heroes" operating by force or shamans via ecstasy or initiates through the wisdom of ritual paradox—traverse the primordial rupture in this life. In any of the cases, the way amounts to passage through a form of death and resurrection.

However, the shaman is one who can construct such a passage repeatedly—by ecstatic technique navigating the space of death him- or herself and by ritual creating the conditions for the possibility for others to dare the venture as well. In realizing (or causing to be realized) this capacity for shape-shifting and transcending time and space, the shaman's own body often becomes a kind of war zone, or a site of combat, with the spirits guarding the terrifying "break in planes" (Eliade, 485, 229). In the process, shamans, in effect, "interiorize" the "cosmology, mythology and theology of their tribes . . . experienc[ing] it, and us[ing] it as the itinerary for their ecstatic journeys" (Eliade, 266).

Anthropologist Joan Halifax elaborates further on the relationship between shamanism and death. The initiatory crisis that opens up the shamanic vocation must necessarily be designated a religious experience in her estimation—perhaps coextensive with the initial awakening of feelings of awe and wonder in primates (Halifax, 1991, 4). Its inception is an accident or severe illness or psychological or spiritual trauma "of such proportions that [the sufferers] are catapulted into the territory of death" (Halifax, 1991, 5). Learning to integrate such experiences of sickness, suffering, dying, and death, shamans in the making learn, as well, "to share the special knowledge of these powerful events with those who face disease or death for the first time" (Halifax, 1991, 5). In some renditions, shamans become observers of their own dismemberment (Halifax, 1991, 13). It is part of the terror of the vocation that such figures will not be able to cure anything "that has not eaten of [their own] flesh" (Halifax, 1991, 14).

At the same time, this experience of initiation intersects with the question of ideology. Halifax insists that the experience does "not represent a rending of the individual from his or her social ground"; rather, it represents a "deepening of the patterns that compose the sacred, ahistorical territory that supports the more superficial and transient aspects of human culture" (Halifax, 1991, 18). In this passage through crisis, "the mythic images woven into a society's fabric suddenly not only become apparent but often enacted and made boldly visible and relevant for all" (Halifax, 1991, 18). The shaman is a figure "balanced between worlds," teaching that trauma can be "a passageway to a greater life where there is access to great power at great risk" (Halifax, 1991, 18). Indeed, the shaman often becomes androgynous, "balancing" or equalizing problematic social roles and creating healing through paradox (Halifax, 1991, 21, 22). The initiatory quest here is one that opens the mystery by "becoming it," transcends death "by dying in life," pierces duality "by embracing opposites," reunites fractured

forms by fashioning oneself as "a double being" (Halifax, 1991, 28).
Halifax offers, among others, the account of one Sereptie whose initiation was conducted by a man who leapt out of the root of a sacred
tree that Sereptie had been commanded by his people to cut down to
make into a sleigh (Halifax, 1991, 38). After traveling through other-
worldly domains and undergoing numerous visionary experiences,
Sereptie is finally left alone at the confluence of all the illnesses devouring humankind where he must submerge himself and either die or
return a shaman, "singing with the throat of nine diseases" (Halifax,
1991, 45, 47). It is there, in that unwanted experience of facing the
most feared thing, that the shaman is "forged" (Halifax, 1991, 44).

The dread usually accompanying such initiations underscores the
element of involuntary selection. Halifax notes, for instance, that the initiatory ordeal most frequently comes on suddenly, "through the action of
total disruption" (Halifax, 1982, 10; Levy, 43). In the useful solicitation
of these comments by art historian Mark Levy to uncover the
shamanic sensibility of some modern artists, the suddenness marks out
a certain terrible elucidation (Levy, 45). Among Levy's "artist-
shamans," Frida Kahlo emerges as perhaps most true to the form in
virtue of the bus accident (at age nineteen), and subsequent thirty-two
operations to slow the deterioration of her skeletal system that transformed her life from typical upper-middle class Mexican teenager to
painter of a precise psychic terrain of great pain and terrifying solitude
(Levy, 43, 49). Celebrated at one point in her career by surrealism's
founder, Andre Breton, as painting "pure surreality," Kahlo responded
with harsh clarity: "they thought I was a Surrealist, but I wasn't. I
never painted dreams. I painted my own reality" (Breton 144; Herrera,
49; Levy, 49). Her "monumental realism," in the opinion of her artist-
husband, Diego Rivera—offering tiny heads on a miniature scale that
was nonetheless "colossal," and sculpting veins and cells as if her interior
was at the same time the exterior of the world—represented not
narcissism, but concreteness (Herrera, 260; Levy, 49–50). In the single
instant of the accident, the world had become old for her, devoid of
secrets, transparent as ice, a painful planet divulging everything to
her at once (Herrera, 75; Levy, 45). Thereafter, her perception was
informed by the "advice of death (Castaneda, 35; Levy, 46). "Shamanic
seeing," in this modern instance, refused modernity's fetishism of
individual choice and intruded itself with horrific irresistibility.

Accommodation between shamanism and individualism, however,
may well point to the future. Stephen Larsen is one scholar of shamanism
who tries to work this out. Building on the works of others like Eliade

and Joseph Campbell, Larsen seeks to address the impulse in modern Western "civilization" to deal with the mythic consciousness of the Middle Ages that would banish myth from history and "never dream again" (Larsen, 4). Larsen is convinced that the new agenda is to work out a reciprocity between consciousness and myth that privileges neither mythic "possession" (or its religionized counterpart, "mythic orthodoxy") nor scientific objectivity (or its spiritualized counterpart, "yogic renunciation") (Larsen, 42). For him, "the force that has been so perennially active throughout human history, informing [human] perception of the world and subtly shaping [our] every dealing with it, is being and must be withdrawn from the theater of history and relocated in the pysche" (Larsen, 6). The error of modernity has been to try to deal with this force "in its formless aspect" as "pure power and meaning" (Larsen, 34). The world of terror and ecstasy given articulation in the vocabularies of myth may indeed have been delusion, but within that madness a kernel of method must be discerned (Larsen, 44–45). The shaman, although not merely a "dressed-up schizophrenic or hysteric," does share with those more pathological responses a deep structural relationship to the psyche (Larsen, 60). Dreams and visions, illnesses and pathologies alike share a common need: they demand, even if only briefly, a moment's realization in "tangible, solid form" within the field of time and space (Larsen, 116). The shaman is the specialist who "ensures that the doorway be kept open, that vision may seek enactment" (Larsen, 117).

In outlining his approach, Larsen arranges West and East in a certain counterbalance. Where the East is not afraid to confront the human being with ultimate reality in its form as absolute terror—Brahman poised like a thunderbolt to enlighten; Shiva dancing terrible and marvelous, at once god of destruction and patron of yoga—the West also offers a necessary element (Larsen, 136, 152, 156). Liberation of the self requires "the cooperation of that aspect of the psyche which is ontologically *other*, not simply an extension of one's own will" or an accident of *maya* (Larsen, 156). Here, shamanic negotiation rather than yogic renunciation is apposite. In its "technique for relating to, rather than vanquishing, the living substance of one's psyche . . . the shaman's symbolic dialogue with mythic beings and events preserves the idea that there is a positive virtue, a magic in the forms of *maya's* dreams" (Larsen, 157). By way of a summary quote of Campbell, Larsen affirms that it is with "irony and grace, not fierce daemonic compulsion," that the "same psychological energies that were formerly in the capture of the compelling images" can "take the images in capture" and be deployed for "life's enrichment" (Larsen, 232).

But just here there is capitulation to a certain unrecognized privilege of position as shown by ecofeminist professor of literature Gloria Orenstein. Orenstein comes away from four and a half years of study with Sami (Norwegian) shaman Ellen Maret with a strong conviction that white Westerners dare study shamanism in indigenous cultures only if keenly aware of the ethical demands of their actions. For her, shamanism is not simply generic across cultures but takes on specific features in relationship to the local culture and place (Orenstein, 174). Indigenous folklore, indigenous ancestral lineage, and the floral and faunal potencies and agencies of the local ecology all require careful study and maximal openness and respect (Orenstein, 175). Not only "spirit journeys to the otherworld" but also political journeys in this one, not only "out of body" visitations with spirits on other planes, but also real-animal embodiments ("of spirit") here and now, must be entertained (Orenstein, 176). Among the Sami, for instance, mosquitoes have become dearly loved not only as protectors of Sami lands from white encroachment and takeover, but also as literal guides and messengers (Orenstein, 187). Against New Age trivialization and dilettantism, Orenstein cautions that shamanism is no less precise or dangerous a venture than surgery is in the West, and requires knowledge not only of how to call forth spirit energies but also how to guard against and dismiss unwanted or harmful incursions (Orenstein, 178). At the same time, exoticizing and romanticizing tribal shamanisms in a search for ready-to-hand "cross-cultural archetypes" leads easily to stereotypical images of such cultures and disregard for real suffering that Western contact has imposed or even that shamans themselves are capable of causing (Orenstein, 179). Orenstein also cautions against imposing Western feminist gender role expectations on indigenous patterns or reading a kind of "macho shamanism" practiced by indigenous females in such a way as to erase the real effects of either indigenous or Western patriarchy (Orenstein, 184). Likewise, Orenstein notes her own difficulties in avoiding reproducing subtle forms of racist superiority even in her attempts not to retaliate when threatened or assaulted by drunk Sami males (Orenstein, 185). Orenstein also argues for a recognition that indigenous forms of shamanism may not differentiate political and spiritual uses of shamanic power, or may equally respond to dreams of "lay persons" as to "professional" shamans (Orenstein, 188). At heart, Orenstein is savvy about the need to guard against one more gesture of appropriation and commercialization of indigenous creativity (Orenstein, 189). Benefit received from indigenous shamanic practices should be foregone unless one can return the benefit in the form of contributing to that culture's survival.

## Shamanistic Insight in the Midst of Slavery

Orenstein's work, in particular, raises questions about the politics of shamanism in a modern social order that has suppressed its own indigenous expressions of shamanic healing and then, unable to live with its own rational disenchantments of the world, has turned to the peoples it has subdued in its colonial takeover of the world for shamanic redress. Such gestures of appropriation point to a peculiarity of modern forms of colonial domination that themselves may well force a kind of shamanistic "initiation" onto the peoples they dominate. For our purposes here, that question of initiation will be focused in relationship to the colonial enterprise of American slavery and its postcolonial offspring of racism and racialization. The reconstructions of slave conversion experiences found in Clifton H. Johnson's *God Struck Me Dead: Voices of Ex-Slaves* supply a first hint of the possible correlation. Very often, the narrative recitations of the ex-slaves recount an experience of death and rebirth suggestive of shamanistic travel and travail. Consider the following:

> When God struck me dead with his power I was living on Fourteenth Avenue. It was the year of the Centennial. I was in my house alone, and I declare unto you, when his power struck me I died. I fell on the floor flat on my back. I could neither speak nor move, for my tongue stuck to the roof of my mouth; my jaws were locked and my limbs were stiff. In my vision I saw hell and the devil. I was crawling along a high brick wall, it seems, and it looked like I would fall into a dark, roaring pit. I looked away to the east and saw Jesus. He called to me and said, "Arise and follow me.". . . We traveled on east in a little, narrow path and came to something that looked like a grape-arbor. (Johnson, 59)

The account goes on to describe a visitation with God, being given "a through ticket from hell to heaven," seeing herself ("in the spirit") going to church, not fully obeying the vision and getting sick until she finally cooperated. Another account tells of getting "heavy one day and beg[inning] to die," being unable to eat or sleep, a light coming down from heaven and splitting the subject "open from my head to my feet," lying dumb and paralyzed, hearing moaning and getting up to travel not as her "natural self but [as] a little angel, journeying straight through fire and hearing the voice of God" (Johnson, 61–62). Yet another recounts hearing a dead person speak and becoming herself a "big-headed beast," being told she must die, watching "little Mary come out of old Mary and [standing] looking down on old Mary lying at hell's dark door," traveling east, being chased by a pack of dogs and "blowed at" by long-horned cows, until finally a voice answers on the inside of her in the same tone as those speaking on the outside and she gradually comes, "through the spirit" in many subsequent travels, to see the "meaning of the thicket briars, the snakes, the dogs, and the cows"—namely, that "they were [her] enemies" (Johnson, 63–64). Story after story of conversion speaks of the necessity or reality of dying, followed by traveling both to hell and to heaven accompanied by spirit-guides (usually in the form of little men), hearing voices, seeing this-worldly phenomena (including the convert's own comatose or "dead" body) from the "otherworld," and eventually returning healed, changed, and subject to future such "travels." Often the visionary travels entail encounter with various animals that terrify or, in some cases, bring messages ( Johnson, 124, 149). And strikingly, again and again, testament is offered to being "split," seeing oneself in "two parts" or "two bodies"—the old self lying dead observed from the vantage point of one's new "spirit-self" ( Johnson, 63, 100, 143, 148, 149, 151, 168).

Theologian Riggins Earl, Jr. culls this material to argue that, in effect, such conversion experiences led slaves to create a profoundly distinct new identity for themselves "inside" of the master's use of Christianity as a discourse of domination. Here, for Earl, is where what Du Bois will later formulate as "double-consciousness" first begins to emerge (Earl, 174). This form of nascent "slave awareness" involves two critical emphases that not only correlate with, but also extend, the shamanistic paradigm. On the one hand, in keeping with the implicit Hegelian theme of "recognition by an other" running through Du Bois's later rendition of the double-consciousness idea, Earl notes that the slaves make a shift from seeing themselves through the eyes of the master to seeing themselves through the eyes of a significant other. In conversion, that other is Jesus Christ, who enables the converted slave to see the "old dead self" through the eyes of a "new revealed self" (Earl, 174, 164). (In folk stories, the other is the imaginary trickster Brer Rabbit, while in ex-slave autobiographies, it is the imaginary free citizen.) While double-consciousness before conversion is a form of debilitating affliction—a looking down upon oneself through the gaze of the dominator—after conversion, it emerges as a "gift" (for Du Bois later, as the "gift of second sight"). Slave conversion parallels shamanistic initiation in affording not only visionary insight and flight *into* the realm of death, but also indeed, visionary insight *from* that realm back into the "living" realm to view the slave's old body as now dead and no longer a constraint. And this very emphasis on subjectivity as constituted through the gaze of another opens up the second area of emphasis. In almost every narrative of conversion, what is revised is the slave view of the self as body. The place or role of the body in these shamanic-like visions of the slaves is somewhat unique.

Earl is clear that, for slaves, the issue in conversion is one of overcoming "oppressive anthropological dualism" by revising one's relationship to one's body as the master's property (Earl, 175). For Earl, the lived awareness "I belong to my master" is tantamount to the confession "I am my master's body"—a merely "subordinate extension of the master's being and will" (Earl, 174). Double-consciousness as a positive critical awareness emerges only when the slave can say emphatically "I am my [own] body." Only when the victim refuses any longer to see the body in a detached fashion does the oppressive dichotomy between body and mind—between the "self as felt selfhood" and the "self as willing and thinking selfhood"—begin to be overcome (Earl, 175). And that overcoming itself is the beginning of a dialectical awareness. For the slave, it is a matter of becoming a "center of one's world experience" by living the creative tension of "having a body" (that remains the property of the master) and "being a body" (as a "recognizable incarnate feeling, willing, and thinking project" of one's own) (Earl, 175).

At the core of Earl's project is a concern to exhibit the ways in which "the theological question of the nature of the slave's being" continually exercised the imaginations of Christian slave masters (Earl, 10). For him, it is abundantly evident from the literature that whites struggled continuously to reconcile their own religious convictions with the anthropological implications of the institution of slavery. For Christian slave masters, the enslavement of Africans could never be merely an economic or political problem. It was rather a "social problem that required their ethical and theological engagement" (Earl, 10). In displaying the anthropological problematic at the core of the ongoing struggle for legitimacy, Earl offers two "antithetical ideal type responses" of Christian masters and their theological apologists.

In what he calls "the soulless-body type of response," slaves of African descent were believed to be devoid of souls altogether (Earl, 5). Physical blackness was interpreted as a metaphysical sign of internal depravity (Earl, 13). The lack of transparent skin pointed to the impossibility of revelation in or to a black soul. Such creatures could not function as "self-determining moral agents": at best, as a "lower species," slaves could only imitate white masters (Earl, 13). In its most cynical versions, this anthropology of slavery implied a natural inferiority that was uneducable and relegated the slave to mere utilitarian value in an agrarian labor market (Earl, 11).

For some slaveholders, however, such a response was both too cynical to be consistent with a Christian worldview and too crass to be politically useful "against the antislavery adversaries of the North" (Earl, 15). The resulting response in this case is what Earl calls "the bodiless-soul type." Part of the picture here was the doctrine of manifest destiny, the "belief that God had called white men to enslave the bodies of black[s] for the purpose of saving their souls" (Earl, 5). The unchangeable blackness of the slave's body continued to signify "the demonic," but theologically, the Christian master affirmed that the slave's soul was made in the image of God (Earl, 15). Such a soul could shed its blackness in the blood of Jesus, which cleansed as "white as snow" even though the body remained anthropologically ambiguous from a biblical point of view. The dichotomy proved difficult to maintain, but for the duration of the institution of slavery, it did allow masters to pursue the Christianization of their slaves' souls while continuing to submerge their bodies in the commodity form.

Further apologetic labors attempted to locate African inferiority in the economy of salvation. In some versions of the second (bodiless-soul) type of response, Africans were understood to have been created inferior from the beginning. In others, they were deemed to have "fallen" out of their original equality with whites by disobeying Noah during the flood (they were, thus, "twice-fallen," according to Earl) (Earl, 27). But in either case, whites measured African being by their own definitions of humanity, and in both versions, white superiority also meant white duty. As Earl notes of the preaching of Bishop Meade of Virginia: "masters could not neglect the souls of their slaves without doing negative damage to themselves spiritually" (Earl, 31). Manifest destiny cut two ways at once: "the soul salvation of the white Christian was invariably intertwined with the soul salvation of the slave" (Earl, 35).

While it is beyond the purposes of this chapter to get into the creative counterresponses of slaves to this bifurcation of the soul and body in white anthropologies of blackness, it is worth noting again Earl's understanding of double-consciousness. For him, it begins in slave experiences of the recovery of their bodies out of the white demonization of blackness. This becomes particularly clear and cogent in Earl's discussion of slave conversion experiences. The narratives of conversion offer a tripartite codification of that experience. The authenticity of slave conversion was said to hinge on "having felt God's power," "seen the travel of one's soul," and "tasted God's love." Earl is clear on the role of discourse in the conversion experience: "It was through this mode of language that slaves experienced having their ontological status radically changed" (Earl, 52).

At the center of the conversion drama, as noted above, was the metaphorical language of "having been struck dead by the Spirit of God" (Earl, 53). The dialectic of Jesus' death and resurrection was (shamanistically?) appropriated from the master's religion as the template on which was cast the slave experience of being struck dead and traveling in spirit to the timeless places of hell and heaven in a form of dream-consciousness. According to Earl, this dream-consciousness was understood in the slave community as a "metaphysical gift from God." It "placed the one experiencing conversion outside of the temporal self for the purpose of turning the universe of oneself and one's fellow human beings into objects of contemplation" (Earl, 53). It conferred on slaves a critical perspective from beyond the point of death. This experience of "dream-travel" radically dissociated slaves "from the untruthful structures of plantation time and space" and from being "perceived as mere objects of their master's gaze" (Earl, 52, 55). Instead, the slave-converts suddenly experienced a form of "subject–object awareness independent of the master's authority," saw their old self as dead at "hell's dark door," and witnessed a new self emerging out of the old as a "little angel" (Earl, 52, 57, 60). They moved through a form of bodily paralysis, in which motor and verbal skills were experienced as temporarily suspended, accompanied by a kind of unexplainable "fear of being," into a "call-response" dialogue with their heavenly tour guide, and finally into a new form of embodied self in which they could faithfully recite the slave formula, "I looked at my hands and they looked like new; I looked at my feet and they did too" (Earl, 58–59). This entire rite of passage is summed up by Earl as the "birth of positive double-consciousness" that freed the slave "temporally from the hegemonic world of the master" (Earl, 54, 60).

What is especially interesting in Earl's reading of Du Bois's double-consciousness idea back into the slave context is the way it articulates a visionary struggle over a question of embodiment In such a retrojection, the idea of double-consciousness is simultaneously linked implicitly with the dualistic structure of a dominant discourse (in white anthropologies of slavery) and explicitly linked with forms of narrative emancipation from that structure (in slave conversion stories in which they consciously appropriate their own doubling). Narrative, here, is the mode of both domination and its overcoming, but it is narrative about forms of embodiment and the meaning of the body inside of its "formation." It is striking—from the perspective of the shamanistic paradigm—that while so much of the material in the slave conversion narratives echoes shamanistic accounts of initiation from other contexts, the one feature that seems to be missing there is explicit talk about dismemberment. The position being explored in this essay is not that the experience of enslavement "is" necessarily an instance of "shamanistic initiation" (whatever that would mean), but rather that shamanistic initiation (and subsequent experience) can perhaps productively signify on the deep structure of slavery and racism. There is, thus, no necessary reason dismemberment should appear in slave conversion accounts. But it is also easy to read this element of shamanism into the situation. The ongoing material violence of enslavement really (physically, psychologically, and socially) dismembered and recomposed the slave body in everyday practice. The tactical forces of dismemberment and discipline inherent in the institution of slavery itself—surveillance, the whip, the shackle, the diet, the work, and (in the case of female slaves) the master's penis—in effect created a collective condition of initiation, indiscriminately "baptizing" the whole group in what sociologist Orlando Patterson has called a mode of "social death" (Patterson, 5). Everyday life was an ongoing and unavoidable initiation into the other world. And indeed "initiation" is precisely the word used by Historian of Religions Charles Long to characterize not only slave experience but also the entire non-Western experience of Western colonialism for 500 years (Long, 1986, 9, 110, 181).

## Shamanistic Insight and the Post-slave Community

Long's work contributes to and informs the question being investigated here in so many ways; the basic theme could almost be said to amount to an inquiry into race and shamanism under tutelage to Charles Long as himself shaman extraordinaire. But such an apostrophe would itself be misleadingly true. Long's work does indeed exercise a kind of relentless "second sight" into academic discourse, uncovering its hidden and incipient violence, its social disease and pirating of soul into the captivations of death. But the relevance of his flights of insight must be allowed to speak without apotheosis.

For Long, history itself is initiation for all of the peoples made to "undergo the West" in centuries of colonial takeover and in the remaking of indigenous culture in terms of scientific (anthropological, economic, philosophical, cartological, political, philological, and indeed, historical) discourse (Long, 1986, 9, 110, 181). The experience was one of continuous rupture, a form of de-construction of indigenous myths of origin that tore open native cultures all the way back to their "primordium," their sense of their initial fall away from wholeness and into pain (Long, 1986, 177). The resulting placement of such peoples "inside" of the West economically, alongside their categorization as irremediably "other" in Western discourses (on the primitive, on the racially inferior, on the religiously superstitious, etc.), meant colonization itself was undergone as a fundamentally "religious" experience. It broke down indigenous codifications of the ultimate such that post-contact "reality" increasingly bore down upon those cultures as inscrutable, overwhelming, and lethal in an absolute sense. "Death" intruded so precipitously, pandemically, and irresistibly in colonial forms of violence that its cultural "grammar" was entirely obliterated. It became an ever-present possibility, ready to fall with unpredictable swiftness, uncontrollable randomness, and indecipherable consequence.

For Long, only a category like Rudolph Otto's *mysterium trememdum* begins to get at the existential dilemma thus imposed (Otto, 13). The instinct for survival meant ever-renewed attempts to render the violent structure of colonial expropriation intelligible in native terms. Fragments of the old myths were mobilized alongside of imposed Western categories in new creole discourses of these oppressed peoples to make such captivity, and the god hidden behind these irresistible powers of domination, comprehensible. Religions of the oppressed appear then, for Long, as new amalgams that disclose the "mythic truth" about Western irrationality that the West hides from itself under its vaunted rationality. In its own religious terms, the Western "God" was codified as eminently lucid and alluring; in the experience of those made to live "underneath" Western economic structures and subsumed into Western scientific categories, this God emerged as profoundly opaque and "terrible." The *mysterium tremendum* points to a quality of encounter with reality that is quite other than the *mysterium fascinans*. It is Long's genius to have broken apart such a totalizing category as the *mysterium* to signify the incomprehensible depths of the "break" Europe's sudden presence constituted for native cultures.

While Long's project as a Historian of Religions mandates comparing religious forms across cultures, not surprisingly, his work has elaborated with particular precision the African American experience of enslavement. The institution of slavery unquestionably institution-alized a form of colonial violence and reinscription of indigenous cultures in extremis. Like Earl, Long invokes Du Bois's double-consciousness formula to give emblematic expression to what, for him, was the paradigmatic experience of the *tremendum*. A "double awareness" exactly described, for Long, the experience of being created "for a second time," from without, in discourses that allowed no room for intimate self-designation (Long, 1986, 166). Africans found their very identities profoundly and irresistibly reconfigured in the scientific discourses of race and evolution, reinforced by the violent disciplines of the plantation. "Seeing oneself through the eyes of this other" (i.e., white society) described not only an existential condition, but also, throughout the time of slavery and afterward in the Jim Crow South, a requisite survival skill, an absolute necessity if one were to have any hope of anticipating and thus (perhaps) avoiding the adventitious and incessant eruptions of white violence directed toward blacks. But Du Bois's aphoristic treatment only gave laconic expression to an experience more eloquently described later in his work in connection with stumbling on a backwoods southern church service. There, the language Du Bois offers is more telling and more suggestive.

> It was out in the country, far from my foster home, on a dark Sunday night. The road wandered from our rambling log-house up the stormy bed of a creek, past wheat and corn until we could hear dimly across the fields a rhythmic cadence of song—soft, thrilling, powerful, that swelled and died sorrowfully in our ears. I was a country school-teacher then, fresh from the East, and had never seen a Southern Negro revival . . . And so most striking to me as I approached the village and the little plain church perched aloft, was the air of intense excitement that possessed that mass of black folk. *A sort of suppressed terror hung in the air and seemed to seize us,—a pythian madness, a demonic possession, that lent terrible reality to song and word. The black and massive form of the preacher swayed and quivered as the words crowded to his lips and flew at us in singular eloquence.* (Du Bois, 1961, 140–141; quoted in Long, 1986, 163–164, emphasis Long)

In Du Bois's rendering, this service initiated him into a new level of black identity. It gave communal and creative expression to a "pythian madness" and a "dread" that, though common to human experience in general, is not commonly expressed in modern formulations in social memory or public practice (Du Bois, 1961, 140; Long, 1986, 165). In Long's reading, what Du Bois later formalized as double-consciousness was first experienced by him in the mode posited here as a form of demonic dread or even "possession"—a "scene of human passion," in Du Bois's own words, that while "grotesque and funny" when merely described, remained "awful" in experience (Du Bois, 1961, 141). For Du Bois, this "frenzy of a Negro revival in the untouched back-woods of the [late nineteenth century] South" reflected an intensity of experience and expression as "old as Delphi and Endor" that was yet peculiarly evocative of the "feelings of slaves" (Du Bois, 1961, 141). For Long reading Du Bois, it was only in this work of ritual re-creation that the slave and ex-slave communities were able to fashion for themselves a means of survival.

At bottom, slave experience of the violence of white supremacy could not be entirely divorced from the experience of ultimate reality. The "demon known," in its very arbitrariness and incomprehensibility, seemed to manifest a "Demon unknown." White violence was "comprehended" in—and most importantly, relativized by—this struggle to grasp a God who could, unfathomably, be "present" in such experience (Long, 1986, 165). Not so much conceptual clarification, but ritual transfiguration, displaced the banality of the violence and reworked the contingency into a much larger horizon. The real "dread" was the one that attached to the primal experience of finitude and frailty characteristic of every human life but patently unavoidable and peculiarly irrepressible in the black condition of oppression. Knowledge of reality itself as *tremendum* came to be virtually constitutive of black identity.

For Long, it was and is this communal mediation of demonic violence into *daemonic* vitality that epitomized the very meaning and structure of African experience of America. It was a quintessentially "religious" experience whether or not it made use of religious idiom in the very fact of its impossible confrontation with human contingency and dread and death. The very incorrigibility of white violence gave rise to an intensity of experience that produced new hybrid forms of collective human being in black religious (and later black music) ritual. What Du Bois found himself confronted with in that backwoods church—and subsequently found himself initiated into—could be described as a collective work of conjure and re-creation. The body of the community became a sort of collective shamanic realization, a theater of crossover between this world and the "otherworld"—a thickness of communion between the living and the dead, between slave ancestors and ex-slave descendants, a rich concourse of historical reality and mythic epiphany made palpable, given voice, full of scent and sound. In that gathered repertoire of historical memory and spiritual mastery, double-consciousness *was* second sight: sacred "flight" materialized in that shuddering woman's body over there; the bridge between sky, earth, and underrealm came to stammering expression in the preacher's shout over here; ancestral gaze fiercely colored a deacon's watchful eye; demon and god wrestled almost indistinguishably for control of the antiphony; death stalked, life quaked, lost souls returned to their owners with a shriek. To what degree such a description is a romantic projection from a position of safe academic hindsight as opposed to evocative effect of the experience itself is probably an irresolvable question. That such services—on the sly during slavery, in the outback after it—did (and do) effect a recovery of souls from the living death of daily life under the whip and the burning cross is indisputable. The effect was shamanic, whatever the appropriate designation of the means.

British culture critic Paul Gilroy (among many others) traces the way this peculiar proclivity, forged in response to slavery, both has been and continues to be conserved and revalorized in black diasporic religions, musics, and popular culture since then (Gilroy, 37, 77, 217). Much like Long, but in a different vocabulary, Gilroy identifies the experience of slavery as having given rise to various ritual competencies that did not just seek to erase the awful memory of enslavement. Rather, slave and ex-slave communities are understood to have, in effect, "done judo" on the violence of the oppression by ritually absorbing the terror, recapitulating its intensity in dramatic forms of mimesis, reworking its absurdity into a strange kind of sublimity. For Gilroy, the result has been a set of communally re-produced "affective structures" that generate various forms of "expressive culture." The constant renegotiation of form, breaking language apart to give voice to an intensity of experience that defies grammar, the improvisation of ever-new hybrid sounds and discourses, the refusal of simple capitulation to modern disciplines of the body as a mere laboring machine by making physicality itself productive of alternative meanings and pleasures, the constant re-creations of community under innovative regimes of antiphony and polyphony, and so forth, are all read by Gilroy as disclosures and reproductions of a collective competence born of the agonies of slavery and ongoing forms of racially coded and structured domination. Blues, jazz, gospel, reggae, soul, funk, and hip-hop are all interrogated in form and function as complex re-creations of communal identities under the duress of modern structures of oppression that canalize violence into beauty.

Here again (as with Long), even though the express language of shamanism is not used, the paradigm all but shouts its suggestiveness. Gilroy's argument is important in moving beyond a certain nostalgia for what may appear to have been more clearly spiritual or religious in slave and black church traditions without getting caught up in some kind of essentialist notion of blackness. The line of suggestiveness is one that asks after the cultural consequence of unrelieved struggle with social oppression and anomie—with what could otherwise be understood as the conditions of both physical dismemberment and soul loss. The thick texts of cultural innovation in evidence all over the black diasporic world point toward something more complex than political combat defined in simple liberal democratic terms. Resistance here is grasped not only as more fragmentary and constrained but also as more opportunistic and subtle than a clearly defined political agenda—or lack of one—would admit. Indeed, the cultural innovations do not simply answer to political necessities but constantly expand political exigency into deeper registers of metaphysics and aesthetics, into the more profound questions of human being and human meaning that trouble and excite every community.

## Collective Shamanism in Black Ritual

The possibilities of a shamanistic reading of such competencies are not sheer invention on my part, however. Theophus Smith reworks the insights of Amanda Porterfield on the shamanic character of individual revival preachers into a notion of corporate shamanism characteristic of the black community in general (Smith, 1989, 384). Porterfield is solicited as observing that revival preaching

> often combines the prophetic activity of making moral pronounce-ments with the shamanic activity of representing dilemmas in bodily gesture. Some preachers go into trances that enable them to act out the intense pain and hope that is represented by their symbols of sin and redemption . . . The compelling power of these preachers is in large part the result of their ability to dramatically embody the emo-tional problems and social tensions besetting their patrons. (Porterfield, 728–729)

Smith paraphrases Porterfield's understanding of such "shamanic preaching" as a matter of "personally *embodied* symbol production for the purpose of psychological and social *conflict resolution*" (Smith, 385). The shaman figure stages the disease in his or her own body in the very act of projecting healing. Both Smith and Porterfield (as also Eliade) note that the shamans "have often been the subjects of their own curative abilities," and thus model a kind of simultaneity of sickness and its overcoming (Smith, 1989, 385).

*Incantation and Transformation*

But it is Smith alone who pushes the paradigm further in arguing that "in Afro-America one observes not only singular individuals but also . . . larger agencies of psycho-social cure" (Smith, 1989, 385). In its life and death struggle with "the disorders generated by the oppression of racism [like] deteriorating self-esteem, internalized feelings of inferiority, and intergroup mistrust," the black community has evolved forms of "corporate shamanism" (Smith, 1989, 385). For Smith, these are found not only in revitalization movements like the 1960s freedom movement, but also in any therapeutic practice materializing in one-on-one relationships, family systems, churches, neighborhood organizations, or larger social events like boycotts, labor strikes, or protests when that practice's "social and political visions display *incantatory* dynamics" (Smith, 1989, 385–386; emphasis added). At the heart of such a dynamic is an interlinkage of social change and personal transformation. The incantatory factor emerges for Smith any time a vision begins to function "as a device for inviting us to 'make ourselves over in the image of the imagery' " (Smith, 1989, 386, citing Kenneth Burke, who borrows from John Crowe Ransom). Historically, "black communities have performed incantations . . . by corporately embodying biblical symbols of suffering and redemption" (Smith, 1989, 386). By "harnessing such symbols to their own socially despised skin color and bodily features," they have acted shamanically to effect a psychosocial transformation (Smith, 1989, 386).

In further appealing to a James M. Glass article on political philosophers as shamans, Smith elaborates the connection between the therapeutic and incantatory elements in black forms of corporate shamanism. He quotes Glass to the effect that "what a shaman does, how he enters into a diseased situation, depends on his capacity to construct signs, to devise an incantation that will reach the unconscious" (Glass, 186, quoted in Smith, 1989, 387). It is an ability that is critical to political vision. Smith argues further that "the incantatory signs that have functioned most powerfully in . . . America, at the level of 'the unconscious', are biblical symbols" (Smith, 1989, 387). And indeed, Smith's own work focuses on tracking the way specific biblical images (such as "Exodus," "Ethiopia," "promised land," "captivity," etc.) have been shamanically deployed in the socially transformative, corporate dynamics characteristic of much black political work.

But much is left unsaid around the claim of what is most powerful in the American "unconscious." Smith's pursuit of black communal embodiments of biblical symbols uncovers a perspective on shamanistic creativity at the level of collective practice that is equally suggestive for black displacements and transformations of the imagery of race itself. While he does not specifically identify such as being "shamanic," in his discussion of black musics, Smith does lift out a formal characteristic that points once again to such a connection. Morton Marks's work in ethnomusicology is invoked to highlight a structure that is common to both sacred and secular ritual events among black groups in the United States and the Caribbean. Marks argues that the alternating pattern of expression known as "style-switching"—building on an aesthetics of polyrhythm widely found in Africa—goes beyond simple "expressive behavior" (Marks, 63–64, 67). This essential black feature of alteration from the forms of one culture to those of a different system functions to induce "trance behavior" (Smith, 388). In Marks's own words, it generates a "ritual event" that can only be called "spirit-possession" (Marks, 63–64). Key to this power of inducing trance states is both the abruptness and the direction of the shift. The switch is sharply introduced with what could be called a "percussive" effect. It breaks abruptly from one style to another, and its direction, according to Marks, is "always from a 'white' style to a 'black' style, from a European to an African one" (Marks, 63–64). It is not pursued (and would not work to induce trance) the other way around.

For Marks, the duality structured by the polarization between the two styles is a by-product of culture contact. It "provides a kind of record or deposit of that contact" and offers "models for patterning other aesthetic productions" (Smith will later concentrate on black discourse rather than music) (Smith, 1989, 388). Once again, Du Bois's language of double-consciousness is cited as the formulaic sign of this complex and compound structure of creativity. Smith notes that Marks's musical insight has been prefigured in that more general recognition of black "biculturality" (Smith, 1989, 388). Rounded out with discussion of the capacity of black musics to offer "transcendent" glimpses of a world far different than the one defined by segregation and of the reliance of such musics on call–response dynamics and improvisation, Smith has, in effect, displayed the rudiments of what could be summed up as a form of incipient and anonymous shamanism at work in the very core of black musical creativity. His final identification of an evident "will to transform" that is emblematic of this cultural competence underscores the shamanic preoccupation with shape-shifting and metamorphosis (Smith, 1989, 391).

Despite his explicit identifications of shamanistic features, however, Smith's discussion of black spirituality in this vein also remains rich with unmined ore. The identification of incantation as a hallmark of a generalized black shamanistic proclivity seems to point to a formal property that shows up regularly in black creativity. Smith has underscored this trance-inducing feature as above all an "invitation to re-make identity inside the image of the imagery" (Smith, 1989, 391). This is exactly the tactic taken with much of the racialized imagery imposed by white culture on black communities. The 1960s transvaluation of the term "blackness" itself is perhaps the paradigmatic example. Rather than resist the term and insist on yet a new one, less polluted with pejorative associations (as, e.g., in the switch from the "n-word" to "Negro" in the early twentieth century), the Black Power Movement of the late 1960s took up the very word "black" with all of its negative valuation by the dominant culture, and remade its content in terms of qualities like "beauty" (black is beautiful), "pride" ("say it loud, I'm black, I'm proud"), and "soulfulness."

At another level, "taking refuge inside the sign" has a long history in black tactics of resistance to white domination. Pretending to be nothing other than white stereotypical images of "negro-ness"—adopting public stances of "innocence," "docility," "simplicity," and "happiness," or, later on in the game, postures of "militancy," "dangerousness," "gangsterism," "unbridled eroticism," and so forth—has been one way blacks have used white ignorance of black experience to forge alternative identities and cultural competencies separate from white surveillance. Underneath such public *personas*, a whole set of subtle and sophisticated cues for communication could be and were and are elaborated. Ironic tonality, parodic gesture, mimetic grotesquery, double entendres of meaning have all become recognized and pleasurable features of black-on-black dialogue in public, constantly innovating ways of "puttin' on ole massa." In shamanistic terms, the proclivity can be understood as a form of homeopathy, subduing the demon by wrestling it into a serviceable form "inside" one's own body (Smith, 1994, 168–169, 213–216).

### Dismemberment and Mastery

But the shamanistic quality of this tactic requires some careful unpacking. Smith notes that historically, black communities harnessed biblical symbols of suffering and redemption, of captivity and freedom, "to their own socially despised skin color and bodily features" to perform a shaman-like psychosocial transformation (Smith, 1989, 386). As mentioned above, the same has been true of the entire regime of racist imagery and imagination. Being "black" is not a natural condition—indeed, very few people so identified actually have skin that is anything close to that color. Rather, the category functions as shorthand for a whole set of negative meanings in dominant cultural discourse and is imposed by that culture on the minority culture. The experience of that imposition has been articulated by numerous authors over the last century. One of the more eloquent comes from Martiniquean psychoanalyst Frantz Fanon in his book *Black Skins, White Masks*, which describes a chance encounter with a white child and his mother on the streets of Paris mid-century (we will briefly examine Du Bois's account of an "American" version of the experience below). As a general rule, Fanon says,

> consciousness of the body is solely a negating activity. It is a third-person consciousness. The body is surrounded by an atmosphere of certain uncertainty. I know that if I want to smoke, I shall have to reach out my right arm and take the pack of cigarettes lying at the other end of the table. The matches, however, are in the drawer on the left, and I shall have to lean back slightly. And all these movements are made not out of habit but out of implicit knowledge. A slow composition of my *self* as a body in the middle of a spatial and temporal world—such seems to be the schema. It does not impose itself on me; it is, rather, a definitive structuring of the self and of the world—definitive because it creates a real dialectic between my body and the world. (Fanon, 111)

But in the moment of encounter on the street, where a little white boy says, "Look, a Negro!" and then continues, "Mama, see the Negro! I'm frightened!," the corporeal schema crumbles (Fanon, 112). For Fanon, the moment is "an amputation, an excision, a hemorrhage that spatter[s his] whole body with black blood" (Fanon, 112). Indeed, the world itself shatters: "All around me the white man, above the sky tears at its navel, the earth rasps under my feet, and there is a white song, a white song. All this whiteness that burns me" (Fanon, 114). His corporeal schema is replaced by an epidermal one. He ceases to be aware of his body "in the third person" and instead becomes aware of it "in a triple person" (Fanon, 112). He suddenly exists triply, responsible at once for his body, his race, his ancestors. No longer able to assemble himself by "residual sensations" and "perceptions primarily of a tactile, vestibular, kinesthetic, and visual character," he finds himself, rather "woven . . . out of a thousand details, anecdotes, stories" by "the other, the white man" (Fanon, 111). Thinking he had merely to "construct a physiological self, to balance space, to localize sensations," he discovers he is "called on for more" (Fanon, quoting and extending Jean Lhermitte, 111). He has burst apart and been reassembled from without (Fanon, 109). In that distance from himself, "afar off," he feels an "easily identifiable flood mounting out of the countless facets of [his] being" (Fanon, 114). He is about to become anger itself.

In the instance at hand, Fanon describes going on and shocking the mother involved by telling her to kiss his rear end. He decides to become the very thing she and her son have projected onto him: a monstrosity of unpredictable blackness. The experience is hardly desirable, but at least he inhabits the image on his own terms once it has been imposed. The moment is patently a real-life "hallucination." There is an uncanny quality in the experience as Fanon describes it. He is suddenly myth incarnate. The question is not how he can halt the sudden metamorphosis of time and space (he cannot, it has already been accomplished), but how he will inhabit the accomplished alchemy. His response could be understood as an example of the kind of thing Eliade identifies as shamanistic combat with the demons (Eliade, 236).

In Eliade's account, it is often the case that the shaman will engage such combat by taking the evil spirits "into his own body" (Eliade, 236). In the employment of ecstatic means to diagnose and counter the condition of soul loss, often enough the shaman will, for a time, be possessed by the very forces he or she seeks to subdue. Indeed, in working with "animal familiars" or "helping spirits," shamanic finesse frequently entails "imitation" of the animal's voice or actions (Eliade, 93). What appears in such cases as "possession by" such spirits, Eliade argues, is perhaps more accurately understood in terms of the shaman "taking possession of the spirits" (Eliade, 93). It is profoundly active. One body becomes the field of combat for multiple forces. We could just as easily say it is spiritual combat in the form of "taking possession of possession."

Fanon's momentary tactic on a Parisian street may be grasped as a less happy version of a similar response. The demonic is finally transfigured by way of imitation and cohabitation of the evil. In this instance, white supremacy and terror have the effect of dis-membering a body and reassembling it as black. For Fanon, it is instantaneous death to physicality on his own terms and immediate resurrection into a (negative) ecstatic body constructed by a spirit, all in a flash. It is shamanic initiation without a choice. But what to do? There is nothing more for it, but to resist by submission, to become the very terror projected. (Bare the teeth and snarl!)

The impulse to overcome by imitating, to tame ideology by taking possession of its own possessing force, remaking oneself in the image, is patently shamanistic. It is also quintessentially a black tactic for dealing with the ideology of racism and the demon of white supremacy. (And this recognition may also go part way toward explaining contemporary black dance innovations such as "the robot"—namely, a creative gesture combating the power of technology to conscript human embodiment and vitality into a meaningless capitulation to the "machine as fetish" by mastering the machine in the body.) Often enough, shamanic initiation gets described in traditional idioms as an experience in which the initiate's soul is spirited away by the devils until the candidate "has learned all of their secrets" (Eliade, 38). Certainly, black expressive cultures have learned much of the secrets of white society and the social functioning of racism. What must be recognized here is that it has often been at the cost of having to live inside of the image.

We can go further. One shaman's account of initiation described the experience in terms of having his head cut off and his body chopped into little bits and boiled in a cauldron the size of half the earth. Afterward, everything was fished out by the (spirit-) blacksmith, the shaman's head was forged anew on an anvil, and he was "taught how to read the letters inside of it"; his eyes were changed to see not so much on the bodily plane but the mystical one, and his ears were pierced to understand the language of plants (Eliade, 42). Keeping in mind Orenstein's caution about the local specificities of various forms of shamanisms (earlier in the essay), it is nevertheless possible to read this episode alongside of African American experiences of racism and their struggle to develop the ability necessary to overcome (or at least endure) it. In this particular account, the shaman-to-be comes out of the cauldron with three bones too many and is told he must therefore go and "procure three shaman's costumes" (Eliade, 42). Concerning these latter "shamanic costumes," Eliade says,

> In itself, the costume represents a religious microcosm qualitatively different from the surrounding profane space. For one thing, it constitutes an almost complete symbol system; for another, its consecration has impregnated it with various spiritual forces and especially with "spirits." By the mere fact of donning it—or manipulating the objects that deputize it—the shaman transcends profane space and prepares to enter into contact with the spiritual world . . . But the costume is not allowed to leave the clan. For in a certain sense it concerns the clan as a whole—not only because it was made or bought by contributions from the entire clan, but primarily because, being impregnated with "spirits," it must not be worn by anyone who cannot control them, for the result would be that they would trouble the whole community. (Eliade, 147)

To what degree can black alchemical work on the categories of their own oppression inside the imagery of race be understood in these terms?

As Smith argued above, part of the "incantatory" creativity of African Americans has been to "harness these symbols to their own socially despised skin color and bodily features in order, like the shaman, to perform a psychosocial transformation" (Smith, 1989, 386). Smith specifically had in view biblical symbols. But it is also the case that "blackness" itself—after the trauma Fanon has described and the various tactics improvised to survive it—becomes a kind of public costume, continuously reimposed in seemingly ever-new negative formulations by white imagination that is just that frequently debrided and refashioned as a black hide of proud elocution, inimitable improvisation, and irrepressible polyphony. Whether in religious ritualization or musical syncopation, whether in sartorial proclamation or rhetorical elaboration, the deep levels of black experience of the meanings of "being black" are regularly plumbed and innovated into fresh dramatizations of "human being." Indeed, we could almost say (Long, in effect, does say) that black skin comes to bear a spiritual force of meaning. Even while it remains really nothing, an arbitrary somatic feature, ebony appearance, in virtue of black creative labor, is impregnated with spirits. Blackness itself, in the collective efforts of those forced to live under the duress of such a category, is forged into a shamanic costume of almost numinous force. Inside of the community, possession is possessed.

Along these lines, even Smith's biblical symbols demand rethinking. Not only are such symbols harnessed to despised skin color, thereby revalorizing that feature as positive, but it is also the case that black skin transfigures the biblical imagery into a new kind of potency. Whence the power of black Christian worship? The vector of transformation is not one way. It is as much the case that ritually re-wrought blackness takes the symbols of salvation into new domains of significance as that the biblical tradition lifts blackness from the pit of opprobrium. Indeed, it is precisely the way the very bearing and demeanor of "blackface" has been intensified with multiple possibilities of significance that gives black worship much of its fascination and vitality. Both terror and its ecstatic displacement, horror and the dramatic overcoming of horror, are made palpable and worked through in the antiphonies of black worship protocols. Biblical symbols become hybrid signifiers in a ritual process in which black possession of the meanings of "blackness" thickens the very possibility of the body as a locus of meaning and history. It is this paradoxical doubling (and quadrupling and quintupling) of the body in its incarnate powers of communication that constitutes "incantation" and "shamanic mastery." Again, it is Du Bois's formulation that hints at the intensity of the achievement.

## Flight and Return

In his description in *Souls* of a boyhood encounter with a white classmate that leads into his double-consciousness formulation, Du Bois offers his readers testament of his first experience of the meaning of race as a child. It is notable that he describes it as a "worlding" event: the "veil" that drops so suddenly and unaccountably does not just separate him as individual from his classmate as individual. It separates—and indeed creates—two distinct "worlds." Ever after, he can see into "the other world." But he cannot live there. Indeed, he cannot *not* see into that world. Life becomes an ongoing exercise in double sightedness; seeing always this world and that one in the togetherness of their separation, seeing his world in light of that other one, seeing himself through the other's eyes. And to the degree white cultural imagination equates blackness with death and then socially, psychologically, economically (and today we should surely say "criminologically"), makes blackness an ongoing negotiation with death in its manifold guises, we could say blackness is a shamanic structure. It is constituted as a living embodiment of a violent rupture between two worlds, one of which is culturally coded as "life" and the other as "death"; it is a form of living flight across that impossible gap, a continuous concourse between discontinuous social spaces, a political condition of ever being forced to inhabit a region of subhumanity and the concomitant struggle to transform that subaltern status into something palpably human.

But here lies all manner of paradox and confusion. When I speak this way, I am arguing largely by way of suggestion. In no way can such a brief essay as this do justice to the historical and phenomenological complexity of the operation and significance of race in this country. Indeed, as a social formation, race does not answer only to the imagination of national boundaries or the pedagogies of citizenship. I am suggesting that historically, the category of "blackness," in all of its popular permutations (the n-word, "Negro," "colored," "African American," etc.), has served to designate a certain ethnocultural domain as so incalculably different from the dominant culture that it has often taken on the force of an absolute other, a kind of Archimedean social reference point leveraging much of the meaning of various other forms of public identity in America. Not least of its purpose has been the consolidation of an ideology of "whiteness" that has served to incorporate all manner of European immigrant groups into the operative hegemony in this country in the nineteenth and twentieth centuries. Indeed, by positing a kind of absolute position of negativity, a social condition to be avoided at all costs, it has also oriented non-European immigrant struggles for a place in the American Dream. As a social signifier encoding political choice at many levels of institutional, cultural, and individual decision making, the label "black" has been made to function simultaneously as both the cause and the effect of a system of exploitation and expropriation.

At issue in this way of thinking is the real and mythic location of death in American society. I am suggesting that in the plantation system, the dominant culture institutionalized death as a mode of living, as Orlando Patterson has argued. In post-slave societies in different forms in the North and the South, "blackness" came to be associated, in the dominant cultural mythology, with death both metaphorically (as a condition of grotesque and terrifying subhumanity) and actually (in the social structures brought to bear on African American existence, such as forced impoverishment, enghettoization, repressive labor and vagrancy laws, denial of educational opportunities, etc.). The category served to implement and enforce various forms or conditions of social and physical mortality.

For the likes of a Du Bois (or in French colonial society, a Fanon), the existential situation is then complex and confusing. Analyzed in light of a shamanic paradigm, the need for travel to the realm of death to reclaim souls from their enslavement there required a convoluted flight from one's condition and community understood as merely accidentally and unimportantly black to this other realm and meaning of "blackness" as that thing that mysteriously mires the community in real tragedy. Here the shamanistic task is as has been analyzed above: it is a matter of learning how to descend into this latter form of blackness as a kind of underworld and find within its opaque and dizzying depths, the strange possibilities of life that the terrors there can be made to yield. It is no surprise that so much of black literature, for instance, has fantastically reworked a Dantesque theme like the pilgrimage into hell in such scenarios as Ralph Ellison's invisible man living in the New York sewer system (in *The Invisible Man*) or Toni Morrison's character in *Beloved*, Milkman Dead, finding salvation in daring to travel back down south to the terrain that hosted his family during slavery, experiencing a close brush with death and coming away from the experience renewed and free for the first time in his life; however, the return from this kind of "hell of blackness" is also not at all guaranteed as Richard Wright made brilliantly clear in *Native Son*.

From the perspective of the black community, however, it is white society that appears, paradoxically, as the land of life and death. It is experienced as both the source of violence, repression, exploitation, and untimely demise and as the place wherein is harbored much (capital, jobs, educational institutions, expertise, etc.) that is necessary for living. Du Bois talks, for instance, in relationship to his boyhood experience of "the dropping of the veil," of finding some way to wrest away and win for himself and his world the benefits of that other world (Du Bois, 1961, 17). He must pass over and win what he knows is forbidden him (and indeed, his life is testament of both the potency and the cost of having done such).

In shamanistic terms, then, we find a very complex form of flight and return illuminated as a theme. Death wears both white- and black-face. Healing involves pilgrimage into and return from both the terrifying depths of black oppression and the wearying world of white supremacy. Life also bears this double aspect. Vitality lies at the heart of transfigured darkness, in the homeopathic gesture of intensifying terror into beauty. It equally lies at the center of the resources and powers that white privilege has gathered to itself as the outcome of a massive global system of defrauding and exploiting the world of color that must be repossessed.

In Eliadian terms, we could perhaps describe this structure of blackness as "second sight" as a complex form of "ecstatic enstasy" or "enstatic ecstasy" (Eliade, 417). It has evolved as a survival strategy that entails external raids on white social capital to take back some of what was and continues to be stolen. And it entails internal flights of creative daring, laboring inarticulable depths of anguish into forms of self-knowledge that continually elude dominant culture categories and understanding. In this vein, we would also perhaps have to recognize a certain novelty of the enterprise in coming to enjoy shamanistic flight for its own sake. What else, for instance, is jazz improvisation but an alchemy of rhythm making new worlds out of (nothing but) novel time signatures and sonic forms of "space travel"? The sax, here, is not only a weapon of assault on the temporal uniformities imposed by the clock, but also a mental probe creating the domain it explores in the very act of exploring it.

## Shamanic Blackness and Demonic Whiteness

What we have, then, in black forms of double-consciousness is the possibility of a kind of "horizontal shamanism." "Second sight," in this sense, is simultaneously a form of diagnosis, mobility, and mastery. It is one of the perspicacious knowledges of the deep meaning of "America." As a form of internalized cosmology, collectively embodied as blackness and shamanistically transfigured in African American ritual practice, it represents simultaneously an exhibition, and an over-coming, of the ideology of white racism. It is "shamanized" white supremacy—a reductive and violently constraining force of evil taken into one's own body, suffered, struggled against, wrestled into creativity, made productive in (and as) one's own flesh that is then complexly re-exhibited and redeployed as a "mastered form of mastery" for the sake of communal healing and survival (Eliade, 229). As an initiative of diagnosis and healing oriented especially toward a radically historical, and not just mythical or spiritual, break in planes, black ritual practice may productively be thought of as a kind of new form of shamanistic combat. It shamanizes across a break in *this* world.

Once again though, there is need to slow the analysis down to let the shamanistic motif signify on the historical division of race. Eliade offers that the "pre-eminently shamanistic technique is the passage from one cosmic region to another" (Eliade, 259). The shaman is the one who "knows the mystery of the break-through in planes" (Eliade, 259). The possibility of communication between these severed cosmic zones arises from the structure of the universe itself. The break between the three levels—sky, earth, underworld—is connected by a central axis. The symbolism surrounding this axial connector itself has a history that is full of contradiction. But essentially, the axis passes through an "opening" or "hole" that allows the gods to "descend to earth and the dead to the subterranean regions" (Eliade, 259). It is through this same hole that the shaman's soul in ecstasy can "fly up or down in the course of . . . celestial or infernal journeys" (Eliade, 259). In the process of shamanizing, however, it is not only the case that shamans traverse these three levels in flight, but also that they come to embody elements of each of the zones in their persons (Eliade, 352). They become living intermediaries.

In later discussion of this phenomenon of the "perilous passage," Eliade notes that whereas *in illo tempore*, everyone could pass easily over the bridge connecting heaven and earth, now, with the advent of a mysterious fall and consequently of death, that passage can be negotiated only "in spirit"—either through actual physical death or in the simulation of death constituted by "ecstatic" practice (Eliade, 483). The passage is now fraught with obstacles and dangers; demons and monsters stand ready to devour; not everyone seeking to cross makes it over. Indeed, in this life, passage is possible only by way of shamanic ecstasy or heroic force, or through the paradoxical wisdom of initiation, which ritually simulates the experience of death and resurrection (Eliade, 483).

The rites themselves build the bridge; their accompanying myths keep alive the prospect of the danger. In New Zealand, for instance, the traveler is considered to face a passage through a very narrow space between two demons: if the *voyant* is "light," the transit is successful; if not, the pilgrim becomes the prey of the demons (Eliade, 485). Other myths envision traveling along a razor's edge or a length of hair or between two constantly moving millstones, or finding the place "where night and day meet," or a gate in a wall that opens only for an instant. What lies at the heart of such mythic passages, Eliade insists, is the "need to transcend opposites, to abolish the polarity typical of the human condition" (Eliade, 485). Transferring from this to the other world or returning therefrom requires passage through "the undimensioned and timeless 'interval' that divides related but contrary forces, between which, if one is to pass at all, it must be 'instantly' " (Eliade, quoting Coomaraswamy, 485). Whoever succeeds transcends the human condition: such a one "is a shaman, or a hero, or a 'spirit', and indeed this paradoxical passage can be accomplished only by one who is spirit. For one functioning as a shaman-in-ecstasy, "the bridge, or the tree, the vine, the cord, and so on—which *in illo tempore*, connected earth and heaven—once again, for the space of an instant, becomes a present reality" (Eliade, 485).

Again, the question here is the degree to which such shamanistic paradigms of action can throw in relief some of the processes by which African American communal practices have transfigured their racial marking as black into an antidote for racial oppression. The argument is not that blacks as individuals are necessarily shamanistically gifted but rather that the experience of slavery and racism has pushed black communities into forms of creative displacement (based on residual memory of their traditional practices in Africa?) of their oppression that begin to look very similar in structure to certain shamanistic strategies. Du Bois's formula highlights the experience as both "affliction" (double-consciousness) and "gift" (second sight). In his discussion of Native

American Ghost Dance rituals, Eliade notes the complexity attending the practices of the secret societies and ecstatic movements that spring up in the wake of colonial destruction of native culture: "The differences between 'consecrated' men and the 'profane' multitude are not so much qualitative as quantitative; they lie in the *amount* of the sacred that the former have assimilated" (Eliade, 314). Indeed, he will argue, "we could almost say that every Indian 'shamanizes,' " even if such is not a conscious "wish to become a shaman" (Eliade, 315). In similar vein, I am arguing that the black community under colonial and postcolonial onslaught has forged blackness itself into forms and practices of communal identification that function shamanically. Double-consciousness can be, has been, and regularly is transfigured into a capacity for second sight.

The transmutation of secular pain into spiritual proclivity, of existential anguish into aesthetic eloquence, of oppressive constraint into political finesse, of all the virtually alchemical transformations of time and space into unforeseen dispositions of humaneness—in black religious virtuosity, in black musical prodigality, in black literary sophistication, in the transformation of simple exercises of walking on the street or conversing in the barber shop or hair salon into expressions of artistry, in the endless proliferation of style that serves the serious end of survival—is strikingly evocative of a shamanistic effect. Yes, the effect is elusive and not productive of an immediate solution to the exploitation. The resolution of division into a momentary communion across the divide does not remedy the ongoing violence of white supremacist privilege. The resulting intimation of wholeness is indeed only for the instant of a majestic and dangerous flight in the face of disaster.

But this particular facility with the instant itself (as is discussed in chapter 4), this ability to create and exploit breaks in the plane of racial domination, to cross over from blackness to whiteness and back again, to invent a music of the break, like jazz, that opens a parallel universe inside of this one, to syncopate postindustrial despair into forms of youth subculture that answer to an expressive need in younger generations as far away as Russia and Costa Rico, South Africa and South Korea, cannot be fully grasped in the languages of quantifiable productivity or scientific substantiality. It is no accident that the American community that, by every measurable index of the material conditions of existence, should be most expected to have lost its "soul" is also the very community identified with having the most of that peculiar attribute. There is also a sense in which African American creativity with the conundrum of racism results in a peculiar refiguring of the American cosmos. It is as if modernity has its own myth returned to it. It is not now a cosmic tree or world axis that is climbed or descended, but an open wound in the body politic is made to reveal itself in the very effort to overcome its disfigurements. It is perhaps most immediately in the black community that one can today draw near to the central axis of American social history. There typically "American" notions of good and evil can be interrogated in their mutual implication and decoded or passed beyond. But now we begin to get into the broader question of our investigation.

If African American appropriations of imposed blackness can be understood as a form of shamanistic conjure, what is appropriated is fundamentally a paradox. Race is simultaneously a *fictional creation* of the European imagination implementing changing forms of domination in history and a *real life effect* carried out on colored bodies in various forms of action and social constraint. Overcoming the latter without succumbing to or reinforcing the former presents the communities under assault with a tactical dilemma. As already noted, the dilemma itself resembles shamanistic struggle with the condition of soul loss. In discussing the latter, Eliade notes that in the process of diagnosis, in order "to identify the author of the trouble," the shaman has to decide between seemingly opposite tactics. On the one hand, it may be requisite "to incarnate [one's] familiar spirit" and go into trance (or sleep) to solicit information. On the other, it may be necessary "to evoke and embody the spirit that is troubling the patient" (Eliade, 243). The choice of which of these two possibilities to employ in any given scenario of healing is part of the problem of diagnosis. Such shape-shifting (into the forms of either one's animal familiar or the alien spirit troubling the patient) is not definitive of the personhood of the shaman nor exhaustive of the shamanistic repertoire of remedy. But it is a useful power of being possessed while maintaining control of what is possessed. In thinking through the racial dilemma in this vein, "blackness" can perhaps be comprehended as a kind of equivalent to a shaman's familiar spirit, a certain kind of vital energy, figured as bestial in white eyes, that is actually tamed into a helping role. However, there may also be need to embody what whiteness means for the sake of overcoming its controlling norms and constraining injunctions. The domestication of white forms of enculturation—learning how to mimic white speech or gestures or imitate white codes of conduct—is a potent form of subversion. In such momentary theatricalizations of whiteness by black people, white supremacy is relativized and, in some measure, detoxified. In this case, by controlling the dosage, the poison itself is made to supply the remedy.

In further elaborating shamanistic practices around the exigencies of soul loss, Eliade continues:

> For the multiplicity of souls [in the anthropology in view here there were believed to be three distinct souls] and their instability sometimes make the shaman's task difficult. He must determine which of the souls has left the body and go in search of it; in this case, the shaman calls back the soul in stereotyped phrases or songs and attempts to make it re-enter the body by gesturing rhythmically. But sometimes spirits have entered the patient; then the shaman expels them with the help of his familiar spirit. (Eliade, 243)

Juxtaposed to the situation of race, the paradigm again is suggestive. Overcoming the effects of racism in the black community inevitably entails developing effective means of combating the inferiority projected by the dominant culture. Almost inevitably, some aspects of the negative stereotypes end up being internalized within the target (black) community. Healing then may require bolstering the sense of black cultural identification, or it could mandate diminishing identifications with certain white codes of conduct and being. Or both. In countering the effects of a schema of identification that is itself an impossible paradox, the antidote will itself necessarily involve paradox. What is important in the shamanic paradigm is recognition that the kind of work to be done is not merely cognitive but somatic; the means are various combinations of possession and exorcism. Gestural rhythm is an integral modality of remedy. In this vein, the ongoing proliferations of style found in black religious and musical rituals could be said to effect a kind of "folk diagnosis" and "vernacular therapy" at one and the same time.

Especially fascinating—and profoundly informative—is the way black forms of black identification do not simply oppose white cultural protocols, but regularly deform the stereotypes. Often enough, black stylistic innovations, in effect, analyze white cultural forms not just in verbal dissections but in gestural and rhythmic send ups that are really breakdowns of the presumed authority of white identity.

Diagnosis here is fully half of the cure. Blackness in this case is not the mere opposite of whiteness but its transcendence—a refusal to accept the polarity as absolute and a reworking of the presumed line of exclusion into a much more complex mode of relative exclusivity, communally validated as black, that also regularly juxtaposes black and white idioms in ever-renewed hybrid forms of expression. In this sense, blackness itself is the transmutation of what would have to be called "white double-consciousness." It is the ongoing volatilization of an imposed polarity into antiphonal forms of communal identification. Du Bois's double-consciousness signifies a sickness that is really of white origin; second sight is the incipient awareness of that polarity that is already the beginning of its overcoming. "Expressive blackness" thus emerges as a thick cultural code that grows out of the ongoing struggle to displace an incessant form of oppression. It is a matter of dealing with paradox not so much by denial and negation as by incorporation. Such a blackness is made to be much more than just black.

## Transnational Gift or Youth Culture Curse?

Thus far we have focused on the degree to which active elaborations of black identity can be usefully analyzed as communal forms of shamanistic transformation. The object of such activity is the oppressive effect of a white supremacist social formation inside the black community. The cure involves both exorcism and soul retrieval, rejection of self-images of inferiority and reinvention of the self, expulsion of white norms and repossession of blackness. But it is also clear that black cultural innovation exercises power far beyond the borders of the black community.

Considered in a broader constructive compass, the question of "black shamanism" can be examined in relationship to the contemporary U.S. social order and African diaspora practices, framed together in consideration of a popular culture quest for altered experience. Without doubt, the 1960s "turn to the east" articulated something at work in the culture that found "other experience," mystical phenomenon, altered states of consciousness, and so forth, both exotically fascinating and (inevitably) economically profitable. At the same time, on the home front, it is also possible to argue that the community recurrently racialized as "black"—with all the associations that color coding has insinuated and enforced historically between darkness, "the demonic," and death—has consistently been made to serve a kind of unwilling shamanic function with respect to the dominant white culture. That cross-racial role has a long history.

Much work has been done, for instance, on the way blackface minstrelsy emerged historically as a white-controlled institution playing with the ambivalences of race created by the dominant culture. According to labor historian, David Roediger, the category of whiteness was first given broad historical force in the nineteenth century as a way to consolidate white industrial interests against wage labor. As an invitation to newly arrived European immigrant groups to buy into a form of psychological solidarity defined largely in terms of a negative reference to blackness (in its predominant social meaning as "slavery"), "white solidarity" effectively co-opted the political energies of white wage labor. Membership in the privileged community of "whiteness" served as compensation for ongoing exploitation as a "wage-slave" (Du Bois, 30, 700; Roediger, 12). Blackface minstrelsy, in this analysis, emerges in the 1830s at the precise moment when public forms of celebration that mingled free and enslaved blacks and lower class whites were legally suppressed.

Minstrelsy, the argument goes, gathers force as a safe form of masquerade in which exploited whites use blackface as license to explore desires otherwise repressed in the daily regime of industrial work. Both actors and spectators alike here engage the images of blackness as a kind of carnivalesque pornography of their former lives working the land in Europe, when the body was less fettered in its responses to the erotic, to nature, to animals, indeed, to time and space in general. Dressing up in "blackface drag," parading and parodying the very meanings of blackness projected by whites (onto blacks) in the first place, "cutting loose" with the body as a ludic instrument of the grotesque, mimicking observed forms of black ritual practice, black dance, and black music—all afforded white immigrant groups a means and forum in which to escape their repression in the industrial order for a short time. They could play with the ambivalence of their own otherness, and then, often after beating up (sometimes even killing) actual black people, in a postperformance climax, reaffirm that they are really "not that" (not black). Minstrelsy can be analyzed as, at least in part, a theater of violent ambivalence simultaneously serving a social function of discharging dissent and a political function of ramifying hegemony.

The history of white uses of blackness in entertainment formats that remain safely under the control of white authority is patent in America. Again and again, black religious and cultural innovation has been experienced as strangely powerful in white culture. It has regularly been appropriated, adopted, adapted to white audiences and performance venues, and indulged in separate from the contexts of desperation in which that innovation was usually first created as a means of survival. Sooner or later, commercial interests climb on the bandwagon and manipulate the new artifacts for profit, diluting and mainstreaming the expressions until their power is finally lost, by which time the black community has usually innovated a new set of ritual forms of protest and subversion, which will themselves be subjected to a similar cycle of appropriation and routinization. This historical pattern can be observed in relationship to the blues, jazz, R&B, reggae, techno, and most recently hip-hop. The question that emerges from this history, in the context of this essay, is the degree to which such black creativity can be understood as also serving a kind of shamanistic role in white society.

And here the question emerges as one having purchase, potentially, with respect to modernity at large. Gilroy has drafted an argument that juxtaposes double-consciousness and modernity as twin offspring of the same globalizing history of colonialism, slavery, and racially coded capitalist takeover of much of the planet. If "double-consciousness," in such a perspective, serves as an emblematic marker of the fundamental and violent ambivalence of Western claims to rationality and rationalization, then "second sight" may well stand elaboration as an incipient form of postmodern shamanism, alive (if not well) in the practices of minority, migrant, refugee, and other postcolonial populations, precariously working out "subaltern" survival tactics at the edges (or on the underside) of the newly emergent global order. In this vein, anthropologist Michael Taussig's work on shamanism, colonialism, and wildness supplies provocation to rethink contemporary discourses of race, urban space, and violence in a shamanic key.

Taussig identifies a recurrent pattern in colonial takeovers of indigenous populations in South America. Once European hegemony has been secured in a given setting, and Western economic and social orientations articulated with local cultural patterns, it is not uncommon for the resident populations, both *criollo* and *mestizo*, to seek out still-practicing shamans in the conquered cultures and solicit healing from the stresses and strains of the newly adopted Western lifestyle (Taussig, 210, 446). Taussig's analysis is complex, layered, and ethnographically postmodern in shape. He includes himself among those pirating "fat" from the conquered (Taussig, 221–241, 438–443). The impulse to identify "wildness" with the losers of modern forms of struggle, to locate "wholeness" or efficacious magical powers with the indigenous colonized, seems to reflect a complex form of projection and subversion (Taussig, 171, 187, 211, 217–220). Terror merges with therapy; dismemberment is made to yield a bizarre re-membering (Taussig, 266–267, 440–445).

In this perspective, the historical victors cannot survive their own triumph, but regularly descend to the underworld of creolized practices that their own forms of domination have forced into being in order to seek healing (Taussig, 230, 256–257, 378–379). A "space of death" underwrites the colonial surface—a terrain of violent promulgation of order that paradoxically renders that very order itself unstable (Taussig, 1, 4, 39, 121, 133, 373–374). Indigenous shamans are deemed to be those who know the truth of such a disordering order and have the ritual means of de-centering the structures of control and recovering a lost vitality (Taussig, 441–446, 448).

In his own experience of night-long marathons of *yage* drinking, vomiting, defecating, weeping, laughing, singing, swooning, dying, and coming back to life, Taussig identified the primary technique as one of "shamanistic montage" (Taussig, 440–445). It was not the case that the shaman cured the patient. Rather, each entered upon a joint creation—the shaman's mute visioning was voiced by the patient, blind but word muttering. The fantasy of the Other that had produced, in the early part of the century, a "cannibalistic form of capitalist practice" (e.g., the Peruvian rubber company whose European employees regularly set native workers on fire and watched them burn to death for after-dinner entertainment) here yielded a form of anti-dote that was itself fantastic (Taussig, 10, 65, 81, 128). Healing was not first a return to homogeneity, but a baptism into the waters of decomposition (Taussig, 328, 344, 412). The doubleness of the historical dependence between colonizer and colonized, represented in the rhetorical ambivalence of bipartite categories like "civilized" and "savage," was ritually revisited in the form of a jointly fabricated space of imputation and otherness. The return gaze of the second-sighted eye, full of plunder and laughter, bearing pain, and revealing price-tags, conjured tongue magic from the grid of "rationality" (Taussig, 78, 94). Healing in such a structure of pain implied "undoing," going under the imagination of order to reemerge in a destabilized form of reciprocity. From such a vantage point underneath the rational mirror of Western confidence, Taussig has sought to reveal social science as itself peculiarly "mythic" (Taussig, 10–11).

Whether or not Taussig's project accomplishes anything like a subversion of Western pretensions to rationality, he has brought into view a provocative question of shamanic structure. Taussig focuses on effect; for him, "shamanism" does not necessarily designate anything attributable to a human subject independent of its others (Taussig, 446). It rather points to an economy of projection and return. What is mythically predicated and then enacted onto a historical other gathers to itself a kind of fetishistic force (Taussig, 95). His own conviction is that the economy in question must be brought into service of a deconstructive possibility. What must be shamanized is the Western category of "shamanism" itself. The center does not hold. The "West" is already an imaginative geography of double-worlds—first world affluence constructed on top of Third World poverty, suburban heaven layered over urban hell—that can only be resisted by means of its own apparatus. Anthropology's new task is one of staging a ritual conjuncture between myth and rationality in reverse of the usual outcome. It is now the academy and its sciences that are to be targeted in a new form of shamanistic warfare.

Leaving the more convoluted question of "academic mythologies" aside, it is nevertheless intriguing to rethink popular-culture practices in light of the shamanic perspective that Taussig offers. Has the shamanistic venture so thoroughly repressed in the scientific medical model of Western healing practices returned from repression in a surreptitious form—in the guise of popular-culture consumption of rhythmic reproductions of vitality and syncopated transfigurations of alienation? To what degree is the whole phenomenon of an intensively creative stream of marginalized musical innovation running through blues, jazz, R&B, and gospel, issuing in the 1950s in a pervasive national rock and roll movement that is itself subsequently taken over in the 1980s by an even more pervasive transnationalizing hip-hop subculture susceptible of analysis as a current of shamanistic "compensation" transmogrifying losses in other social quarters? Why is the population in our midst that is recurrently made to undergo the most violently immediate confrontation with death in its multiple social forms (today, in the physical form of gunplay, in the socioeconomic form of enghettoization, in the political form of imprisonment) also the population most recurrently productive of those cultural forms of Americana internationally selected as carrying especially vital intensity? Do "we" (who benefit from such arrangements) fail to recognize—and thus valorize—our own social forms of a shamanic search for healing? Or is our current practice of nonrecognition, but not nonappropriation, too effective a solution for those who benefit from these "mediations from marginality"?

Here the question can only be posed. Diasporic innovations of black expressivity like hip-hop show obvious powers of making the postindustrial cultural landscape yield something other than just quiet despair. While their harvest hardly warrants the label "healing," they do register various measures of transformation, rendering steel girders, for instance, and silicon cables eloquent in unforeseen and not fully controllable idioms of human reappropriation in dance forms like the "robot." Is this a form of shamanic retrieval of soul from the heart of the machine? Unquestionably, the forces of co-optation ever more quickly reestablish the regnant hegemony. But for a pause of time, for the interval of a gesture, something more than mere commodity logic shows its face—before the value of exchange again whispers its all-encompassing song. This may be a postmodern version of shamanic homeopathy, operating in the language of bricks and cement, police and poverty. But if so, the aim of its intention of exorcism should not be mistaken. On the dominant side of the equations of control and profit making, the effect is not blessing. It is a curse-form whose exposé assumes the shape of a rhetorical grenade. The language is dismemberment, and it is the young who find the code true to the social reality. For the marginalized, a few smoking brands are pulled from the fire before the burn is total. There is celebration of finesse, even in the face of terror and profound trauma and ultimate capitulation. But for the dominant, this shamanism is a force of prophecy. The aim is not reconsolidation of lost energy or recovery from soul loss, but breakup of the lie. The demand is for an initiatory death to the illusion that society is working. The gift is only such on the far side of a journey through dissolution and a reorganization of resources in wider circuits of reciprocity. Second sight is first of all the efficacy of a curse. But damnably, in our world, even cursing is now able to be bought off. There may be nothing sacred left.

# 4

# Constructing the Break

*The African singer alternates head and chest voice like a game of hide-and-seek in a labyrinth of rhythm. . . . and it throws open the gates of time to reveal a glimpse of the future.*

—*Francis Beby* (African Music, *132*)

In modern European discourses of the humanities and social sciences, ocular understandings of knowledge have dominated perception in ways that ramify the parsing and policing of social space by means of the categories of race. In response, oppressed African diaspora communities have repeatedly mobilized an alternative *episteme* of the ear to carve out hidden life-worlds inside of Western hegemonic formations (Berendt, 21–23; Esteva and Prakash, 75–76; Gilroy, 1993, 73, 198–202). Time (!) and again, Afro-diasporic political and cultural resistance has exploited *time* and *timing* as a modality of innovation "inside" the modern capitalist project of rationalizing labor and routinizing the body through the envisionments of race (Gilroy, 1987, 197–209). The result has been trickster-like alterations of a construct so thoroughly subjected to the regime of production as to be almost unthinkably unalterable (Gilroy, 1993, 37; Hopkins, 100–106; Willis, 37).

In European colonial venues, the clock emerged as almost equally efficacious in conquering indigenous populations as the cannon (Comaroff and Comaroff, 12, 64, 191–194). Time—as uniformly organized in a relentless sequence of homogeneous units, parsing human creative activity into calculable units of productive output and thus of capital accumulation for "owners"—emerges in modernity as one of the primary structures of ideology. That the flow of time came to be understood in Kant and Bergson as profoundly subjective only further reinforced the grafting of modern "humanity" onto the grid of modern capital.[1] It has been the singular savvy of slave communities and their descendants to rework the regimen of work into a regime of "workin' it" that reinvests infinite possibility inside of the space of racialized oppression (Gilroy, 1987, 202–210).

More particularly, slave populations in the Calvinist-dominated United States were subjected to a religiously valorized project of labor and a theologically scrutinized project of culture that allowed very little room for public display of antecedent "African" practices (Bynum, 252; Herskovitz, 214; Murphy, 1994, 190, 198–200; Raboteau, 64). Even more than in Roman Catholic organizations of enslavement in the Caribbean and Central and South America, North American versions of the same were "rationally" ruthless in breaking up shared cultural patterns in slave communities and breaking down religious practices (like drumming and dancing) "read" as idolatrous (Spencer, ix, xiv). In consequence, ancestral memory has been forced to work the interstices—of the black body, of the white plantation, indeed of the fleet momentariness of audition itself in the spirituals, the blues, jazz, gospel, soul, funk, techno, and hip-hop (Coleman, 50–52; Gilroy, 1987, 153–222; Hall, 27). Where James Brown could pride himself on always being "right on the one" (hitting the beat precisely "on beat"), this was already an improvisational "riff" on a growing African American tradition of syncopated explorations of the intervals between the beat(ing)s of order (Gilroy, 1987, 212–213; Spencer, 143).

The argument elaborated here is that this sophisticated laboring of time into alternative spaces and delirious places is quintessentially "political" and functions as a form of de facto tricksterism that holds up to the community the arbitrary and constructed nature of the very forms by which it is controlled and dominated (Babcock-Abrahams, 182–185; Siems, 148–149).[2] Such a sophistication makes resistance a possibility even in the tightest tenement, the most meager interval. By itself, of course, such a resistance does not translate into an alternative world, a utopian realization of, say, Martin Luther King's "beloved community." But it does point up one of the fault lines in a totalitarian project.

## Resistance in the Key of Temporality

Globalizing capital seems virtually irresistible in its powers of organizing. "Everywhere" appears to be vulnerable to its drive to monetize, its logic of "putting up for sale." The efflorescence of visual culture to which we stand not only as witnesses today, but also in which we are interpolated as participants is only the latest extension of the logic of accumulation (Kroker, 1). The late Middle Ages shift in Europe from "production for use" to "production for exchange" would almost necessarily require hypertrophy of the eye (Foucault, 1980, 92–100; Marx, 71, 85, 360).[3] The market is not an institution of patience; it does not tolerate a long period of assessment of a possible buy. It relocates value toward the exterior of the object, toward what can be taken in by a glance, toward a surface equality of appearance, formulated as a price (Marx, 90, 95, 102–103). Yes—the real marker of value, I believe, continues to be labor's surrogated surplus as Marx so tenaciously taught—human effort surreptitiously submerged into a homogenized quantification of time (Marx, 38, 91, 210; Postone, 150, 189, 202). But increasingly in postmodern rationality, it is the sign itself that sweeps all into its magical sway (Baudrillard, 143). Hilfiger and Nike rule by sleight of hand.

And indeed capitalism's reconstruction of the human subject is similarly driven toward a surface reorientation. The schema of racialization that emerges as modernity's organizing taxonomy for colonial trade in property and person is the most obvious signal of this supremacy of sight. As has been well clarified in postcolonial historiography, the first assessment of indigenous populations by European colonists was leveraged by theological categories: the meaning of observable differences in skin and religion, coiffure and culture, was decided in a spiritual projection (Dussel, 54–55; Omi and Winant, 60–61; Perkinson, 1999, 439; White, 160–164). If immediate preaching did not result in immediate conversion, the outcome was all too frequently assessed as an absolute augury (Earl, 13; Wessels, 60). Obduracy of the heart toward God, in European theophany, was thought to have been psychosomatically signified on the body surface as a predestination to perdition (Bastide, 270).

This spiritual assessment was also quickly integrated into the European perception of white skin (Mills, 13, 21, 53; Pagden, 1–2). Pallor supposedly predicted valor and favor in the courts of deity. Two hundred and fifty years down the line, this theological supremacy emerged from the crucible of the European Wars of Religion as a metaphysical hegemony. "Enlightenment" designated not only a mental condition but also an epidermal destination (Mills, 44–46; Omi and Winant, 61–64; West, 1982, 47, 51). Anglo-Germanic philosophical predominance supposedly predicted evolutionary trajectory.

The whole world trudged toward the apex of universal development that stood revealed in the halls of Jena. White supremacy pretended to scientific progeny.

The ascent to world-historical dominance of the all-surveilling eye of Europe did not only show up in overtly racist taxonomies, but it also coalesced with no less insidious effect in the "common sense" of the day (Gramsci, 330; Mills, 53). The breakup of village communities characteristic of modernity, the erosion of extended families, the more recent atomization of urban neighborhoods that are all recognizable effects of the carrot of upward mobility backed by the stick of unemployability are predicated on the notion that a human being is primarily an individual. That predication is perhaps the quintessential myth of modernity. The "individual" celebrated as the subject of human rights in democratic political revolutions is a fictional creature of the law (Bellah, 80, 84; Esteva and Prakash, 11, 51, 76–77, 91, 121–125). In the United States, this legal power is imaged as a blind lady holding a scale—the obstruction of the eye indicating exactly the domain of the proposed formal equality. In the conceit of common sense, individual faces individual before the sightless "citations" of justice.

But clearly global capital has been a prodigious power of dismemberment, cutting "the person" out of the thick web of relationships that have sustained identity around the world up until the modern period and relocating personhood inside the fetishized construct of autonomous individuality. Today, the fetish reigns supreme—imaged in the market, eroticized in the commercial, empowered as "citizen," privatized in the dwelling, euthanized in slow motion in nursing homes or the warehouse of the wearied wealthy called "Florida." At the turn of the millennium, that individuality is primarily an entity of the fast moving eye,

> scouring the surface of significance,
> constructing meaning from a momentary fleetingness,
> concerned for the appearance,
> the sign, the scheme, the "isosceles-rhomboid" flair of the hair,[4]
> the slant of gait, the lime green lip,
> the well-pierced tip of the tongue,
> the landscape of leather shape, the gothic cape, the nape
> of shaved neck, the alligator-ed step, the heft of furred drape,
> the deft dip of the diamond-studded wrist.

It is all about the visual package, seeking to register its hungry difference in a flickering second on the surface, in the consuming eye, before the advertisement disappears back into the noumenal density of the unmarked sameness of humanity in modern form. In the legal construct, the formal equivalence of every person to every other person, the sameness of rights, proposes a visual tautology, an utter symmetry, a total replaceable-ness, the complete homogenization of producing or consuming units. Never mind that the actuality is anything *but* equality. The ideal is the universal human observed in the mirror of Immanuel Kant. Humanities and social science departments are themselves simply academic constructs of that very vision (Rorty, 181).

That historically we should find some of the sons and daughters of a duskier family tree coding their own critiques of such in the key of polyphony should not surprise (Bynum, 77–102). Merely to stay put on the inside of the discourses of the eye is already to lose the game in the very act of playing it. Part of the potency of indigenous palaver around the world has always been the social mobilization of the role of trickster, marking the cultural boundary of that society as itself arbitrary and contestable (Gates, xxvii, 4–6, 47, 49, 59, 76). Here is consciousness in front of itself, aware, able to smirk. Sometimes tricksterism is the only possible space of politics that can be pried open. Even then, it can serve a broader initiative when conditions conduce to more organized resistance.[5] But at the least, it keeps the door to alternative existence an open allurement. In modernity, inside the academy, piquing policy by way of percussive antiphony has been the particular tactic of those enculturated in the algorithmic probabilities of African improvisation. Western African explorations of syncopation, central African systems of percussive attack, all of the stylistic strategies by which multiple meter and offbeat phraseology, ironic allusion and layered profusion of impertinence, have been elaborated into durable forms of cultural memory are the base-beat for the melody line offered here (Thompson, xiii–xiv).

## Postcoloniality in the Key of Mythology

In mapping out such a piquant tricksterism (African American historian of religions), Charles Long's revision of (European philosopher of religions) Rudolph Otto's comparative categories will supply the first moment. Otto came to prominence in the first half of the twentieth century as a compelling voice in the newly emergent discipline of History of Religions. His self-assigned task was that of developing a method of comparison for anthropology's growing wealth of information on the colonized cultures it had invaded and studied.

The phrase he innovated for a cross-cultural intimation of God— "the mystery that is simultaneously tremendous and fascinating, terrible and desirable"—was then employed to line-up religious data from diverse cultures on the ledger of academic comparison to clarify commonalities and differences (Otto, 13).

Charles Long's genius is to have raided the raiders and used their own categories against themselves. Otto's *mysterium tremendum et fascinosum* becomes, in Long's work, a divining rod, dividing the religious experience of the West from the rest (Long, 1986, 9, 137–139). European culture indeed knows the ultimate as "the fantastic" (Long, 1986, 137, 169). Having succeeded in conquest and capture on an unprecedented scale, Western mythology, in the short term, experienced no rupture of its basic myth, no disconfirmation of its pretension to universality and supremacy (Long, 1986, 123). Indigenous cultures, on the other hand, almost without exception had to survive a cataclysm at once material and ideological (Long, 1986, 9, 110, 177, 181). Not only were their physical bodies violated, but their mythic membranes of meaning also were annihilated (Long, 193). "Enduring" meant profound ritual work to reconstitute a cosmos that answered for—or at least mysteriously allowed—such irresistible trauma and terror (Long, 1986, 166–170). Unavoidably, they became intimate with the ultimate under the force of inscrutable ferocity. "God" had to be somehow "comprehended" in the midst of, in spite of, even perhaps in collusion with, the terror.

It is such cultures alone, in the modern era, that "know" reality in its aspect of utter opacity and terribleness, according to Long (Long, 1986, 123–125, 178, 197). What for the West is sheer frivolity and take-it-or-leave-it religious "play" on the surface of existence is for the rest, a matter of a life-and-death struggle with irreducible dread and violation (Long, 1986, 165, 196). The ensuing ritual labors to remake an inhabitable life-world and liveable self-image meant transfiguring violence into vitality (Long, 1986, 170). Native American Ghost Dance practices, Pacific Island cargo cult activities, Jamaican Rasta resistance, Haitian Voudou revolts, African American Black Church, and Black Muslim innovations alike are read by Long under this rubric of the *mysterium tremendum* (Long, 1986, 110, 139, 166–167).

By breaking open Otto's cipher for ultimate reality into a devilish signifier of the breakdown of colonial domination over traditional religion, Long lampoons the will-to-compare itself. His tactic is "tricky," revealing impassable boundaries where ideology claims unity, calling both European colonial Christianity and Western

Enlightenment philosophy on stage in all of their constructed "supremacy" as fictions of "fascination" lacking access to the "tremendous" and tremulous depths forced upon the indigenous (Long, 1986, 139, 146, 153, 167). Long's genius is to have grasped that colonization for the colonized amounted to an experience of rupture the size of the cosmos itself, calling in question aboriginal myths of origin and demanding, as the only possible antidote, ritual reconstruction (Long, 1986, 123, 139, 167, 179). Academic study of such in one or another discourse of the humanities or social sciences fails to the very degree it succeeds (Long, 1986, 9, 110, 166–167). The key is not academic clarity, but the core impulse to survive at any cost.

## Epistemology in the Break

It is this plunge into rupture, into the break, theorized by Long as global in extent and now paradigmatic in effect, that will underwrite the particular genealogy of creativity I want to explore in what follows. I am arguing that the long tradition of Afro-diaspora embroidering of breaks with eloquence, of populating small gaps with the groans and growls of multiple identity, of prying open the present to host visitations from the past (in possession-cult-like ritual activity) and hauntings from the future (in prophetic social movements contesting the current order of things) is a form of Nietzschean "idol sounding" (Anderson, 130; Nietzsche, 31–32). Sounding out the fetish, striking its fixed form from varied angles such that it yields motion and oscillation, making the idol divulge its wood and metal are the tenets of a spirited politics elaborating its polemics in the cracks of temporal conformity. The idol sounded here is, of course, the pretended supremacy in forms both overt and invidious.

The great question in the precincts of academe is the degree to which the humanities or social sciences, as part of a culturally particular *episteme* of "knowing the human" that is constituted precisely in the imperialistic pretension to know "universally," are themselves idolatrous. The focus I want to propose is one that succeeds the Enlightenment's "turn to the subject" and Deconstruction's "turn to language" in what I would call a "somersault towards rhythm." To some degree, Foucault's notions of naïve and subjugated knowledges are helpful in catching a glimpse of the bounded and policed terrain of knowing that is in question here (Foucault, 1980, 82–83). What must be "highlighted" in the envisioning processes characteristic of *theoria*, though, is exactly a turn away from the eye toward the ear.

## Ironic Polyphony

Henry Louis Gates, Jr.'s work in *The Signifying Monkey* offers a helpful cipher by which to query the history. He emphasizes the capacity for ironic improvisation characteristic of "black" language use as the requisite "trope" requiring attention. Ironic and parodic improvisation opening out the paradigmatic register of speech underneath the syntagmatic chain emerges, in his analysis, as a primary political tactic for a people under surveillance (Gates, 49). The considerable skill with double-voiced discourse that has been so evident a feature of Afro-diaspora survival tactics gained street-level recognition in the United States by the late nineteenth century as a collective capacity to defy oppression through signifying, specifying, and lying (Gates, 54, 77; Willis, 1, 45). "Capping" on one's enemies, inverting insult and aggression into a masterful "put-down" that was simultaneously a "put-on," served the need to find ways of preserving dignity while also preserving life in a hostile world. What was heard simplistically and eagerly in one way by the Master or Boss could be made to encode an altogether different and even opposite meaning for those in the know.

More often than not, the space of public speech, in such ritual revisions, was transvalued in terms of a different time code. The jerk of a neck, the bob of a head, the flash of an eye, the arch of a back created instant syncopation in the visual mode—a matter of "troping" the words actually said with two, three, five, or fifteen alternative inflections by way of the timing of the bodily gesture on top of or underneath the speech. Such an exercise is a savvy "volatilizing" of the solidity of dominant organizations of space, and of the flow of meaning through space, by way of an act of multiplication in the dimension of time.

In this sense, African American creativity inside the disciplinary domains of the academy has often taken the form of a subversive "mathematics." Not only in oral presentations, but also in written interventions as erudite as those of a Du Bois or a Cornel West, as aesthetically stunning as those of a Hurston or a Morrison, or as politically cunning as those of a King or a Baldwin, words have been made the reservoir of a promiscuous wit. There has often been, in academic interventions culturally coded as "African American," a proliferation of meaning that can be experienced as simultaneously "dense" in depth and "dazzling" in intertextuality. Wrestled into the language of a sine curve and sound, the impression is one of a mixing of high frequency melodic lines with low frequency base-beats that grip the mind and grope the trunk all at once. How does such a claim register in the protocols of knowing that carry the imprimatur of "higher education"? It registers in the body, even when that body is white, and male, and afraid of itself.

My argument is that the Western university is generally not, however, able to recognize such within its own protocols of "knowledge." The white male body remains normatively "regnant,"[6] as erect as a tree stump and as (im)mobile, focusing all its lights in the surveilling eye of objectivity, ignorant of the night inside its own cells. "Identity," in my experience, is not first of all a word, but a rhythmic resonance giving rise, eventually, to a groan (Perkinson, 2001, 96, 112). When James Brown screams "I," "I," "I," nine times in a row on his hit record, "Please, Please, Please," before moving on to the next part of the sentence, he is trying to say something about the core of human being that the first person pronoun (or indeed, language in general) cannot say except through its own rupturing (Gilroy, 213). Clear "articulation" and certain "identification," on the other hand, are much further down the line and "conceptualization" is at an even greater remove.

Deep thinking begins with a plastic body, capable of exploring the cadences of a quiet timbre, the caterwauling of an unmet desire, the catharsis of a whole community of ancestry still locked up in silence inside a moving bone (Brandon, 142; Goodman, 219–221; Murphy, 6–7; Walker, 1972, 104–115). Cut off from a wide-ranging repertoire of gestural performance, thought is easy prey to the design of domination, the fixation of meaning in a single reference, the mistaking of map for territory (Esteva and Prakash, 76–77, 145–146). Having a body that is freed for more full-bellied forms of expression is by no means a guarantee against take-over by dominating categories. But neither is gesture accidental and incidental to thought, as recent studies have made clear.

The kind of body offered as the preferred signifier in most academic departments is a living icon of ideology and dominant class hieroglyphics (the history of affirmative action efforts and multicultural initiatives aside, the statistics still descry the facts: university departments remain reflections of the white affirmative action that has characterized this country from its modern inception) (Mills, 53). This body's typical "white maleness" is not merely a function of appearance, but of a whole cult and culture of controlling norms (Dyer, 44–45). It works not only at the level of sight, but also in quite ruthless pedagogies of time and timing. That it is schooled to understand its own peculiar disposition as "universal" and "exemplary" is the very substance of its sense of entitlement and apotheosis. Never mind that society today is avowedly color blind and secular in its public practice.

The absolutizing of white privilege that began with Columbus, was given explicit theological valence in Puritan color-codes, and found institutional investment in the southern plantation and the northern suburb, today remains a "sacred" inscription in and on the typical middle-class body, in spite of a more recent training in race neutrality. Since the emergence of the ethnicity paradigm for explaining socio-cultural difference beginning with the University of Chicago in the 1930s, it has become *de rigueur* to educate dominate class people in the designs of the color-blind eye (Omi and Winant, 15, 40, 69). But the body habituated in white upbringing carries a deeper memory and an older code. Light skin today is a social palimpsest—bearing contradictory witness to the racial project—even when the *persona* is committedly antiracist.

And the double inscription of the history of the country on the normative white body is also the place where a different regime of knowing can be and regularly is opened up. Caught between the contradictory social inscriptions of white supremacy and color-blind neutrality, the white body is often (im)mobilized in a not quite nameable tension in situations of racial encounter. The tension is the product of a conscious commitment to equality underwritten by an unconscious conviction of superiority. And that double aim is the precise structure of much of our social process. Almost inevitably, the rhetoric of parity becomes an ideological mask for the institutional practice of disparity (Frankenberg, 135). But that very contradiction is also a space of opportunity. Gates recognized that space as the place of a possible irony—the possibility of working a significance in two directions at once (Gates, 49, 50, 76).

Irony, at one level, defines the (im)possibility of occupying the place of blackness in America—a place that is indeed the Archimedean point for the whole social order of the country. Irony is really the linguistic equivalent of Heisenberg's uncertainty principle regarding matter. Its effect is to render space duplicate in the near unity of time: in an ironic mode of signifying, a thing can be either this or that (its exact opposite), with only a blink of an eye intervening. The oscillation between the two possible choices of meaning takes place at the speed of thought. For dominant culture observers of such a tactic, this is like suddenly seeing everything as if ghosted by a "double" that is its photographic negative. How does one know which is the real picture? The dilemma in a nutshell. The deeper discovery? Both are pictures!

The reality underneath the metaphor is unknowable except as part of everything else. Black is part of white, white is part of black! And yet . . . the oscillation continues. The effect is a slight hesitation, a minute paralysis. Domination is made unsure of its target. Listen to Kristin Hunter Lattany for a moment, in her article called "Off-Timing: Stepping to the Different Drummer," for an anthology dealing with Du Bois's notion of double-consciousness:

> I use off-timing as a metaphor for subversion, for code, for ironic attitudes toward mainstream beliefs and behavior, for choosing a vantage point of distance from the majority, for coolness, for sly commentary on the master race, for riffing and improvising off the man's tune and making fun of it. (Lattany, 165)

The "off-timing" of such an irony exactly identifies the mode of the method of survival it represents: it works time into a disruption of the intention to dominate by hitting "off" the beat, "syncopating" meaning by introducing uncertainty as to whether it signifies "this". . . or its exact opposite. Later, in lamenting the loss of bilinguality and biculturality on the part of some black Americans as throwing the ability to survive seriously in question, Lattany continues:

> Once, we danced off-time when the beat of jazz was too fast, employing cool, casual movements that seemed—but only seemed—indifferent to the music. We slipped in and out of the various verbal modes at our command with the same dexterity—most notably, using a white voice to talk their talk at work and slipping fluidly, instantaneously, into the race vernacular one minute after quitting time. (Lattany, 172)

### Percussive Fluidity

It is this slippage back and forth, this knowledge about time as a "tactical weapon" in the battle for survival, that art historian Robert Farris Thompson has taken up and elaborated, ironically, in a visual key. In the opening to his 1983 publication, *Flash of the Spirit*, he says,

> Since the Atlantic slave trade, ancient African organizing principles of song and dance have crossed the seas from the Old World to the New. There they took on new momentum, intermingling with each other and with New World or European styles of singing and dance. Among those principles are *the dominance of a percussive performance style* (attack and vital aliveness in sound and motion); *a propensity for multiple meter* (competing meters sounding all at once); *overlapping call and response* in singing (solo/chorus, voice/instrument—"interlock systems" of performance); *inner pulse control* (a "metronome sense," keeping a

beat indelibly in mind as a rhythmic common denominator in a welter
of different meters); *suspended accentuation patterning* (offbeat phrasing
of melodic and choreographic accents); and, at a slightly different but
equally recurrent level of exposition, *songs and dances of social allusion*
(music which, however danceable and "swinging," remorselessly
contrasts social imperfections against implied criteria for perfect
living) . . . *Flash of Spirit* is about *visual* and *philosophic* streams of
creativity and imagination, running parallel to the massive musical and
choreographic modalities that connect black persons of the western
hemisphere, as well as the millions of European and Asian people
attracted to and performing their styles, to Mother Africa. (Thompson,
xiii–xiv)[7]

The sensibilities here organize the visible on the basis of the temporal.
Even in visual mode, the instinct is that of figuring rhythmic differentiation into ocular sameness. Spatial art is rocked by an aural beat.

British cultural critic Paul Gilroy offers a similar commentary in his
first two books: *There Ain't No Black in the Union Jack: The Cultural
Politics of Race and Nation* and *The Black Atlantic: Modernity and
Double Consciousness*. Music, in particular, serves as his metaphor
for political resistance in the mode of double-timing syncopation.
Beginning with black church traditions working overtime in the slave
era, alchemically operating on the violence of the institution to con-
serve the memory of terror in the sensorium of the groove, black
Atlantic musics represent an ongoing communal transfiguration that
Gilroy labels "the slave sublime" (Gilroy, 37, 73, 77). The rhythmic
intensification of the recollection of agony becomes a weapon of survival, invigorating efforts to elaborate alternative identities in varied
spaces of industrial hegemony.

Cultural critic Tricia Rose likewise elaborates on percussive strategies
of transformation. Hip-hop culture is her terrain of investigation—a
love–hate labor at the core of contemporary globalization. She tracks
the innovations of "flow," "layering," and "ruptures in line" (Rose, 38).
The "stylistic continuities" between break dancing, tagging, MC-ing
(rapping), and DJ-ing yield a style "nobody can deal with": visual,
physical, musical, and lyrical lines are set in motion, broken abruptly
with sharp angular breaks, yet they sustain motion and energy
through fluidity and flow (Rose, 39, 61).

[G]raffiti [works] in extreme italics . . . letters double or triple
shadowed, suggesting [both circular and] forward or backward
motion . . . Popping and locking are moves [in breakdancing] in which
joints are snapped abruptly into angular positions [but in such a serial

manner that the effect is] a semiliquid flow toward the fingertip or toe . . . [R]appers stutter and alternatively race through passages, always moving within the beat or in response to it, often using the music as a partner in rhyme . . . DJs layer sounds literally one on top of the other, creating a dialogue between sampled sounds and words. (Rose, 39)

And Rose is savvy about the significance.

Interpreting these concepts theoretically, one can argue that they create and sustain rhythmic motion, continuity, and circularity via flow; accumulate, reinforce, and embellish this continuity through layering; and manage threats to these narratives by building in ruptures that highlight the continuity as it momentarily challenges it. These effects at the level of style and aesthetics suggest affirmative ways in which profound social dislocation and rupture can be managed and perhaps contested in the cultural arena. Let us imagine these hip hop principles as a blueprint for social resistance and affirmation: create sustaining narratives, accumulate them, layer, embellish, and transform them. However, be also prepared for rupture, find pleasure in it, in fact, plan on social rupture. When these ruptures occur, use them in creative ways that will prepare you for a future in which survival will demand a sudden shift in ground tactics. (Rose, 39)

Rose's "reading" of the urban politics of visual iconography, bodily negotiations of public space, and sonic contestations of air waves exhibits once again the priority of time and timing in African American survival strategies. When geography and architecture cannot be successfully taken over, they can be rhythmized and made to yield a different set of meanings in an alternative economy of power.

Anthropologist Morton Marks takes the analysis into a sustained examination of the phenomenon of "the break" itself as a characteristic mode of mobilizing African American vitality. Here emerges a more explicit articulation of the way African cultures have themselves tended to evaluate this kind of work with temporality—an invocation and evocation of ancestry, the "possession" of the present by the past, the warp of time in the woof of space, the trick of "passage" in the tricksterism of tradition.

### Code-Switchery

For Marks, the primary characteristic that must be grasped is a phenomenon he calls code-switching—the propensity of Afro-diaspora rituals to generate meaning through the alternation between European and African-derived styles (Marks, 61–62). Its important quality is abruptness, the percussive edge of difference it brings into play when it appears (Marks, 62). What he recognizes as an irruption of private identities into public spaces in Afro-Brazilian celebrations of carnival and of possession-behavior in the middle of popular culture in Afro-Cuban traditions of singing, he also glimpses in North American gospel forms of preaching (Marks, 90–91, 112–115). The move is from order to noise, from a European "white" stylistics to an African "black" one, from the uniformity of a singular melody line to the complex polyrhythms underscoring and, at times, overriding a more autonomous melody line (Marks, 64, 66, 96, 98).

Marks thematizes what he is observing as the suddenly produced emergence of a different set of performance rules that is not mere ritual *communitas* in Victor Turner's sense, not mere liminality, but the breakout of one set of identities from a hidden zone of privacy into a communally valorized public expression (Marks, 75, 113). Marks is careful to emphasize that, in Africa itself, this style "does not represent transition from one cultural style to another," but is "simply a part of composition technique" (Marks, 66). However, what is probably a "widely distributed West African speaking convention" involving con-trapuntal forms of argumentation (or an "oscillation between 'noise' and 'order' ") in the New World is actively redeployed as an "expression of cultural duality" and a "communication strategy to represent, dramatize, or bring about transitions (rituals) of various kinds" (Marks, 64–66). Afro-diasporan assimilations of European patterns of belief suddenly disclose their inverse when performance is studied: it is European content that is taken up within and subsumed under African rules and grammar, when code is analyzed (Marks, 67). Marks comprehends the style change as "generating a ritual event [that is essentially that of] spirit-possession" and tracks that trance-work in multiple forms (Marks, 67). Sound is rendered the site of agency both socially and psychologically (Marks, 67).

For instance, in his analysis of gospel, Marks emphasizes that whereas the code-switching in relationship to Brazilian carnival is primarily a matter of musical codes and with Cuban song that of linguistic codes (from Spanish to Lucumi), in North American black church, the focus will fall on "style-switching within a single language" (Marks, 87). Here the cues for a "switch of channels" include changes in intonation pattern, rhythm, and breathing rate, which together effect a ritual induction of trance (Marks, 87). Compared with the Brazilian and Cuban examples, the trance behavior in gospel preaching has become much more covert, referencing no African pantheon of deities and using no African-derived liturgical language (Marks, 90). The markers of the appearance of an alternative set of performance rules are largely those of "trance-produced vocalizations" (Marks, 91).

The gospel-preaching process begins in call–response, the speaker answered by congregational "helpers." But as the preacher heats up the venue, the orderliness and musicality of the antiphony between leader and helpers is itself "attacked" (percussively) by the dissociation of the leader's entry into trance. The "preacher" begins to give responses as well, becoming a syncopated participant in his or her own production (Marks, 94). Hyperventilation, constriction of the vocal cords, shifts of a full octave between beginning and ending words in an utterance, signal the arousal toward a peak experience, the preacher becoming host "site" of a multiplicity of voices, both speaking and commenting on the speaking in an overlapping refrain with the congregation (Marks, 94).

> [T]he unpredictable speech-accenting of the preaching-melody line, along with the over-breathing which marks the lead singer's [preacher's] phrase and sentence junctures, clash with the regularly stressed background rhythms. (Marks, 97)

The multiplication of time sequences into a thickened texture of different times creates uncertainty; it simultaneously represents a cultural patterning that marks a point of "crossover," inviting the audience into a form of what might be called trance-travel (Marks, 98).

Marks exegetes such a moment under the rubric of ancestor worship (Marks, 98). Encounter with departed kin "waiting on the further shore" may or may not be thematized explicitly in such preaching, but the trance induction does facilitate a "going home" that is both "return to Africa" and "aspiration to the land of Promise" (Marks, 99). Here, gospel is elaborating a context that can "hardly be called 'Christian' at all" (Marks, 98). The references are as layered as the music. The African place names and tribal designations that, in carnival, santeria, and voudou, have transmuted into deities (*orisha, loa*) and become ciphers for psychological states of transition in gospel are all sedimented together to return from exile (Marks, 99, 100).

The whole can be summarized as the "activation of a metaphor": a performance rule in which the "first part of the song talks about an action which the second part carries out" (Marks, 104). "Home" is created through music; the switch both represents and effects the "Africanization of performance rules" (Marks, 105). The unison of the opening chorus switches to call-and-response, which is itself undercut by broken rhythmic patterns elaborated over a metronome beat, with the leader embroidering fragmentary formulaic expressions overlapping with the chorus that is as much about creating percussive sound as meaning, and the like (Marks, 105)—the entire performance emerging as a welter of contrasting rhythm patterns in which individual improvisation is licensed as an echo of the overall communal complexity, not as virtuosity on its own. The setting thus becomes the "home"[8]—the move from introductory melody, through a complexion of melodic line on top of percussive underpinning, to the final loss of melody altogether in a dense rhythmic body of sound, punctuated by staggered vocal embellishments and clashing percussive contrasts is the ritual process that builds "Africa" on the spot in the liminal state known as trance (Marks, 106).

It is no accident that the style-switching is unilinear—from European cultural codes to African ones (Marks, 64, 69, 81). The issue is not mere oscillation or back-and-forth "play" with diverse cultural orientations. The transition is rather significant of "war." A preference is stated, a coming out is enacted: "you (observer) may think we are acculturated, but beware, the real deal is the ancestor grin that emerges in the trance moment." Simply to state such, however, merely to articulate such an identity in the key of antinomy, to argue descriptively for a preferred understanding, would already signify capitulation. The engulfment of European protocols in African codes—figuratively "eating up" the individual performance body in a larger complex of rhythmic structures and resonances—signals a different order of order (and relates intimately to our discussion of "witchcraft" practices and fears in chapters 2 and 8).

Marks notes the salience in musical contexts: the switch implies that "an extra-musical event is taking place" (Marks, 110). This is the incarnation of "more" in the key of complexity. The switch is a disordering of order in service of action, of history and memory in the mode of ritual work (Marks, 110).

> The Africanization of performance rules is also a performative, since it is this process that creates the ritual setting and/or event. In other words, what I am terming Africanization always carries with it whole domains of behavior and structures not present when the "performance" begins. Thus the study of the ordering of the elements is crucial; performance rules themselves may be said to have a staggered entry. Performances must therefore be viewed as processes and as totalities whose multiple codes form coherent systems that generate meaning. (Marks, 111)

Here is an ironic elocution—the uncanny echo of "Africanness" as that which gathers up non-Africanness into a larger comprehension.

The opposition "European/African" is itself overcome by being embraced *as* a rhythmic structure, *as* syncopation, "staggered" meaning. It is processual, the "very model of a liminal event" (Marks, 111). It is the introduction of a break, the ritualization of transition by transitioning one mode into a multiplicity. The mathematics is not "one replaced by one is one," but "one broken open to many is one."

As Marks says, this is "a different view of Afro-American public festivities" (Marks, 111). They have typically been dealt with either as "copies of European counterparts . . . temporary lapses from 'civilization,' " or as "more or less purely 'African' events . . . ambulatory open-air museums of bygone primitive customs" (Marks, 111). Here, however, the emphasis is on a group of performance rules governing "linguistic, musical, motor and religious behavior" that "come out" in a place of structured liminality, breaking open public space to the expression of privately held identities, engulfing social boundaries that reflect cultural dualities in a code-switching tactic. The boundary itself is thus refigured as a percussive structure. The performance rules of different cultures are encompassed in a ritual "passage" that leads to trance—to the takeover and possession of the one set of rules by another. The boundary is not so much opposed as it is rhythmized, gathered into a paradox of behavior that is simultaneously liminal but rule-bound. The emergence of African performance rules—first inside and then alongside and on top of European ones—effects a break which itself contributes to trance. As trance takes place, it "creates" a ritual setting, triggering possession behavior in others as well (Marks, 113).

Thus, while its public profile is certainly less overt than Brazilian processions or Cuban popular performances, gospel, for Marks, remains "the repository of African-based performance rules in the United States" (Marks, 114). And it has itself issued in popular culture manifestations in the style of soul singers such as James Brown, Aretha Franklin, Wilson Pickett, and the like. The easy and rapid "feedback" across the boundary supposedly separating "sacred" and "secular" in black culture foregrounds Marks's emphasis on the formality of what constitutes "Africanness" (Marks, 115). It is the introduction and integration of altered states of consciousness and trance behavior into performance, whether located in the church or in popular culture venues, that points to the influence of African cultural forms on New World cultures (Marks, 115). It also augurs a different kind of cross-cultural identification in the African diaspora, a sharing of trance-cues that remain intelligible across different language systems and religious idioms (Marks, 115). For Marks, the shared trance features encode both common origins in Africa and historical connections in the

New World. They also query theories of one-way processes of acculturation, revising the idea that black has simply adapted to white.

## Rhythmized Intensity

If Marks's analysis points toward "Africanization" as a proclivity for "empowerment through possession," Thompson's work on textiles provides an interesting syncopation of the same in underscoring the way the work with polyrhythm can be made to function as a tactic of resistance even in the mode of the visual. Citing the creolized cloths of Bahia, the capes of Surinamese maroons and the string-quilts of the black South in the United States as evidence of a Mande influence in diverse regions of the New World, Thompson also emphasizes this "love of aesthetic intensity" as "an autonomous development in the history of Afro-American visual creativity" (Thompson, 208). The "deliberate clashing of 'high-affect colors,'" in willful, percussively contrastive" multistrip compositions constitutes a form of "vibrant visual attack and *timing* of these cloths" that is simultaneously traditional and novel (Thompson, 208; emphasis added). The precedent is clear: a seventeenth century textile of Benin, in which patterned and unpatterned strips are deliberately clashed and the broadloom cotton indigo-dyed strips are "cut down" to the cultural size of the narrow loom, multistrip style (Thompson, 210). For Thompson, this is technique—a "breaking" of the "bulk of received foreign stuff" that grants "freedom to the maker of the costume" (Thompson, 210). Similar techniques of "frequency modulation" and "metric play," of staggered accentual patterns and "rippling effect[s]" can be found in Mali and Senegal, surcharging the cloth with "visual syncopation" and vivid phrasing (Thompson, 211). Thompson "reads" this staggering of strip relations in terms of a comment of Owen Barfield on "poetic diction":

> Imagination . . . lights up only when the normal continuum . . . is interrupted in such a manner that a kind of gap is created, and an earlier impinges directly upon a later—a more living upon a more conscious. (Thompson, 295 quoting Barfield, 179)

Here is a partial intersection with Marks's emphasis on "the break" as inculcating trance-connection to ancestry, opening the living community to a "present possession" by the past.

But grasp of the meaning of this gap is not left simply to academic interpretation. The "frequent, seemingly imperative suspension of expected patterning" invokes an old folk tradition of relativizing evil by interrupting it, fracturing its lines of control. Patchwork dress, in the British West Indies, "keeps the *jumbie*, a spirit, away from a resting place" (Thompson, 221). In Haiti, vibrantly striped shirts procured from ritual experts are used to break up the evil eye—entrapping the eye in a visual field of staccato contrasts that admit no easy escape, no simple flow to the edge and beyond (Thompson, 222). Mismatched socks in rural Ohio, and jumbled wallpapering of cabins in the South both served as Afro-American innovations to "keep spirits away" (Thompson, 222). In Senegambia, this impulse was understood as a necessary randomizing of flow paths, fighting against the propensity of evil to travel in straight lines (Thompson, 222). Thompson himself apostrophizes the pattern as a "history of resistance to the closures of the Western technocratic way" (Thompson, 222).

## Syncopated Trickery

Adapted to a discussion of the social sciences and humanities, the analysis yields numerous questions. To the degree the "knowledge industry" that begins with the European Enlightenment and continues through contemporary Western academic influences worldwide is based on a scientific paradigm, it is part and parcel of the capitalist mode of organizing time in uniform units of empty and formally equal duration. "Knowledge" as a process of testing discrete portions of the universe in controlled experiments designed to yield "objective" data works off of a principle of elaborating a certain kind of distance between the knowing mind and the thing known. The eye is the bridge of that distance, concentrating the vibratory patterns of light into snapshots focused on the die molecules in the retina.

Compared to the ear, the eye is an organ of stasis, of quanta, organizing the universe into synchrony and synoptic stability (Berendt, 16, 22, 27–32). The ear, on the other hand, serves diachrony, movement, wave patterns, organizing vibration into a kind of focus that animates the entire body, which invites resonant reciprocity, movement in kind, which invokes the body's own ultimate identity as itself a peculiar pattern of motion (Berendt, 17, 19, 43). To the degree that the humanities (for instance) represent a final focus on texts, on knowledge that can be written down, stored for the eye, quantified at least in terms of pages, commodified and circulated through the market place, academic study of humanity is already a deformation of the subject, indeed a "subject-ion" of the phenomenon to the hegemony of vision for the sake of capital accumulation.

As with textiles, so with texts: the texture must be broken. Ironically, Thompson underscores the function of contrast opened by introducing *time* into the visual, while Marks could be said to thicken the perception of the possibilities of an alternative temporal occupation of shared *space*. Each is instancing the advent of a tricksterism.

In some sense, the trickster figure is precisely what modernity's turn to reason attempted to exorcize from the self-reflections of many traditional cultures. The Enlightenment idea of a universal form of subjectivity pretended that culture was only skin deep (unless that skin happened to be dark, in which case it was not yet fully "human" skin), and that underneath the accidents of enculturation, the human subject was everywhere the same. The pretension was quintessentially European and in no small measure, the reflex effect of capitalism's emphasis on exchange value (the interchangeability of everything through the market) at the level of humanity.

The trickster-hero, in most cultures, functions as a polyvalent figure of serendipity and soliloquy whose antics underscore the contingency and contradictoriness of that local culture's codes. The trickster embodies the consternation of limitation—the messy malleability that forms the uncertain margin of any identity, the incoherent place where one thing slides over into and becomes another (Babcock-Abrahams, 148). The figure is thus the marker, at the level of culture, of the same kind of boundary that death delineates for the individual and tissue realizes for the body. Here is where both wisdom and foolishness emerge, the mystery of being something distinctive and the fallibility of the drive to try to absolutize that difference. In that sense, modernity in its imperial drive in general, and capitalism in its global metabolism in particular, represent precisely the refusal of what trickster mythology tries to teach.

Indigenous cultures the world over give evidence of myths about culture-heroes who have been (rightly or wrongly remains an open question) classified as "tricksters." Exactly how to "read" this has exercised the imagination of anthropologists and historians of religion alike. Barbara Babcock-Abrahams emphasizes that the trickster myths are "preoccupied with those areas between categories, between what is animal and what is human, what is natural and what is cultural" (Babcock-Abrahams, 147–148). The trickster lives "interstitially," "forever betwixt and between," a

> "criminal" culture-hero . . . embody[ing] all possibilities [positive and negative], "paradox personified" in the ability to "confuse and escape the structures of society and the order of cultural things." (Babcock-Abrahams, 148)

As icon of marginality—"hobo, bum, outsider, expatriate, underground man, Okie, clown, Bohemian, hippy, thief, 'picaro,' knight-errant, bastard, rogue, Don Juan, Prometheus and Hermes"—the trickster emerges, in sociological imagination, from the situation of culture-contact in which an occupying group is more or less forced to combine traits of both cultures (Babcock-Abrahams, 148–149). Such peripheral figures emerge as what Mary Douglas would call the "dirt" of the social system, the fictional equivalents of Hobsbaum's anti-structural social bandits who embody the dream of reversing oppression (Babcock-Abrahams, 151–152). But contra real champions of marginal-ized peasant groups, tricksters shadow tragic heroism with a comedic tendency to "dissolve" rather than focus events, breaking down the con-structed opposition between stage and audience (Babcock-Abrahams, 154). With respect to issues of time and timing, tricksters gather to themselves a question of ultimate ambiguity: what happens when the peripheral figure becomes central to the action, while retaining "the ability to 'dissolve events' and 'throw doubt on the finality of fact' "? (Babcock-Abrahams, 157)

Babcock-Abrahams underscores the radicality of the inversion here—tricksters do not just stand for the liminality phase of irreversible processual forms like rites of passage, wherein "anti-structure" is merely a temporary condition (Babcock-Abrahams, 157). They rather partake of the more cyclical ritual instinct for endless caricatures, rever-sals, negations, violations, and transformations (Babcock-Abrahams, 158). The trickster represents a dialogic "coincidence of opposites" that cannot be synthesized, an irresolvable polyphony (Babcock-Abrahams, 161). Indeed, both Arthur Koestler and Henri Bergson, Babcock-Abrahams notes, have understood human creativity itself as dependent on what the former calls the "bisociation of two matrixes," the negotiation of perception and expression in terms of "two self-consistent but mutually incompatible frames of reference" (Babcock-Abrahams, 184). The trickster is "finally" (!) the ever-recreated figure of that "creative negation" that introduces death into the world and with it *all* possibilities, the assertion of a certain indissoluble simul-taneity in the coproduction of sacrality (as the "violation of taboo") and profanation, the revelation of "our stubborn human unwillingness to be encaged forever within the boundaries of physical laws and properties" (Babcock-Abrahams, 164, 185).

What Babock-Abrahams hints at as human impulse, cultural critic Donna Haraway wrestles as "coyote and protean embodiments of a world as witty agent and actor" (Haraway, 298). Here, the trick is total.

Haraway is trying to admit to language a ribald "artifactualism" that tropes nature as "made" in a way far exceeding European pretension to production (Haraway, 297). Her language is admittedly difficult, but the attempt she engages cannot be engaged outside of difficulty. She offers, for instance,

> In the belly of the local/global monster in which I am gestating, often called the postmodern world, global technology appears to denature everything, to make everything a malleable matter of strategic decisions and mobile production and reproduction processes. Technological decontextualization is ordinary experience for hundreds of millions if not billions of human beings, as well as other organisms. I suggest that this is not a *denaturing* so much as a *particular production* of nature. (Haraway, 297)

She is not unaware of the strangeness with which this assertion may strike the eye/ear, but she is adamant in refusing to fall into the very thing she seeks to critique.

> I think the answer to this serious political and analytical question lies in two related turns: 1) unblinding ourselves from the sun-worshipping stories about the history of science and technology as paradigms of rationalism; and 2) refiguring the actors in the construction of the ethno-specific categories of nature and culture. The actors are not all "us." If the world exists for us as "nature," this designates a kind of relationship, an achievement among many actors, not all of them human, not all of them organic, not all of them technological. In its scientific embodiments as well as in other forms, nature is made, but not entirely by humans; it is a co-construction among humans and non-humans. (Haraway, 297)

Haraway's project is to try to rewrite science in a manner that makes its "generativity" and its interdependence with all manner of actors and "actants" productive (Haraway, 299). This involves a revisioning of the world as "coding trickster with whom we must learn to converse" and a rearticulation of agency in terms of actants operating at the level of function, not character (Haraway, 298, 331). She continues,

> In considering what kind of entity "nature" might be, I am looking for a coyote and historical grammar of the world, where deep structure can be quite a surprise, indeed, a veritable trickster. Non-humans are not necessarily "actors" in the human sense, but they are part of the func-tional collective that makes up an actant. Action is not so much an onto-logical as a semiotic problem. This is perhaps as true for humans as non-humans, a way of looking at things that may provide exits from the methodological individualism inherent in concentrating constantly on

who the agents and actors are in the sense of liberal theories of agency. (Haraway, 331)

And in this key, science, then,

> becomes the myth not of what escapes agency and responsibility in a realm above the fray, but rather of accountability and responsibility for translations and solidarities linking the *cacophonous visions* and *visionary voices* that characterize the knowledges of the marked bodies of history. (Haraway, 299; emphasis added)

In such an orientation, "interference patterns, not reflecting images," "monstrous pregnancy," not "luminous technologies" of the "sacred image of the same," "articulation, not representation," take center stage (Haraway, 299, 331). Things, in this compass, do not "pre-exist as ever-elusive, but fully pre-packaged, referents" for the names assigned them in the "passionless distance" of science. They are rather things that (in the cited notions of Gayatri Spivak) "we cannot not desire, but can never possess—or represent" as silent objects or stripped actants (Haraway, 313). What we have in such a profile is a tricksterism in which "boundaries take provisional, never-finished shape in articulatory practices," in which the "potential for the unexpected from unstripped human and unhuman actants enrolled in articulations— i.e., the potential for generation—remains both to trouble and to empower technoscience" (Haraway, 313).

Haraway's verbal profligacy notwithstanding (and perhaps even necessary given the argument), what emerges in this riff on Western humanistic endeavor is indeed the kind of protean play with language that laughs at humanistic certainties and attempts at control. Haraway obviously delights in invoking the aboriginal American trickster figure of coyote as a sign of the semiotic/material intersections she is exploring. Here, not only is the cultural boundary displayed as arbitrary and bathetic, a place of picaresque absurdity and ridiculous policing, but it is also offered as "intimately ultimate"—a feature of every "thing" on every side, inescapable, a tricky allure to desire and dread that is in some nonessential quintessence, the very modality of humanity in its struggle to make meaning, the very "ground" of place, the polyrhythmic structure of an irreducible universal improvisation. Of particular note is Haraway's brief hypostasis of "cacophonous vision," of that work of the eye animated by the ear, vision dethroned from its surveilling pretension to survey indelibly and instead jammed into "concert" with a hearing function that multiplies the recognition of motion ten-fold,[9] beyond the violence of the "line," dazzling sight with the un-site-able "break" that is difference itself. This is tricksterism as the final dialogue, the ropey sinuosity of desire as the thick thread of string-galaxic generation of space and time in the inseparable braid of now, the Om of erotic night inside of flashing light.

With Haraway's work in hand, we can perhaps wonder if the Afro-diasporan delight in trance-possession is not the real premonition of reality, the offering of embodiment to regimes of off-timed presences that open any given "place" to its disparate times, that crack the instant into simultaneously resonant and clashing continuities, that populate the body with more than one. Sex, hunger, blunder, laughter, and death itself are bundled together in indigenous myths of trickster antics and in modern interventions inside of humanist assertions of dominating ocularity. Mac Linscott Ricketts elevates the theme of "theft" as one of the recurrent trickster motifs in aboriginal myth—the wit of the wily hero overcoming greater power by deceitful cunning, often at price of self-wounding, but nonetheless defiantly making off with the "bacon" (Ricketts, 334). Afro-American double-timing can certainly be postured—if not posited—as one modality of meeting supremacy with its undoing by way of "stealing back" the stolen substance of one's self (from the institution of enslavement early on or from the hegemony of white supremacy in subsequent history) in the irretrievable form of the trick. Haraway's argument allows a vague intuition that perhaps this tactic is not mere tactic, not even invocation of an ancient historical invention, but in some manner the mode of "matter" itself (see our explorations of a similar line of thought in chapter 6). If so, the uncovering of humanist hubris as racist in its syllogistic seriousness is not simply making a virtue of necessity. It is a matter of adverting to an inescapable primordiality that is truer to the "fact" than science has heretofore foreseen.

That Haraway also relates this cacophonous vision to "the marked bodies of history" points straight toward the claim here. It is these bodies in motion, swinging their marking into motions that defy the eye, introducing syncopation into sight, that we are attempting to unmap in the revelation of humanism's misrule by means of category. Tricksterism taunts by demonstrating the hidden limits of a power claiming more than its due . . . and then doubling the demonstration in defying the marking of the limitation itself. The gesture is hard to write about. In marking limitation as such, the war is lost in winning the battle. Limitation is identified by way of a delineating and delimiting category. This too must be queried and tricked into its unstable

relativity. And yet, we cannot settle simply for the celebration of insta-
bility, or we merely underwrite the status quo. Here, the tricksterism
of our particular topic—African American improvisational intervention privileging time and timing—is pushed toward its possibility of
apocalypticism.

## Apocalyptic Profundity

The Euro-Christian myth of time as fundamentally "apocalyptic" in
its structure and the Western humanistic myth of rationality as fundamentally linear in its process are patent features of the modern
construction of time. Historian of Religions Mircea Eliade made his
career out of arguing that "history" has been a "terror" visited upon
indigenous cultures taken over by the West which, prior to such contact,
structured their engagement with temporal passage in terms of a
sacred revisiting of their temporal primordium. The orientation
toward an absolute future (of paradise or perdition) developed in
Christian intimations of judgment fundamentally altered that more
cyclical orientation to the past. Western takeover was not only a battle
of physical bodies and spiritual beliefs, but it also involved a restruc-
turing of space in a different intuition of time. The clock was eventually
made to order economic effort as ruthlessly as any fort refigured political place. Johannes Fabian has tracked the resultant ideologies of
temporal triumph in his deconstruction of anthropology as part of the
colonial-imperial aggression of the West.

Fabian's work offers a convenient opening for the final general
construction of this essay. For Fabian, the history of salvation that is
secularized and naturalized in the Enlightenment project into a history
of reason remains the great colonial adjunct to dominated space
(Fabian, 154). Time is made to encode space in the direction of
unbridgeable difference. The conquered Other is distanced and
denominated in a politics of temporal "mapping" that is fundamentally contradictory. Anthropology emerges as the academic discipline
embodying the contradiction perhaps most intensely. At the heart of
modern constructions of "other" cultures, according to Fabian, is
a denial of coevalness, of occupying the same time (Fabian, 34).
Evolutionary thinking wields discourses of civilization, development,
acculturation, modernization, industrialization, and urbanization in a
manner that constructs time as the great gap of difference appearing in
the interval of opposition thus created (over-against the implied or

expressed correlative qualifiers like "primitive," "underdevelop-
ment," "savage," "tribal," "traditional," "Third World," etc.)
(Fabian, 17). Recapitulated notions of physical time and mundane or
typological time concentrate anthropological perception on the value
of "objectivity" in a manner that fundamentally denies the shared time
of intersubjectivity (Fabian, 31).

The result is a discipline structured in paradox (Fabian, 64).
*Anthropology* itself places its referents "in a time other than the
present of the producer of anthropological discourse" (Fabian, 31).
Yet, *ethnography*, as the basis of the discipline—as its condition of
possibility—requires the anthropologist to submit to the demand of
coevalness with his or her interlocutors (or admit to entirely missing
the object of re-search) (Fabian, 32). Thus, anthropology denies as its
very form of knowing the shared time that ethnography requires for its
production of knowledge. Fabian is clear that coevalness is a creation
of human agency, a praxis of intersubjectivity that is not optional to
communication, but its basic condition (Fabian, 31–32). It is precisely
that reciprocity that is abrogated in so many colonial and now postcolonial "recipes" for how to use anthropological knowledges of
others "so that *their* behavior can be tricked into serving *our* goals"
(Fabian, 51). It is also interesting to note the degree to which Fabian
will emphasize that the ideal of "participant observation" shades over
into an *observational* eclipse of participation that virtually requires
native society to "hold still like a *tableau vivant*" for the ethnographer
as "naturalist" *voyeur*, watching an experiment (Fabian, 67).

The result is a certain cannibalization of the other in ethnographic
discourse (here again, the connection between this language and our
discussion in chapter 2 is patent) (Fabian, 94). Western anthropological
schemas of the other have refused the reciprocity of hermeneusis in
establishing a structural hierarchy by means of time that ordered the
relationship in an irreversible sequence (e.g., of development toward
the West and away from the primitive, etc.) (Fabian, 91–94, 99, 102).
In this hierarchy, the hegemony of the visual operates "first, to detem-
poralize the process of knowledge [by denying coevalness] and, second,
to promote ideological temporalization of relations between the
Knower and the Known" by taxonomizing the relationship in an
asymmetrical chain (Fabian, 102, 160). The fundamental rule underwriting such a temporal taxonomy is that "no two members of the
chain can precede and succeed each other at the same time" (Fabian,
102). The taxonomy maintains hierarchy in whatever way it is turned
or employed.

For Fabian, the only remedy is reconsideration of the fundamental character of consciousness and (thus) of human being. Consciousness, here, is "consciousness with a body," "sensuous production of meaningful sound" (Fabian, 161). The emphasis is not on expression of a preexisting modality of awareness, of its representation in language, gesture, posture, attitude, and the like, but on a "speaking and hearing self," on the communication that *is* the human being (Fabian, 161). Rather than solitary perception, the social production of communication, embodying consciousness in the material medium of sound, is what constitutes humanity for Fabian (Fabian, 162). Human beings do not first exist and then find themselves in need of language to express their existence; they *are* the language they coproduce in a growing awareness of themselves as articulated in a "dialectically transitive" process of becoming (Fabian, 162).

Fabian is clear that language thus understood is a creature not so much of spatial properties like volume, shape, color, and the like, but of the frequencies, pitch, and tempo that are indicative of *temporal* materiality (Fabian, 164). The fundamental condition of epistemology is the "cotemporality of producer and product, speaker and listener, Self and Other" (Fabian, 164). Anthropology—as the study of cultural difference—is productive only to the degree its studied difference "is drawn into the arena of dialectical contradiction" in which neither party to the encounter is temporally ascendant over the other (Fabian, 164).

But such a politics of time points toward an uncanny possibility of meaning for the off-timing we have been considering. The disruption of linearity can be hypostasized as a kind of relativizing of apocalyptic premonition in a modality of insurgent reincarnation. The resistance to the taxonomizing gaze that various African American tactics of code-switching or syncopating tricksterism embody is apocalypse made quotidian. The possibility materializes exactly at the node of hierarchical ordering proposed by colonial domination.

Colonialism gave political expression to the ancient rule that said "it is impossible for two bodies to occupy the same space at the same time" (Fabian, 29). When the Western colonial body took over the space of an autochthonous body, various strategies implemented the rule: in North American and Australia, *indigenes* were simply forcibly removed elsewhere; in South Africa, apartheid simply pretended that the space was divided and allocated to separate bodies (Fabian, 29). But most often, the easier remedy was to manipulate the other variable in the equation and deploy time as the category of difference. As we have seen in Fabian's explorations, the basic corollary of this gesture is the claim that "no two members of a [temporal] chain can both precede and succeed each other at the same time" (Fabian, 102).

But it is precisely the work of polyrhythmic off-timing to subject space to multiple time signatures in the same temporal interval in a manner that relativizes origins and ends. Marks noted that style-switching always works from a European code to an African one—in trance, populating the living present with the ancestral past, opening one body to occupation by another. Where Western evolutionism seeks to lock African culture into a temporal position downscale from European development, code-switching inverts the sequence. "Africa" thus emerges as both before and after—as the "before" that the European "after" can nonetheless be made to yield. In so doing, the effect is a kind of (oxymoronic) "apocalyptic repetition" in the key of the everyday. The "end" is tricked into yielding a different "ending." "Africa" precedes "Europe" which precedes "Africa." There is perhaps even room in such a construction for entertainment of John Mbiti's notion that traditional African cultures in many places lived temporal passage in the direction not of the future, but of the past (Mbiti, 23).

This is an "end" of the future orientation of Western society that is certainly unanticipated and perhaps even ungraspable in its own terms. The end of history here would not then be a function of Western victory over the Soviet Union in the cold war, but of a still surfacing repossession of its present by its (supposedly subdued and dismissed) past. Robert Farris Thompson argues that far from erasing "Africa" in the diasporic displacement of populations effected by the European slave trade, the most palpable effect of that domination has been the rocking of the entire Western hemisphere in an African beat. Yes, capitalism has continuously commodified the creole productions of the displaced populations and made their innovations serve capitalist accumulation. But history also discloses a tricky unruliness in which intended actions regularly yield unforeseeable consequences. This entire essay is adding to that intimation "and unheard syncopations."

Historically, Western notions of temporal change have coupled with an obvious commitment to developmental evolution a hope for apocalyptic revolution. Although both are patently specific and limited cultural constructs, underwriting Western perceptions of space as split by subject and object and of the species as split by race, the apocalyptic fascination yields an especially interesting counterintuition. Biblical textures of the apocalyptic genre weave a single injunction into the anticipation of world-collapse: when time appears to be ending and the world is falling apart, the possibility of refusing fear and resisting power is won or lost in the first moment of "seeing" (i.e., the biblical imperative is to "Watch!"). I am arguing that African American and Afro-Jamaican practices, in effect, rewrite such resistance in the idiom of sonic rhythm. When the eye is inundated with images of a cosmos increasingly troubled by cataclysm—and contrary to Gil Scott Herron's idea of the revolution, in our day, as recent events have indicated, the apocalypse *will* likely be televised—it may be the ear that offers hope its only possible ground. Ishmael Reed's *Jes' Grew* may well intimate the surprise-shape of the revolution that capitalism in our day seems to make increasingly unthinkable. It may already be seeping up into the cranial control room in the mode of an irresistible timing whose effects of difference will coalesce into "visible" change only when a certain kind of critical mass is reached.

The ear can remain unbowed even when the eye is colonized by disabling categories. This is indeed what I take to be the ongoing testament of African American creativity in dire circumstances. Yes, "acting a fool" in black church, losing oneself in a boombox bubble on the street of poverty, clubbing when one should be climbing into a book or a bed can be enervations of needed political action. In a Marxist sense, they may well be a kind of "opium." But they are not necessarily simply that.

The capacity to deflect the eye of surveillance by hiding inside a culvert of cadence is also a political resource. It is not an accident that large-scale movements for change in black conditions worldwide have built on the syncopated structures of alternative collective identities: the witness is similar whether we speak of the role Haitian *voudou* drums in the eighteenth century slave revolution, singing in the Civil Rights era, or stomp-stepping in Soweto's challenge to apartheid. Hope is given a slender "space" to stay supple inside of the concrete walls of constraint, uniform time remains vulnerable before the uncontrollable rhythms of off-beat timing. Whole new worlds can be opened inside the structure of an old one; "New Jerusalems" can be made to descend inside the time signature of Babylon. Time itself can be made to release its terror (Eliade) and bend to a "will-to-syncopate."

And Marx himself indeed allowed for such in comprehending the drug of ritual celebration as not merely the "expression" of real suffering, but as simultaneously also the *protest* against such. While that protest factor begs analysis in relationship to the possibility of resistance, *so does the simultaneity*. The sigh of the oppressed creature is *at the same time* the beginning of the will to resist. Inside such an inchoate "no-saying," the sound of an alternative reality is already materializing sonically. While I can offer no quick and easy formula for converting the energies of such a syncopation into clear political alternatives, I refuse not to testify to the elusive power of such in my own groping struggle to try to imagine and work toward a better world (i.e., not simply to resign myself to a lifestyle of enervating consumption and planet-destroying upward mobility). That the social science disciplines (as indeed the humanities) of Western *epistemes* of knowledge should have trouble accounting for the power of the aural inside the hegemony of visual should perhaps not be cause for dismissal. It might be precisely the cause for hope.

# III

# Hip-Hop Ferocity, American Mortality, and Trance Trickery

Each of the essays in this section elaborates the construct of "black shamanism" in the direction of hip-hop's rhythmic interventions in American popular culture and characterizes the resulting influences as a certain kind of resurgence of repressed memory in the society at large. The tack here is not to focus on lyrical content, but on percussive effect, in situating rap in relationship to broader issues like the denial of death and the commodification of matter. The claim here is that, at core, hip-hop represents a form of adolescent defiance of postindustrial developments that encodes, rhythmically and psychically, both an augury of social demise and a prophecy of spiritual "resurrection."

The first essay, "Rap Rapture" (chapter 5) was first given as a paper entitled, "Rap as Wrap and Rapture: North American Popular Culture and the Denial of Death," for the Religion and Popular Culture Group at the 2000 American Academy of Religions conference. It invokes rap music as a kind of "return of the repressed" in late-twentieth-century American culture. The degree to which the culture has attempted to deal with mortality by simple fiat of banishment is analyzed as the counterpoint to the ferocity with which hip-hop culture emerges. The phenomenon of the ghetto is represented as effectively a modality of quarantine, a projection and imposition of the social conditions of early demise (impoverishment, exposure to environmental toxins, drug trafficking, etc.) by middle-class society that constitutes itself, in opposition thereto, as the dream of an antiseptic life lived free of the realities of death or the images of dying. White skin emerges here as encoding, at some inchoate level, both a denial of mortality and a demand for control of contingency. In this view, rap is the reassertion, back in the face of the dominant culture, of the fact of death, offered by urban adolescents of color, forced by oppression to face the likelihood of an early demise, who refuse to "go out" silent. That hip-hop is appropriated by big labels and white youth is underscored as a kind of impossible prophylactic hope, a desire to "wrap" oneself in the scintillating vibrations of mortal encounter without actually facing the conditions of desperation that give rise to the art in the first place. As such, rap represents, among other things, an interesting site of popular culture commentary on more theological notions like "crucifixion" and "resurrection."

The second essay (chapter 6) was crafted for a conference on the religious imagination of matter, in honor of the work of Charles Long, whose theme was entitled "The Stuff of Creation." "Manic Matter" (originally titled, "From Mega-Lith to Mack Daddy: Hip-Hop Mantra and the Hidden Transcript of Matter") examines hip-hop in relationship to racialization by situating its work in juxtaposition to shamanism's beginnings in cave art and to modernity's peculiar fetishism of the commodity. Here again, the design is not one of focusing on lyric content but rather rhythmic effect—understanding the cultural work and spiritual import of rap as a matter of trance and entrainment. Modernity's notion of the object as above all a phenomenon of exchange—in which objects are stripped of the patina of memory by which they function liturgically and secure identity—is brought sharply up against paleolithic visions of the cosmos as animated. Shamanistic trance-work inside caves, "pulling" parallel universes of hybridized (human–animal) creatures out onto the surface of the walls, is understood as "underworld work," necessary for human vibrancy and destiny. Hip-hop is here refigured as trance-work performed on the inner surface of black social constraint, making it dance with hybridity and mythology, transforming the incarcerating category of race and the cave-house of the ghetto into an alternative universe of meaning and pleasure.

# 5

# Rap Rapture and Manic Mortality

*[People] make their own history, but they do not make it as they please . . . but under circumstances directly encountered, given and transmitted from the past. The tradition of all the dead generations weighs like a nightmare on the brain of the living*

—*(Marx, 1963, 15)*

Postmodern culture emerged around the globe in the latter half of the twentieth century as, among other things, an increasingly intensified metropolitan social order structured (in part) around a profound denial of death. Twentieth-century America in particular witnessed a sustained expulsion of the reality of mortality from public life, and an uncompromising attempt to manage some of the more obvious "re-arrangements and enforcements" of mortality (i.e., social structures that concentrate wealth, power, and life chances for some at the expense of others) through popular discourses of racialization and institutionalized tactics of racism. Within such a purview, hip-hop creativity in general and rap ribaldry in particular can be comprehended as a kind of "return of the repressed." They represent a popular culture fascination that mediates the unconscious of the social order, emerging from the marginalized core of postindustrial desperation. Rap's rhythmic structures and ritual stridencies—underneath its often less than scintillating lyrics—encode the underground energies of a culture otherwise gone antiseptic in aspiration. Far from only misogyny and foolery in adolescent dress, rap percussion sounds out depths of experience and memory that do not find ready expression in middle class discourse and preoccupation. Rap refigures the denial of death, the racialization of context in black and white, and the banalization of neoliberal conquest and control.

As many youth seem to recognize—without either the analytical resources to theorize or the ethical motivation to politicize their visceral recognition—hip-hop channels a message whose import addresses the entirety of the country (indeed, now the totality of a globe). High tech fantasies of cyborg destinies, middle-class concern huddled against the globally growing hordes of "displaced-workers" and struggling refugees, terror-struck testosterone and enervated estrogen in industrial park boardrooms and suburban bedrooms—all find themselves solicited in a beat that sounds out the savagery under the civility. America comes face to face in the mirror of a harsh self-revelation. The death-mask is perforated by a syncopated mantra. The postmodern shaman gestures an inane solemnity. Below the insanity is an insurgent polyphony and the ancestry of the entire race. What such a litany of claims might mean is the subject of this chapter. Rap, I argue, reflects and reconfigures a now (inter-) national malaise.

## Adult Allergy

Those who study the phenomenon of cultural attitudes toward death have been unequivocal in their characterization of the alteration of modern human congress with mortality. Modernity does not sit easy to demise Philippe Aries works through the epochs of Western history to characterize the twentieth century as "death denied" (Aries, 1974, 1981). Elizabeth Kubler-Ross has thoroughly underscored the degree to which modern society uses its technology to flee the ubiquitous fact (Kubler-Ross, 1969, 7–11). Colleagues Joseph and Laurie Braga begin their Foreword to a later Kubler-Ross work with the assertion: "Death is a subject that is evaded, ignored, and denied by our youth-worshipping, progress oriented society. It is almost as if we have taken on death as just another disease to be conquered" (Braga and Braga, 1975, x). Sherwin Nuland explores (and challenges) the resulting sense of failure when the disease cannot be defeated by a medical profession driven by the imperative to "solve the Riddle" (Nuland, 223, 248, 255). Ernst Becker traces the way the general phenomenon of denial underpins specific practices like American funeral efforts to present the dead as merely sleeping. David Chidester details the shifts in language serving to mask mortality in euphemism, accompanied by increasing professional control over actual dying and dead bodies, removing such dissolution as a reality from ordinary experience and creating a "buffer between the living and the dead" (Chidester, 280).

It is this buffering effect that will especially occupy our attention—not only as a "spiritual" intervention between the living and dead, but especially as a material realization of that intervention in the parsing of social space into antiseptic middle-class enclaves of "normally" enculturated human and racially "othered" spaces hosting communities living closer to nature's predations and mortalities.

## The Great American Denial that Rap Denies

It is curious, however, that this euphemizing of death seems to operate by a law of compensation. Yes, as Aries has emphasized, death is now a hidden fact—the "dirty and ugly" secret of modern society that in contravening the aseptic values of bourgeois hygiene, medicine, and morality, must now be secluded and sequestered. So the hospital indeed emerges as the new bureaucracy of ultimacy, advertising care, promising cure, and providing quarantine when the smells and sights and sounds betray the promise. Whereas at the century's onset, eighty percent of Americans died in the company of family and friends at home, at the other end of the era, eighty percent now are quietly managed into the grave by the white robed children of Hippocrates (Corr et al., 45). Death incarnate has largely left the community and added solitude to its repertoire of terrors.

At the same time, however, death as "eloquence" has gained a proportionate following (Corr et al., 86–89). At least in popular culture, the fact has reemerged in drag, offering its emoluments as both visionary experience and elocutionary emphasis. Where it has become *de rigour* to dress and address the fact of mortality in such soft figurements ("laid to rest," "called home," "gone to their reward," etc.), death as a metaphor has emerged as perhaps the most "dead on" intensifier of meaning or dramatizer of effect of our time ("I am dead certain," "dead tired," "a dead aim," etc.).[1] On the other hand, it is extremely old news that death sells (Corr et al., 89–92). The media has marketed out-of-the-ordinary mortality (plane crashes, industrial accidents, war brutalities, overdoses of movie stars, etc.) as the bread and butter of its business. At the same time, the entertainment industry capitalizes on "splash and gore" in big-butted bottomline figures.

But in any case, what is clear is the contradiction. Death is not allowed to offer its body in public except through a surreption. It is not the slow accretion of death's small triumphs over a lifetime that fascinates (for "death as aging" we have reserved a great huge warehouse called "Florida"), but its sudden swift descent on still vigorous flesh. The horror of ruptured vitality is packaged as pleasure.

The other side of this masking of mortality is the elevation of adolescence to a heretofore unattained preeminence. Western industrial and postindustrial commodity cultures can indeed be analyzed as, in part, representing a concerted attempt to marginalize and even eliminate (old age and) death as a meaningful constituent of metropolitan social life. Death is consigned to "nature" and to older forms of human existence—part of what has been left behind on the farm or screened away from the more developed metropolitan life-worlds in various strategies of bionic intervention. But in the very turn away from age and mortality, youthfulness has now been fashioned as the new fetish, marketed as the ultimate image of a humanity on the rise toward a biotech immortality, and sold as the constituting aim of middle-class leisure activity. The incarnate orthodoxy of this newly "christened" image of erotic youthfulness is a metropolitan lifestyle driven by the privileges and powers of accumulation, organized into exclusive enclaves of shared interests, and committed to forms of identity constituted in consumption (Bellah, 71–75; Dumm, 189).

Rap will be seen to emerge as precisely the conflation of these two seeming oppositions; a body of youth augering the reality of death.

### The Great American Denigration that Rap Displays

But this contemporary orthodoxy also has its necessary heterodoxy. The brokering of resources, opportunities, and statuses that allow for such a pursuit (of eternal youth) is partially moderated and manipulated by the assignments of race. To the degree poverty, high incidence of disease, unemployment, "ill-literacy," uncollected garbage, abandoned buildings, and so on represent "specters of death" in social form, the racialization of lower-class urban experience in dominant culture discourse has arguably functioned as a form of social *prophylaxis*. In simultaneously constructing and imposing irremediable forms of "difference" (e.g., "blackness," "Latin-ness," etc.), racialization and its accompanying structures of racism can be partly understood as forms of quarantine imposed by the dominant culture (Haymes, 5). They function to reduce contact with the social "body" of death. Institutional practices (in the real estate, housing development, banking, and insurance industries, for instance) that function disparately to rearrange resources and opportunities (in part) on the basis of race, are, in effect, so many processes of "ghetto-creation and maintenance." They forcibly concentrate in particular areas of the city and forcefully cordon off from middle-class lifestyle venues the forces of impoverishment that constitute an early, prolonged, and unmistakable encounter with death in manifold forms.

People racialized as "black," for instance, suffer (a long with native communities) the highest disease and mortality rates while society's dominant "white" community lives longest. (Indeed, so much so that the 64.8 years average life expectancy of black males in this country means that black male labor is a bulwark of social security support for all other groups in this society—since, on average, black males do not take out any of the monies they have contributed!; Parker, 15.) A recent *New England Journal of Medicine* article offered evidence that racism continues to inflect the delivery of health services, directing more palliative and less radical therapies toward white recipients and more radical and invasive procedures toward darker skinned sufferers of the same symptoms and disease stages (Geiger, 815–816). At the same time, demographic surveys indicate the greater concentration of toxic waste processing plants and polluted industrial properties in or near communities of color—a demography whose disease incidence is correlatively higher as well. Add into this mix the very evident stress accompanying the ongoing experience of racism (an average of 250-plus personal incidents of white racism experienced by black people per year according to a recent study of the black middle class) and a certain picture becomes evident.[2] Mortality is not simply "indiscriminately" distributed across class and race lines; it is "concentrated," to a degree, in certain social-class locations.

Quarantining of lower-income populations of color in areas of concentrated poverty targeted for various kinds of illegal drug and legal alcoholic beverage marketing has, in fact, *not* resulted in higher percentages of use when compared to white population segments. But it *has* translated into differential policing tactics, known in polite society as "profiling" but more accurately described by its sufferers as brutality. The profoundly racist operation of the criminal justice system—in effect using the so-called war on drugs as the neoliberal equivalent of enslavement, arresting black and latino youth with virtual impunity in many urban centers and contracting out the incarcerated populations as the new, cheap labor of the age (along with various migrant populations)—both directly and indirectly influences mortality rates (Chomsky, 6; Rowan, 193–199). (When coupled with awareness of the recent emergence of the "prison–industrial complex" as the largest scale employer in the country, granting host communities jobs and stockholders high-end returns on investments, the "profile" becomes all the more sharp [Schlosser, 51–79].) It is no accident—and not yet outdated—that James Baldwin wrote in 1963: "White Americans do not believe in death, and this is why the darkness of my skin so intimidates them. And this is also why the presence of the Negro in this country can bring about its destruction" (Baldwin, 1963, 106).

Baldwin perhaps embroiders on Hegel's master–slave dialectic here (or gives Hegel true grounding in modern history!). Human being (or perhaps more accurately, male human being) is constituted in a freedom struggle that finally risks even death itself (Fanon, 216–222; Hegel, 117–119). For Hegel, to emerge in truth, one must insist on recognition even to the point of death. In the (inevitable?) struggle for survival, someone "wins" and enslaves another who is then made to labor over nature to produce the substance of living for the winner. At the heart of that relationship between the master and the slave is death—a death risked, a death avoided, and, for the slave at least, a death reconfigured into a form of living-death.

But Hegel's genius is to have hinted at a surprising reversal in the equation. The master who appears to be independent and "free" is, in the sublation of the dialectic operating between opposites in human language and experience, finally dependent upon the slave and unfree. And the slave who has been reduced to a mere shadow of the master— to a form of labor for the latter that is, in reality, a mere delay of death or its elaboration into a mode of gradual demise—is, in reality, the one who emerges into the truth of death defied and of "being" ramified. The slave, says Hegel, has been struck to the core by the terror of unremitting contingency, of the possibility of life being ended at any moment by the whim of the master. In the face of such, the slave has been forced to carve out from hard soil, by hand, a facsimile of human substance, an objectified version of subjective being, that, though owned by the master, nonetheless bears the stamp of the slave's own personal impress of work and wit. It is the slave who has descended into the void of nonbeing and come up knowing truth. It is the slave who has looked the end in the eye and is still breathing, chastened, shivered, struck profoundly awake to the utter delirium of a life that is standing on the back of death. The slave *knows* what the master has managed to hide from. The death-defiance involved in the original moment of struggle is masked and manipulated in the subsequent enslavement. The master lives mastery as untruth and "knows," in an unconscious gesture of denial, the reality of destiny only in the eye of the slave. The slave becomes, for such a one, both the prophylactic against, and the sign of, the end both share.

This too, rap will adumbrate: a reversal, not of fates, but of fear and its fixations in a certain narrowness of experience.

### The Great American Projection that Rap Protests

James Baldwin was not hyperbolic. "Black" skin, in America, is the uncanny figuration of what lurks dragon-like and unfaced, beneath white skin. ("Black" here is being used in a metaphorical sense for a complex and contested set of meanings and practices of exclusion that are also operated, with more or less similar effect depending on circumstance, by other ethnically specific forms of stereotyping.) Blackness projected onto darker hues by a desperately anxious dominant culture yields white skin as a structure of denial. To be white in America (to date) is to be caught up in deep-seated cultural constructions—and contradictions—of the social meaning of mortality. Middle-class lifestyle is, in part, an imagination of life as antiseptic, ordered, upwardly mobile, volitionally amendable, protected from violence and chaos, and free of victims (Albrecht, 113). Suburban residence is assumed to be tranquil, tame, tidy, and untainted by the "problems" observed elsewhere. The gated communities that have come increasingly into being in recent decades by way of well-monitored points of entry and well-policed "exteriors" have successfully exorcised the sights and sounds and smells of death from their daily regimens.

Such structures are constituted in contradiction. They represent profoundly powerful concentrations of carrying capacity gathered from beyond their borders (Rasmussen, 120–121). They metabolize resources garnered from their "elsewheres" by means as diverse as gulf wars aimed at uninterrupted oil flows, NAFTA treaties opening up desperate labor situations and unregulated environmental conditions to instant exploitation by unrestricted investment, world and local banks whose loan strategies in final effect (not in publicized rhetoric) rearrange capital out of communities of poverty and into communities of plenty, large corporations whose financial departments participate in a $300 billion a year "shadow banking" industry (in this country alone) of "legal" interest scams operating by way of alternative credit institutions in disadvantaged communities, a federal government whose tax concessions and subsidies amount to a $450 billion transfer payment in the direction of "wealth-fare" for hard-lobbying corporations and well-connected individuals, and so on (Hudson, 1–6; Zepezauer and Naiman, 6–13).

The favored lifestyles and residences carefully screen out the blight and the bluster left in the wake of their predatory reach—except when they want info-tainment relief from the pressures of counting money and courting power, or a quick adrenaline shot by way of the mesmerized eye with no risk attached. But the "inclusive" economics is obviously complemented by an exclusive sociopolitics. Such communities consume the living substance of others but refuse a shared sociality or a reciprocal exchange of spirit. And much of the rationale for the refusal goes by way of the tacit function of *racial* perception. Projected "otherness" ("blackness," "brown-ness," "red-ness," "yellow-ness," etc.) is the great unexamined *apologia*, in the cultural common sense, for the impoverished living and early dying structurally imposed upon various elsewheres (around the world and on the home front) in the process of enhancing accumulation and longevity inside the gate.[3]

And even as the gated community can thus be analyzed as a socioeconomic *structure of denial* of the decay and death "exported" elsewhere, so white skin serves as the individual correlation for that larger demographic prophylaxis. (In rap "crossover," as we shall examine below, the prophylaxis is decisively broken.) In the operations of the racial imagination, whiteness emerges, in one sense, as the social artifact of a cultural quest for "clarity," "definitiveness," "intelligibility," "order," "form," "freedom" (Dyer, 44; Harris, 1; Kochman, 16–42). It gains force as an elusive index of identity whose substance is largely that of a silent negation of imagined darkness, a kind of lived denial of many of the social conditions imposed on communities of color (Roediger, 12). As the "color" of a psychic gesture, whiteness abreacts "away from" the formless fact of mortality, the beginning of life in dark intimacy, the reproduction of life in a merging that muddles boundaries between bodies. It promises control; it organizes sight as "reflection," as light bouncing off of surface. It resists opacity, interiority, the density of contacting surfaces, the proximity of perishability, the permeability of the body to all other bodies, the wetness of exchange, the "surrounding-ness" of the ground of incubation and end (Bakhtin, 27, 29, 32–33, 53; Bynum, xxiii, 79; Long, 1986, 133–157). The attributes listed above are not so much immediately obvious as the surrogates of white identity, but rather accumulate as the epiphenomenon of imposed darkness, in all of its powers of containment and quarantine. Projected color "identifies," contains in a category, ramifies an invisible wall around an impossible geography, mobilizes the policing eye on the street and highway, guards the gate against intrusion. All the silent attributions of whiteness are the payoff of that projection.

Such an understanding of "opacity" as a social hieroglyph, produced and reproduced in various forms of cultural discourse to reinforce a simultaneous exploitation and exclusion, need not imply that its significance is simply an imposition from without on communities of color.

The "blackface" put on the institutional structures of violence giving valence to white desire and concreteness to white interest is not simply so much charcoal and elbow grease exercised by white imagination. The category has necessarily been taken up by communities of color in various forms of agency and refigured in various forms of positivity.[4] The 1960s, for instance, especially witnessed a weariness with trying to side-step white modes of categorizing African American appearance and a new tactic of reversing the valence. "Blackness" was taken up by Stokley Carmichael and SNCC, by Angela Davis and Black Nationalist groups, by Albert Cleage and black religionists, by Amiri Baraka and black artists, by James Brown and black musicians, by Gwendolyn Brooks and black poets, by James Cone and black theologians, among others, as a public badge of pride precisely in counterpoint to its public purveyance in white media as a surreptitious sign of shame.

But that moment of explicit reversal of a contested category—that rap itself will also recapitulate and resyncopate with profound public effect—had a long history of reversal and revisionment behind it.

### The Great American Transfiguration that Rap Transposes

Historian of Religions Charles Long has provocatively sounded out the way slave communities refigured the violence of their enslavement. In his collection of essays entitled *Significations*, Long offers academic finesse in the key of vernacular redress. He signifies on the signification that seeks to mark and locate him as "non-white" (Long, 1986, 7). He does so by way of a History of Religions discourse, broken open on the anvil of colonial historiography, yielding, in the process, "strange fruit." The chain and shackle, the sardine packaging of the Middle Passage, the hulk of ship, the hurt of whip, the phallic burst of cannon, the fanatic thirst for conversion—all of these Long reads through the lens of mythic reconstruction. Colonized communities and enslaved sodalities, the world over re-created themselves recurrently from the shards of ritual and the ashes of story left them once they had been effectively metabolized in the growing world economy and reclassified in European taxonomies. They did judo on genocide, taking up their shattered cosmograms and refiguring "fate" in the fantastic shape of a Divine Grotesque.

Rudolph Otto's *mysterium tremendum et fascinosum* gives Long his academic ammunition (Long, 1986, 163). The concept is cracked in two by Long to differentiate the religiousness of the experience of destruction from the mundane hollowness of the experience of conquest (Long, 1986, 123). What, for the West, seemed to be simple "confirmation" of its own myth of superiority, was, for "the rest," a plunge into terror. The terror was not only physical but also primal. Indigenous myths of origin were peeled back to their articulations of the original rupture of creation, when sky separated from earth and deity from humanity. Here was the original faultline of chaos slipping again in seismic ferocity. This was the earthquake of beginnings all over again, when the Force behind the world made its potency palpable and its meaning incomprehensible. This was no tame experience of divine intention; this was a "fall" into utter contingency—the "taste" of the hard tooth of mortality crunching one's own bone.

The religions of the oppressed that resulted—the native Ghost Dance, the pacific Cargo Cult, the Rasta reiteration, the ring shout, the hoodoo root work, the voodoo *veve* revolt, all the riot of ritual ribaldry—are read by Long in terms of the *tremendum* (Long, 167). "Fascination" with deification is the luxury and necessity of the culture of domination (Long, 1986, 137, 169). For those who lose history, however, "God" must be wrestled with in inchoate forms of darkness. It is this face of divinity that Long tries to render "thinkably unthinkable" in the cozy denials of the academy. Indigenous religion in general, and black religion in particular, cannot be grasped solely in terms of surface feature. The deep quest beneath the detail is a matter of touching unbridled terror. The Ultimate offers no decipherable physiognomy, only sheer opacity. And yet, it is precisely this opaqueness that is given embodied dramatization in communal celebrations and there is re-wrought into an intensity of vital identities. The possession-cult of the colonized and perishing is the vibrant taming of a two-faced force: God and the Devil, Life and Death in syncopated lockstep, where each is made to "sound out" and signify upon the other.

Numerous other scholars have worked this same angle. Paul Gilroy's writing is a virtual elaboration of these insights under the rubric of the "slave sublime" (Gilroy, 37, 55). Toni Morrison, again and again, manages to conjure the "unsaid unsayable" in her liquid prose (Morrison, 1). Bell hooks "talks back" to white arrogance in apostrophizing black experience of white presence as almost universally that of "terror" (hooks, 1992, 169–172). From Jamaica Kincaid to Angela Davis, from Ellison back to Hurston, from Wright forward to Walker, the struggle is to write apocalypse under the twin sign of violence and "vibrance." What has been damnably suffered has also been astonishingly transfigured. The "deep throat" of ritual intensity must be read on many levels at once.

It is this that is also the deep-throat "word up" on contemporary rap. It is not surprising that young people on the contemporary scene of holocaust would innovate new riffs on the old theme. Folk forcibly "baptized into" an unavoidable encounter with mortality on a daily basis in our postindustrial landscapes of abandonment must either reinvent their world or resign to despair and dismemberment. Hegel (by way of Fanon) offers a point of interrogation (Fanon, 216–222). What rap constitutes can be partly explored as a peculiarly male mobilization of the "recognition economy" animating the master–slave dialectic (George, 184–188; Hegel, 117–119).

In our contemporary urban wastelands, the death-struggle definitive of Hegelian dignity and human "truth" has not ceased to define a necessary transcendence. B-boys and boasters, gangstas and other west coasters, live crews and posses of every cry and hue, give continual exclamation point to the strange truth Martin King discovered after Watts erupted in 1965 in defiance of his own counsels of nonviolence: despite thirty-four dead bodies and a burned up community, young blacks told King that they had "triumphed in the streets" because "we made them pay attention to us" (Cone, 1991, 99, 223, 292). Malcolm had understood—better than King—that the first and most important step in the freedom quest of any community is "pride": the self-esteem that accrues to the first taste of beginning to decolonize one's own mind and demand a hearing. Early rap reverberated as a form of cultural self-exorcism writ large.

But the "devil" in global capital has learned quickly. Hegemony today resists resistance by way of capitulation: any gesture of opposition capable of gathering a following is quickly bought off with success. With rap music and hip-hop culture in general, the big label companies and fashion moguls rapidly got over their sense of offense once the smell of big money came around the corner. The dominant culture today is fat and absorbent. It enfolds with immediate comfort and cash. As Fanon lamented regarding the freedom "won" in French colonies in the 1950s, so too in turn of the millennium "AmeriKKKa": there is no opposing "eye of desire," no face-to-face challenge, auguring death, offering life, exposing the lie of mastery (Fanon, 219–221). Instead, under the rhetoric of "rights," impersonal bureaucracy, indefensible brutality, incomprehensible policy increasingly represent the blank face of control and containment. There is no hot form of struggle discernible, only a domestic "cold war."

In consequence, it is no surprise that, more often than not, the death-struggle today is "black on black" (or "brown on brown," etc., or a very complex slamming together/exploding apart of racilized identity: "black on yellow" as in African American/Korean American economic conflict in inner city Los Angeles; or "olive on black," as in similarly structured Chaldean American/African American encounters in inner city Detroit). The resistant arm-blow most frequently lands on a homeboy (Rose, 141). Kool Moe Dee, for instance, captures both the instinct for battle and the flip of resistant bombast back on itself in his one-liner from Stop the Violence Movement's antiviolence all-star jam *Self-Destruction*: "I never ran from the Ku Klux Klan / so I shouldn't have to run from a black man" (George, 199). The bigger enemy of white supremacy and overclass hegemony is (seemingly) out of reach. But each of these forms of the "opposing other" are also mediums of projection. At another level, the bulls-eye is a mysterious "Something" just beyond consciousness, hovering, suffocating, unanswering, defiantly "not quite there" (Long, 1986, 116). The mortality and contingency that slave and ex-slave ritual arm-wrestled into a kind of "body-knowledge" in the antiphonal sweat of a four-hour worship service, hip-hop now communalizes as a competitive contest (Gilroy, 102; Long, 1986, 169; Rose, 61). "Knowing" oneself as alive is no longer codified in the trance-breakthrough of conversion, but the break-dance of bodies and words on the concrete (Rose, 48). Ritual combat here mobilizes a new street corner culture of rhyming recognition: words fly, rhythm cries, eyeballs see into the beyond on the horizontal plane of defiance and def-jam self-dependence. Robert Bellah is right when he underscores urban survival as a big daddy arena of resourcefulness at the turn of the millennium. In the Hobbesian world of late capitalism, he says, "far from breeding dependency, life in the ghetto . . . requires the most urgent kind of self-reliance" (Bellah, xiv). In this world, rap can easily be read as the new recognition ritual of urban male initiation.

Saying such is not to deny the frequently puerile cant of repetitious rap lyrics today. Nor is it to dissemble before its often misogynist preoccupations and adolescent grandiosity. But the interrogation here is aimed at a different trajectory. Where else in our death-denying culture is face-to-face confrontation with human contingency as raw-ly engaged in a ritual form? That these expressive modalities would find a huge crossover market among middle-class youth of various cultures (including its majority market in this country among white suburban kids) as ritual significations engendering something like "religious response" is also not surprising. Hip-hop has become the adolescent idiom of choice the world over, today, for negotiating questions of iden-tity and desire. Adolescence is a new wrinkle in the human life cycle.

A definitive creature of capitalism's erosion of the family and simulta-neous elaboration of technology, bureaucracy and the commodity, the teenager is a new phenomenon on the horizon. As a kind of living embodiment of temporal disjuncture, contemporary youth are a sign of the times. In them, we face our own dissimulation.

## Adolescent Entropy

The adolescent body is a clear augury of capitalism's fundamental contradiction. It emerges in our pedagogy as a physicality shot through with hormonal insurgency, enjoined to multiple and indeed continuous "orgasms of consumption," while simultaneously derided when it dares consummate "intercourse with the image" in actual physical copulation. A virtual crock pot of chemical potency—

> suspended between mom and the mall,
> heated daily in the commodified blaze of the social,
> tipped at every turn,
> dipped in the commercial,
> sipped in the sample,
> rippled in the visual river,
> slipped the trip of "ecstasy" everyday from twelve to twenty five

—and yet expected to hold back the fluid like a tantric hero! "Adolescence"—the long stretch of amplified arousal denied any real prospect of a "family values" form of satisfaction until social maturity somewhere around twenty-eight years of age on average in our culture—is a mirror of the impossibility of our society.

Youth are also a site where the surreption of death in our culture shows through. In their bodies, time disrupts its own capitalist codifi-cation as continuous, uniform, and infinite. It bulges with differing frequencies, aches with tumultuous temporalities, each demanding its own separate hearing. Without the necessary "concept" and ritual ram-ification, youth nonetheless "know" that time possesses sharp edges and ends, social disjunctures and physical dismemberments. They know that the body of childhood has "died"; they know "death" in the body. They are made to live in such a space of death, in the gap between the child and the adult—the body of the carefree learner long dead, the body of the responsible producer still far ahead, offered con-sumption as their only solace, besieged with the siren-call necessity of re-embodiment without release or prospect. It is no wonder youth are fascinated not only by *Eros* but also by the great, banished "dark" one of the West. They know what "we" adults have hidden—precisely in being unable to know.

Rap gives that subjugated knowledge of endings, and of death itself, a social body.[5] While much of hip-hop culture has indeed been subverted (from both within and without) into a preoccupation with machismo, misogyny, and predatory violence, there remains at its core a codification of death both "dared" and "defied" that continues to echo with transcendent and tragic power.[6] Jon Michael Spencer offers analysis of the phenomenon under the twin rubrics of "mastery of form" and "deformation of mastery" (Spencer, 5, 136, 144). Applying these concepts, borrowed from literary critic Houston Baker, to probe the rhythmic structures of rap, Spencer also mobilizes Amiri Braka's play, *The Dutchman*, Fanon's *Wretched of the Earth*, and Nietzsche's notion of religion, to underscore rap's insurgent aggression (Fanon, 52–57, 147; Spencer, 136, 142, 145, 149). Lyrics alone only tell a piece of the story. The driving base-beat, the syncopated production of "breaks" in the time signature, the sampling of the melodic harmonies of soul redeployed in service of percussive lower frequencies all contribute to rap's hidden intentionality, according to Spencer and others (Rose, 75; Spencer, 165, 173). This intention is one of "murder" (Spencer, 143–144). Much as Fanon read the release of muscular tension in rites of possession in colonial Algeria, Spencer reads rap's microstructures as a "canalizing of the impulse to kill" (Fanon, 203, 220, 241, 291; Spencer, 145–146). Razor blades on throats can be heard in the undertones (Spencer, 145).

Hip-hop does not simply gesture in idle boast: it both "places" and "displaces" death. Its aggressive modalities (of scratched vinyl and stone-faced denial) are not innocence but augury. Yes, they serve to contain what might otherwise break out in blood. They release the violence brought down on a community by invisible policy and all too visible policing. They play out what might otherwise remain pent up, subject to sudden earthquakes.

For the dominant culture, such displays of musical mastery function like religion in the sense in which Nietzsche says religious belief is really a masked belief in the necessity of police (Spencer, 149). The serrating sounds of rap both exhibit and allay fear of what is masked. In part, they "civilize" the severity of the eye that gazes back from the ghetto. Pull away the mask, however, and the grin is a cracked skull, likely to rise from the grave with war in its eye sockets. The cracked bone is just as likely to provoke living mourners to take up rocks like Palestinians. Or Glocks and Uzis. The dominant culture not only prefers rap to its alternative, but it also hears and fears this alternative in the "allaying" tones.

But the rhythms of rap also "entertain." They "host," give physical form to a desire that does not just want to penetrate the other genitally (Spencer, 169–171). They do not only mask, but they also make palpable. They partially produce what they placate. They are not far removed from South Central when the outrageous verdict of "innocent" comes back from Simi Valley. Literary critic Baker wrote, after the 1992 upsurge, that the voice of the violated on the street of the ghetto could not be heard by going directly to a Rodney King. There, one only encountered the ventriloquized voice of "the massah" (Baker, 45). The unvitiated verb has to be heard in the sounds of choice produced away from the scene of surveillance. Rap represented the kind of sound that could be "sounded out" by the articulate and attentive pedagogue. It had been hammering away at the deaf ear of the nation for long years prior to King's beating (George, 143). Yes, video supplied necessary evidence. But the eye by itself is deceptive. Human beings are complex creatures, requiring audition as well as vision. The voice is far more capable of nuance than the eye (Berendt, 14–19). And hearing it demands attention to depth-resonance as well as surface-sonority. The depths of rap harbor a truth about America never yet heard by America. That truth is that it will not last forever. Empire never does. It will die. One day.

What Tricia Rose calls "Black Noise" is far more than meets the eye. Even when organized in terms of Spencer's "mastery of form," making use of hearer-friendly cadences and offering parent-friendly pacifisms, rap can still open the underworld. Underneath the "pirating" and repackaging by mainstream firms, and the promotion and promulgation by major broadcast forums, DJ scratches still undercut MC moderation.[7] Middle-class premonitions of mastery are deformed. The beat breaks down the gate. The neighborhood is penetrated by a sonic intention. White youth sample a flavor they can't find at home. Affluent alienation finds, not quite a voice, but a texture of pain and its posturing that catches the breath.

The death that haunts adolescence like a nightmare that can't quite be remembered suddenly re-presents itself. There is an edge that vibrates dangerously here, an abyss that opens, beckons, terrifies with its strange allure. The vibrancy and vitality that mark the inner resonance of rap that is not simply "wanna-be repetition" is compelling. What is it that compels? The power that is typical of all spiritual work. A "close encounter of the ultimate kind" at the threshold of nonbeing, looking over the cliff-edge, stripped down to the essential realization of being alive in spite of destiny. Incomprehensibly, Life "is," in spite of, indeed, *because of*, the close proximity of Death. And it is so, right here, right now, in this body moved in-itself beyond-itself. There is, in rap, that does "keep it real," that stays close to the bone and honest, a kind of inchoate transcendence, a form of rhythmic resurrection, potent precisely because it has one leg in the grave, a nascent knowledge of nirvana, on the cusp of extinction, still flaming in spite of the wind.

## Shamanic Augury

While such a construction can be read, in a modernist frame, as sheer romanticism, it can also be comprehended, in older indigenous idioms, as shamanistic work, opening a crossover point between "this world" and the "other side" (Eliade, xiv, 243, 259, 355). It begs to be comprehended as, in its most incandescent moments, a postmodern form of incantatory conjuration. It returns what the mainstream culture tries to hide: the grotesque grin of universal desire in the face of demise. But it does so in a *living* form of grotesquery—of artistry performed on the ugliness of destruction that renders it strangely beautiful and vital (Anderson, 129, 139). Rap, in this revelation, straddles life and death by refusing the quarantine. Something of the animation of human "being" in general—alive to its own paradoxical impermanence and improbability—is damnably and yet irresistibly revealed in this particular body of articulate aggression, gesturing under duress in a social topography of desperation, refracted in a sensibility rooted in (West and Central) African explorations of percussive polyphony, intensified in histories of enslavement and enghettoization (Long's *tremendum*), inflected in *griot* traditions of rhyming narration, spiced with the digital amplification of trance-rhythms (Thompson, xiii–xvii). Rap growls with an aliveness common to every "awake" human existence. It is no mystery why it sells in the suburb. Ironically, it offers an intimation of wholeness. Rap's market crossover mimics an older instinct to facilitate passage between "upper" and "lower" worlds.

### From Shamanic Healing to Prophetic Hardening

Historically, human healing has often involved flights of at least fancy, if not fact, to "other" realms. Trespass of boundaries—between human and animal domains, between living and dead bodies, between the temporal divisions of ancestors and offspring—is definitive of the shamanistic vocation (Eliade, 6, 34, 89, 314, 376). Rap, in this compass, can be read as a raid on ultimate destiny for the sake of a proximate deliverance. It gives urgent expression to what can't be avoided if life is not to be lived in a state of somnabulence or "living death."

Many of death's urban signatures, for instance, were given haunting eloquence in Grandmaster Flash's early 1980s "Message" in the forms of sharp-edged sound, broken syntax, burned-out-building-and-vacant-lot imagery, and the intonations of street-corner predation. Hip-hop has certainly gone global in market and manner since, treating not just the savage inequalities of ghetto "realities," but softer topics like romance, finance, and freelance humor. But its root remains the anger and attitude of a harsh confrontation. Young lives planning their own funerals; jail as school; gender as the jaded space of an intimacy war; education as an initiatory beating; home as hell; old age as twenty-five.

The "Death Row" label named the experience both figuratively and really: rap is the tongue-riot of the anteroom of ultimate negation, whether this room is called "prison cell" or "ghetto corner." Ice-Cube's *(AmeriKKKa's) Most Wanted* album and Public Enemy's self-signification underscored the outlaw ambience. The jail style of baggy pants half-way-down the butt adopted by early 1990s urban youth faced with the decimations of crack and the defamations of drug arrests—whether dealing or not—defined the defiance.

Especially in the 1990s "high gangsta" period, rap refigured the elemental nihilism of a crack-sapped community, speaking far beyond its borders. It was able to do so because it reflected what writer Nelson George described as "the mentality and fears of young Americans of every color and class living an exhausting and edgy existence, in and out of big cities" (George, 49). In figures like Tupac Shakur and Biggie Smalls, the country heard an impulse already coursing "deep in its soul" (George, 49). For "poets of negation" such as these, George says, "black male pride was a weapon and an attitude," both "an attack on the negative" and "a way to spin the negative on its head" (George, 51). Their antiheroism took root in more than just urban concrete.

To the degree that the social conditions giving rise to rap have not been altered, however, but actually in many situations worsened, the soil remains stone-hard. The plant forced to grow in such conditions inevitably adapts to the hardness. Hip-hop culture is the "tag" on the American Dream, intimating the stark underside of the boom, blooming in black and red. For its own ghetto practitioners, this culture serves a sense of independence, of communal creation "in spite of." It is the equivalent of blues-song growling love–hurt into the joy of "still breathing."

For the suburb and other sites of consumption of urban desperation, however, rap is a young man's opium. Defiance and dare are packaged as rage, offered as sage commentary, staged as "revolution." The rhythmic structures "sound out" suburban alienation and wrap emptiness in a vibration of power. The result is a ritual experience of insurgency that portends, but does not deliver, revolt. Rather, the product is a blunt blend smoke of hallucinogens. The promised potency is impossible in the mode of consumption. White youth see a face of grimace that resounds in deep truths that have no social tangibility in the gated community. The video flash, the MTV finesse belie the struggle observed. No site of contestation is identified. No connection is drawn between the "thump of baton on black back" that the music mimics in its pumped up percussion and the middle-class lifestyle of living high on a hog raised and killed elsewhere (Spencer, 143). The very dollar plunked down to purchase the sound is not innocent of the scent of blood on ghetto streets. The open maw of capital is the real grin behind the grimace. But the Mask remains intact. And Death is left laughing on the side, still unrecognized. And still triumphing *in* this life, not just at its end (Lattany, 164).

If a collective effect of shamanistic healing was hip-hop's early possibility, its reality is real loss in the war of competing witchcrafts. White supremacy continues to infiltrate much of the private talk in this country. Capitalist intimations of unlimited accumulation and unbridled concentration of wealth continue to determine much of the social organization. And patriarchy continues to recruit new fists in its rapacious construction of woman as object.[8] Where rap's exploration of human resilience at the abyss-edge between life and death could have resulted in a new confrontation with the history of this nation, a new depth of encounter with all of our ancestral voices, a genuine "baptism" in our genuine possibilities, the result has been instead a deepening of the crisis. Healing "demand" has been swallowed up in harrowing denial. And the shaman's face has hardened into prophecy. Death increasingly disappears as the mysterious force behind ritual fantasy and is left ever more naked on the horizon as the sheer fact of our fate.

## Postscript Summary in the Sound of Syncopation

Hip hop has brought America a new language of rhythm, speech, and movement that has inspired a generation to take to verse to say what was too long unspoken about this nation. If rap went away tomorrow, would the discussion disappear too? Or would it just come coded in an alternative form? . . . *Hip Hop America* . . . chronicles a generation coming of age at a moment of extreme racial confusion—in these years since official apartheid was legislated out of existence and de facto segregation grew—that has been grappling with what equality means during the worst economic conditions for the underclass since the Depression. Hip hop is . . . the spawn of many things. But most profoundly, it is a product of schizophrenic, post-civil rights movement America. (George, xiii–xiv)

In this quote, Nelson George is tracking a development that is quintessentially "American." It signifies on America. This is its object, its topic, its material condition. It speaks "out" of as well as "to." It represents the breaking open of a sealed space, the arising of a body locked away as terminal if not dead. It is the grave lid sliding back and the ghost stepping forth. But the body that is spoken through is not the ghost. Urban youth are very much alive. What emerges in their staccato gesture is a deeper truth. Their hard staring eye does not simply codify their own reality. It unleashes a laser of dark light. They are the possession cult of the national history in the present, the place where America can be encountered in its own intention of violence, its own structure as supremacy beating the "inferior" to death, its own constitution as rape, as "rigid force of plunder" sanctified by a price tag, sold in a Benetton's ad.

And here responsibility falls on all of us to read rightly, to "be read," ourselves, irresistibly, to enter into an alternative economy of recognition. It is a national schizophrenia that appears here, a national confusion. Hip-hop speaks the unspeakable. Yes, it is immediately bought off. Yes, it is commodified in the icon, eviscerated in the visual facility, telemarketed into the medium of "more of the same." But its mediation as medium is not entirely lost. It augurs depth. It gives edge to what order wants to deny or deify, but not deal with: the fact of demise. The truth is in the base-beat. The melody of American fatuity is stripped. It is the thump of the bottom, the vitality of being alive in the face of not being at all, that is coiled in on itself, intensified, interrogated, elaborated in a long growl of defiant irony. This is the face under the face.

In Zen terms, this is what the face of America looked like before America was born; this is the sound of one hand clapping. All manner of spirits fight for expression in this young body besieged with too much truth in too short a time in too small a space. Time and space are reconstituted here. This is not the mall. This is not the suburb. This is not the green lawn, the ripe vine, the waft of delicate scent of daffodil. This is the grunt of groan. This is the funk of fomenting brain on fire, the ice of hawk-faced wind without a coat, the slide of syncopated step avoiding the rat-tooth. This America doesn't smile in high alto giggle. This America is "destiny" for all of us, a "guerilla art" articulation of our ultimate deposition (George, 11). What will we answer in that final moment? Martin Luther King went to the mountain, peered over into the Promised Land, and came back shouting. Hip-hop goes to the basement, peers over into the Other World and comes back harsh. Both are the truth. America only believes in the former.

Rap, however, is the strange rapture of unwrapping the nightmare inside of the Dream without flinching. It is the embodiment of the other ancestor that Thomas Jefferson denied. It is the code of contemporary healing, offered in the key of challenge. The sample is the metaphor of the meaning of "America." The sharply tensed edge between the beats is the place where the past surges up, unrepentant and raging. Will it find us at home? Or only creating another structure of denial?

6

# From Mega-Lith to Mack Daddy

*Its like you're the instrument and the universe is playing you*

—*DJ Qbert*

## Manic Preleude

This is a probe of planets, of skin, of worlds between words, of sympathetic-sonic-soul-magic trapped in a def-shout, caught in a jazz note, locked inside a horn, layered in a rainstorm, rocked in a vibrated cave of rave-dancing bison, fried in the pie of sky, in the high-rising laminate of syncopated fate, of fight, of starlight, of night, inside your head, crawling out your eyeball like a misplaced squeal, like a earful of warring colors, like sex inside a sentence, like a seismic serration of the world-code, seeking healing in the sound, seeking five bodies to live in, seeking to "synctify" soul through a world-whole, seeking to probe the primal lobe of strobe-truth, through every layer of cell. This is the jack-up of get down, the frown on the face of god, the laugh of the dead, the grin of Goldilocks at the top of your head, bleeding red over the midnight bed of lost lovers and flavors of pulled back covers, revealing the dread of black at the bottom of the stack. This is the lack of limitation, like matter musing on its own beginning.

## The Modern

In our time, the "stuff" of creation has increasingly become subject matter for the creation of stuff. The relationship of the human community to the rest of the created order is increasingly mediated by the commodity. Matter no longer matters; it is simply there to be altered, picked, dug, designed, molded, modified, manipulated, masticulated, metabolized, minced, mythologized, mercurized, monumentalized, and made over. The last 500 years have witnessed a scale of human intervention into the biosphere and its mineral substrata that is patently unprecedented and practically lethal. In the mix, what might be called the "religious imagination of matter" is no longer merely a matter for religion. The apocalypse is upon us and its name is the machine. It has perhaps already won. At least such is the "post-human" view from inside the centers of Western cultural domination of the planet. Columbus, in this take on fate, unleashed a genie of technological takeover (via ships, cannon, bullets, and swords) that continues to reorganize organic life in service of the social triumph of silicon and steel. It answers to no captain save that of growth and recognizes no limit save that of the globe itself. The enshrinement of commerce and the fetishization of commodification that have resulted have indeed emerged as the new religious fundamentalism of the age. Capital commands devotion like nothing so much as "God." But it is a god unnamed as such, mystifying its monstrousness in pursuit of the trivial, claiming its legitimacy as merely the engine of scientific objectivity, refiguring the human as cyborg.

The matter of human meaning-making in such a takeover has increasingly turned to the margins of material wherewithal to find its inspiration. It is now patent that conquerors solicit the conquered for healing of their own viciousness; civilization turns to "the wild" for respite from its tame propriety; conscious ideation seeks animation from the unconscious dream world. Western rationality has found cold comfort in its drive to control; older intuitions of destiny and ultimacy—of human purpose and divine presence—have attracted prosaic interest. Boardrooms dress their walls in batiks of Balinese spirits. Bored wives solicit crystals and hang dreamcatchers in middle-class windows. Evangelical Christians play with Jungian shadows (in the Myers-Briggs popularization) and Sufi obsessions (in Enneagram charts). Zen rock gardens "grow" in uptown buildings and downtown parks. "Rednecks" sing the blues. The fickleness of fashion finds piquant comeuppance in white "dreads" and punk "mohawks." Sushi and burritos go mainstream in the metropole. But the paradox of such a global paroxysm of culture remains caught in the contradictions of global history. Something like a "return of the repressed" (or perhaps more cogently, an "insurgence of the suppressed") has begun to appear on every side—an underworld of ancient rhythm and archaic vision erupting with bombast and whisper from the peripheries of global capital and its metropolitan citadels. In the contemporary "word up" of hip-hop palaver—the beat of the ghetto has penetrated the seat of the suburb.

## The Meaningful

The essay that follows tracks one strand of this resurgent riot by asking after the fate of the age-old human drive to find deep meaning in heightened perception. Ecstasy and alternative consciousness have long characterized human activity to create significance. For long millennia, the species inhabited an ecology entranced in its finite features of mountain and shore, rock and river, with halo and aura of the uncanny (with "hierophany" Mircea Eliade would say). Flora and fauna instructed. Fish flashed omens in stream shadows and dream deliriums alike. Lightning spoke, clouds talked, rain regaled with ancestor message, with an "other" meaning of history. When history incarnate in the guise of Columbus and crew arrived on American shores and began to knit together a world system of conquest and commerce, this older indigenous orientation found itself rapidly "de-flowered," dismembered, and derogated into outlaw existence in the back corners of the new world system as mere "detritus."

However, as religious studies scholar Charles Long has so tirelessly taught, its adherents neither capitulated nor retreated, but recreated. The hybrid heurisms that resulted—"oppressed religions" cobbling together ancestral tradition and Euro-Christian vision into depth-probes of the new existence forced onto the survivors of colonial cataclysm—augured meaning in the modality of myth. They constituted new myths—of new origins in a world brought forth in blood and death. The practices ensuing in places of unrelieved contact and conflict (various colonial and postcolonial "theaters of the absurd") worked fraught experiences of passage (like the Middle Passage) into new meanings of initiation, embroidered harsh rims of difference (like those of the Atlantic and Pacific) with new symbolics of exchange, and displaced borders of conquest (Mexican American, Canadian American, etc.) with *boudoirs* and *bordellos* of mixture. At the core of such "living hypotheses of survival" (new religious syntheses such as Haitian Voudou, Melanesian cargo cults, Filipino *Pasyon*, the Native American Church, etc.) is the cultural elaboration of delirium into dynamism, duress into finesse, hypertrophied consciousness into clairvoyant insight.

Within the cultural codes thus reconfigured, the new rituals often got it more right than Western academic stylizations of the meanings of contact in the machinations of science. For cultures made to "undergo" the

West, the experience really is a matter of "possession" (and the possession of "matter"); the mystery, an indecipherable power of "cargo";
the meaning, a *mestizaje* combination of elements that resist both grammar and control. Far more than the cold calculations of "primitive" and
"civilized," "archaic" and "modern," "matrilineal" and "patrilineal,"
the hot intimacy of danced excess (in Voudou), the concrete cantilevering
of hope-for-provision into bridge-work and warehouse-construction
(in cargo cult), the practical juxtaposition of both flagellant bloodletting
and faithful blood drinking (in *Pasyon*) or Good-Friday-hell-harrowing
and peyote-hunting (in the Native Church), provide idiom and energy
for forging new identities in a hard circumstance. Human consciousness
is in part constituted *as* alternative consciousness.

At least such is the thesis here. The basic intuition is that trance and
its stimulants have been definitive of human being and becoming as far
back as the hand can grope and the eye gaze. The search of consciousness
for alternative consciousness may well be formative of the phenomenon
itself (Goodman, 219–221). Not only have we been (thus far at least)
in our short blip of history, *homo religiosus*, as Eliade et al., would opine,
but *homo "tranciosus."* Shamans have "shaped"—and "shifted"—all
up and down the bloodline.

But modernity has represented a certain attempt to obviate the
excess in human meaning-making, to subject the alterity of ecstasy—
and agony—to the identity of the everyday. Part of what happened in
conquest and colonization, arguably, was the subjugation of bodies to
barometers (in scientific calculation) and skin to vision (in "scientific"
racism) (Davis, 1993b, 149; Du Bois, 1961, 16). Nietzsche marked the
resulting obsession with measurement as the triumph of grammar over
God. Gone was the wild. Fixity reigned. The idol took over with a
map. Race organized the hierarchy of opportunity into a fantastic—
and frenzied—apology (with dire consequences for told and untold
millions of indigenous inhabitants across an entire planet). Matter was
made the mere handmaid of an intractable light-supremacy (Berendt,
21–23, 27–31; Esteva and Prakash, 75–76; Rorty, 181).

But Western humanity also chafed under the bit of vaunted rationality.
While eschewing the myths animated by the trances, contemporary
society has been relentless in pursuing the experience it associates with
indigenous ritual. Whether stomp-stepping in the stadium or popping
and locking under the strobe light at night (Rose, 39), quaffing liquid
transcendence in the bar or shooting up substance in the back room,
the drive to dive headfirst into some kind—any kind!—of delirium has
been irrepressible (Reed, xi). It is this irrepressibility of the attraction

of trance—as complexly crosscut with projections of allergic otherness and primitive pathology as it has been historically in European reactions to contact with the so-called primitive—that exercises the effort to follow.

In seeking to open up imagination about alternative vision, and its profound relationship to the mediation and meaning of matter, I propose to juxtapose the oldest testament of the drive to contrive the trance—rock art of the Paleolithic era among South Africa's San and Europe's clans alike—and the latest wave of raving desire to rock, bop, hip-hop the "material surround" of human becoming with resonant meanings of rhythm. The chosen code here is not visible text, but aural texture, not the hieroglyphs of the roving eye, but the slips, slides, and glides of the unclose-able ear. And here, obviously, the license taken is laughably large: rock rhythm of the entranced cave-dark (presumably giving rise to "third-eye" visions that *cannot* be seen by the physical eye) and hopped up rhyme of the stark ghetto. But the urge is itself urgent: matter is fast becoming our last enemy in the form of ineluctable pollution and intrepid reformulation at the level of the nanocrystal. My claim is that we are fast losing the modality of the multiple, under tutelage of hard matter, in opting for an easier, but deadly, mathematics of the Monolithic One. The number here cuts across physics and metaphysics alike. In reducing everything to the modern Same—in locking into the imperative of growth alone and at any cost, in taking over the host body of the planet like a renegade cancer cell, converting all other tissues of life into that one logic of expansion, and quickly eliminating any other life projects and dalliances (eliminating biodiversity and "difference from" the modern human, that is)—we may well be evolving into our mutational dead end. But matter will continue, even if we do not.

Situating rap music and hip-hop culture in such a cosmic frame is not mere romance but prosaic observation. Quantum mechanics makes clear the centrality of aurality in the human (as well as galactic) universe: vibration finally defines not just hearing but even sight itself (in the oscillation of retinal dye molecules at the back of the eye). That a sonic "cultural" explosion like hip-hop should code its novelty primarily not in lyric but *rhythmic* virtuosity and *mimetic* intensity (the claim of my argument) puts it in direct continuity with both shamanic therapeutic and cosmic micro-phonic "mutations." Shamans shape-shift experientially in pursuing psychic and physical healing and matter itself apparently oscillates its way into new evolutionary forms through subtle revisions of frequency (according to string theory). Rap is merely a resonant reconfiguration of an ancient "incantation" of the universe itself—a tattooing of an objective condition with a subjective innovation that breaks open new possibilities (and failures). But mapping the affinity will require slow-walking through the mire of history (modern and paleolithic) first.

## The Market

In *nuce*, my argument runs like this: A century and a half ago, Karl Marx tracked the way exchange value effectively evacuates the "object" of capitalist enterprise of the human love and labor that produced it in the first place (Marx, 38, 91, 210; Stallybrass, 185, 196). For Marx, the resulting commodity fetishism is precisely anti-fetishistic. That is its problem. It is a European fetishism of fetishism. In calling the pot "black," the kettle has thereby masked its own copper tone. Sixteenth- and seventeenth-century European labeling of certain objects of trade on the West African coast as *fetissos*—as objects revered and ritually palavered into potencies of protection and power by their wearers and bearers—codified an intra-European discourse that marked such a (African) mentality as "dupable" (Pietz, 1985, 10; 1987, 23, 37). It could easily be sold a bunch of beads in exchange for gold—the supposedly valuable secured for a slight sum of the valueless. But the "slight," here, is really a sleight of hand, says Marx, an Invisible Hand orchestrating a global blindness. What disappears behind the calculations is not just the object. Strangely, the human subject, made to appear for the first time ever as "individual," standing out from the communal network of nature and nurture that produced it, also disappears. It becomes the mere "place" of a market price, the appendage to the commodity, the name of a meaning that is no meaning, but mere accumulation (Marx, 102–103). Even as every object becomes exchangeable for any other object, every subject begins to suffer a slight suspicion of being the same—and can thus be sold the latest sign of substantiality, the latest confection of salvation and wholeness inside a plastic box or card (Kilbourne, 3; McGrane, 4).

Much titillating work has been done since, in the name of Marx, on the social dynamism thus unleashed as a new form of global dis-ease. The confusion that human beings take their meaning from the sheer size and novelty of the objects they own. The mobilization of dollars as the digits of a divine arrival (Frank, 1). The cutthroat competition cantilevering technological advance out over an abyss of self-consuming suburbs and warring Third Worlds. The emergence of advertising as the new discourse of deliverance, provoking awareness of the slight Flaw—

> I don't
> smell well (enough),
> dress dope,
> feel fly,
> scope like eye-candy in the appraising gaze,
> drive the real deal,
> live large enough
> inside the gated domain of gain

—and then promising the impossible paradise inside the package.

But, as Peter Stallybrass opines in recent writing, the actual chuckle of Marx over the fetish-phrase is frequently missed (Stallybrass, 184). Marx was not pillory-ing the genuine thing at all. Actual fetishizing of objects—granting them the power of mnemonics, investing them with the love of a lifetime, the handling of a lived history, the wear and tear of trouble and endearing touch and the tears of rending loss—all of that kind of conscription of objects as living embodiments of human meaning, Marx argued *for* (Stallybrass, 184, 186–187).

The fetishism of the commodity was exactly the loss of that kind of relationship with matter. It was rather a remaking of the material thing as void of any particularity and history, as a mere sign of exchange, a mere harbinger of the great invisible growing "something" that answers to nothing identifiable. Marx decried the fetishism of *commodities*, not fetishism per se, argues Stallybrass (Stallybrass, 184, 186). It was the eclipse of the object as bearing the marks of subjectivity that draws out the troubled gaze, and troubling word of ire and analysis, of Marx. Modernity is actually the first form of society that tries to opt out of materiality in favor of an invisible calculus of widgets and digits and all manner of charade and parade of empty velocity, pretending to be important, but going . . . where? As Stallybrass says,

> It is profoundly paradoxical that widely antagonistic critiques of European modernity share the assumption that that modernity is characterized by a thoroughgoing materialism. The force of that denunciation depends upon the assumption of a place before the fall into materialism, a society where people are spiritually pure, uncontaminated by the objects around them. But to oppose the materialism of modern life to a nonmaterialist past is not just wrong; it actually *inverts* the relation of capitalism to prior and alternative modes of production. . . . The radically dematerialized opposition between the "individual" and his or her "possessions" (between subject and object) is one of the central ideological oppositions of capitalist societies. (Stallybrass, 185)

The later fulmination of eighteenth-century political revolution that grounds this highly touted, objectless "individual subject" (sitting alone inside the head of Descartes thinking clear and distinct thoughts of himself) in a juridical elaboration of celebrated rights, perhaps realizes its quintessence in the late-nineteenth-century ascription of those rights to the real individual of the age, the corporation. The advance of the agenda of this "One" continues apace, in our new century, in the promulgation of the transnational agreements that supersede every national sovereignty in the name of liquidity and investment rights. But note even the corporation pretends to be without matter; it begins to disclose its essential grin in the PIN number on the plastic ticket to a digitized heaven of Infinite Possession. As the president of one of the prime industrial giants offered as early as the Youngstown, Ohio, plant-closing struggles in the late 1970s, "The real business of US Steel is not steel, but money." Nike and Hilfiger today do not even pretend: the sign, itself, is the new name of the divine (Baudrillard, 143). The product is otherwise just a nondescript body barreling toward its predestination as garbage. The screen of ever-flowing green finds its dream in a simple binary—if not the One, then nothing. Thus, modernity.

## The Material

But if the fetish of the commodity is actually the mark of a regress in society—as it is for Marx—it remains apposite to demarcate the kind of regression it represents. The word itself, according to William Pietz, quoting one John Atkins writing in 1737, was "used in a double signification among the Negroes: It [was] applied to dress and ornament, and to something reverenced as a Deity" (Pietz, 1988, 110). Indeed, from the first in such colonial encounters—in contrast to the freestanding idol—the fetish "was associated with objects *worn on the body*," such as leather pouches strung around the neck containing passages from the *Qur'an* (Stallybrass, 185). The discourse of the fetish—developed in European concern to demonize the practice thereof—delineated a deep distrust both of material embodiment itself and, says Pietz, of "the subjection of the human body . . . to the influence of certain significant material objects that, although cut off from the body, function as its controlling organs at certain moments" (Pietz, 1987, 37). The *fetisso*-object thus represented a threatened "subversion of the [European] ideal of the autonomously determined self" (Pietz, 1987, 23). But its elaboration as a European concept seeking to demonize whatever powers might be attributed to its display on the body (through the association of the *feitico* with witchcraft), ironically emerged exactly as Europe accomplished the real material subjugation of those same bodies. The very identity of "Europe" itself—as a project of subjectivity loosed upon the world in a practice of unbridled rapacity—was constituted precisely *in that* contradiction. It comes into being as the subjective delusion of a vaunted freedom from material objects leveraged by the enslavement of other material *subjects*.

And here we begin to assemble the necessary pieces of thought to rethink our history. Marx marks modernity under the sign of the commodity: a slippage of the primitive fetish into a new form of duress. Now no longer mere dress, no longer the power of what is caressed close to the skin for its compulsion of protection—the drive-to-fetishize invests skin itself with augury. The slave is the commodity form of *human* matter. Europe-on-the-rise dons Africa as its cloak and disguise, wearing the dark amulet like a bonnet of light, hiding the bite of its own tooth. The white colonial body vaunts itself free from materiality, binds its body in breeches and trusses, boots and hoops, cravats and slats, and all manner of windings, while living on the fat of the other body. Cinema studies in our day, for instance, are savvy about the degree to which the modern Euro-American identity has composed itself reflexively and really as a white "talking head" propped up on a black laboring tread (Dyer, 48, 58, 63). Modern subjectivity is, and ever has been for 500 years, a mentality of light feeding on dark substance. The fetish, however, is Europe itself, in the form of its projection of pallor as power, holding "white" to its quivering naked breast like a charm.

But the tack of this tactic is full of turns and trickery. Yes, slavery emerges in modernity as the new form of witchery, the consumption of "other" flesh in the name of progress. Early Europe mistook impatience for conscience, refused its reflection in the eye of the other subject, submerged the slave in the object, confused the animation thereof for an animality it obviously thought it had tamed, wrote off materiality as that necessary substrate of human becoming that was the lot of mere labor, sat down fat, flatulent and blind on the stoop of the world, as if it were divine. Marx indeed marks the evacuation of the object, in that history, as the ascendance of the commodity form. But it is equally cogent to mark the evacuation of the subject in the form of the slave. Hegel perhaps understood this, without understanding that he understood, in virtue of his (in)famous master–slave dialectic. In the process, Europe (thought it) watched itself emerge from the duress, conscious, clean, white, purely itself, basking in utter aloneness, stripped of all dependencies:

> the titan of all,
> striding tall over the supine dark body of the slave,
> giant of the granite globe,
> gripping hard metal in hand like lightly squeezed mud,
> shaping a sun,
> groping the world-groin,
> full of bombast and belligerence,
> lost . . . in the mirror of its own inverted cornea.

In that same process, it fundamentally misperceived its own body. Intimacy between the body of the human being and the body of everything else ceased to be immediate and became a surrogated experience. Concourse with matter came to be mediated, first by the slave (from sixteenth through the eighteenth centuries) and then increasingly by the machine (from the nineteenth through the twentieth centuries). Marx's unmasking of technology as essentially "dead labor"—as the modern form of intercourse with the ancestors, no longer kept tucked in a canister in a spirit-cabinet in the shrine room or in a small stone in the peristyle, but locked in the form of an ever-growing prosthesis, simultaneously extending and attenuating living bodies on the surface of the planet—is seminal to think with. It also supplies insight on what was made to inhabit the slave body, and all of its racialized, blackened, queered, dolled up, stripped down, eroticized, exoticized, gladiator sports-ified, conscripted, incarcerated, McWorld-ified successor bodies since then. "Between me and the other world is ever an unasked question," once wrote Du Bois (Du Bois, 1961, 15). "Between me and the other world," I would agree, "is a whole history of questions, of dead and living embodiments of questions." The modern body is nested in nature in the form of a profoundly powerful, and profoundly silenced, tech-network of living and dead ancestors. I am not simply, and never have been merely, my own body.

The intuition, here, is that the human body is—like all else that is—essentially holographic in nature. It hosts everything. It needs all. By its naked self, it is, literally, nothing. Modernity has operated, in this view, as a huge category mistake, the erection of a conniption as a basic condition. The hysteria, the tantrum of desire drunk on its own infinitizing appetite, found a hole in the wall of its own European world, crawled through, dared the wave, delivered itself unsuspecting and ignorant into a dazzling domain of unsecured "American" artifacts, circulating in low tech habitats, declared thanksgiving, set up the table, pulled out the gun, hired the Middle Passage, and sat down. It did not so much trade as take, it did not so much make as mystify. But it also mystified itself. The body is and needs a world of bodies, it needs matter, it needs others that matter. It is not, has not ever been and cannot ever be, an "individual," whether in its own physicality, its own spatiality, its temporality, or its speciation. We are part of all that is. Period. But in the frenzy of fantasy, we have fallen headfirst into a fallacy. As Marx, both laughing and lamenting, says, we have tried to fetishize immateriality itself, to lock up infinity inside of a spirit called "exchange," and pretend that the commodity-body does not matter. But infinity, actually, is always a matter of matter.

## The Mega-Lith

An earlier age of the human rage against demise figured the matter differently, however. It is here that we perhaps need to turn to catch reflection of our own image in a mirror that clears the smoke, rather than invites us to disappear. Strangely that mirror was rock. In the title of this essay, "mega-lith" is technically a misnomer. I am not so much concerned with standing stones as with hollowed shelters. It is the word "lith" that does the necessary work. But here the emphasis is not on erection "up" so much as initiation "down." Paleolithic cave art supplies a piquant witness to ancient activities that remain largely a tease. From 37,000 until roughly 11,500 BCE, human beings the world over sought sanctuary in rock wombs that bear the marks of their meaning in modalities that defy the modern eye. Why paint animals inside the bowels of the earth? Why such fantastic creatures bearing monstrous features of hybridity and elision? Bodies half appearing out of cracks in the wall, bodies morphed into bison walking upright, bodies of humans wearing hoofs, bodies not fully there? The history of the industry seeking to decipher the mysteries has gone through its own shape-shifting process of explanation: art for art's sake; totemism; hunting magic; destructive magic; fertility magic; the modern magic of structuralist fame; solicitation of premodern modalities of shamanism (Clottes and Lewis-Williams, 61). No expert in the eloquence of such arts, I am simply here taking up the last and latest favorite as offering a quixotic angle on our own quandary.

There is much to respond to in the allure of these silent graphics of gleam on the sheen of rock wall. Apparently, in some cases, the place was the space of a vaunted kill of feared/loved animal—and the blood of that primal encounter mingled with paint to trace the matter and consecrate the memory. In other cases, it may have been that the place itself communicated, that its cold, its dark, its fantasy-scape of protu-berances and indentures, lines and lips and drips themselves "initiated," or at least induced the kind of body-coma that led easily to trance-vision. In the flicker of candle- or torch-light that must have been the mode of apprehension initially, many of the animal bodies seem to move, disappear, materialize out of nowhere. One supposition is that the first encounter with rock-become-roll-of-revered-deer-flesh was by way of hand, fingers finding seams that suggested beasts-behind-the-basalt. But in any case, thus far, it is shamanic investment that seems best to hint at the meaning of the haunt.

David Lewis-Williams has probed South African San art for decades to try to decode the delirium registered there. Situated in sight of what is now known about trance-experience by way of both ethnology and neurobiology, he offers a tripartite model of the process. Whatever the "trigger" for trance used (hallucinogenic plants, fasting, sleep deprivation, sonic entrainment via drum rhythm, etc.), a preliminary stage of the search for an altered sense evokes altered vision: "geometric forms, such as dots, zigzags, grids, sets of parallel lines, nested curves, and meandering lines," as his collaborator Jean Clottes writes. "The forms are brightly colored, and flicker, pulsate, enlarge, contract, and blend one with another," as they are projected, open-eyed, onto walls and ceilings (Clottes and Lewis-Williams, 16). (And perhaps here we need to make a brief mental note of modern teens tagging urban scenes with screams of shouting syllables, oscillating like dream. But in any case . . . .) A second stage has the subject wrestling these geometric percepts into intelligible shape by way of culturally coded analogues: a round luminous form may suggest a cup or a bomb for Westerners; in the native southwest of this country, shimmering zigzags may become writhing snakes. The real deal lies ahead, however.

If a third stage is realized, the precepts swirl into a whirling vortex, condensing toward an endpoint of light that opens out into full-blown hallucination. The vortex is itself shamanic text, the geometrics of the first stage often coalescing into identifiable animals, birds, and people in the curling lattice-like sides of the funnel. At the far end of this mental-tunnel materializes the "bizarre world of trance" (Clottes and Lewis-Williams, 16). As Clottes says:

> The geometric percepts are still present, but chiefly peripherally. With one's eyes open, Stage Three hallucinations are, like the geometrics of Stage One, projected onto surrounding surfaces. Western subjects liken these projected images to "pictures painted before your imagination"

and to "a motion picture or slide show." They seem to float across walls and ceilings. At the same time, the surfaces themselves become animated. A picture hanging on a wall, for instance, will be seen in three dimensions and with heightened colors, and it may start to move, to come alive. In Stage Three people feel that they can fly and change into birds or animals . . . Sometimes, they believe they actually become a geometric percept. (Clottes and Lewis-Williams, 17)

And the trance is not simply vision. A Westerner experiencing an altered state said, "I thought of a fox, and instantly I was transformed into that animal. I could distinctly feel myself a fox, could see my long ears and bushy tail, and by a sort of introversion felt that my complete anatomy was that of [such a creature]" (Clottes and Lewis-Williams, 17). And so, too (this theory then holds) with San and cave art depictions of bipartite bodies: an initiate may morph into an eland, antelope head perched on top of human trunk. A shaman becomes snake, or seal, or bison looming large. But where the propensity for such altered experience seems to be hardwired into the human nervous system universally, the actual materializations of the manic-mind are culturally particular. San see eland, Inuit become bear, Jivaro jerk into jaguar. Power-animals take possession of the pried-open psyche according to the fauna and flora peculiar to that particular ecology. (And we might add, with just another slight peak ahead: "When b-boys wrestle robotic "machine-power" into break dance "pops" and "locks" of muscle, is this the postindustrial equivalent of being possessed by the power figures of their environment?)

Clottes notes that the shamanic world traditionally was three-tiered (Clottes and Lewis-Williams, 29). The ordinary world was cushioned above and below by overworld and underworld, and the journey-agenda was often imaged accordingly. Where ascension was in order—to search for a cure, retrieve the soul-on-leave, wrestle the dawn-demon—the shape-shifting demanded insight, flight, and a bird-body. Where descent was the demand, however, cave-crawling suggested snake-skin and wriggle-vision (Clottes and Lewis-Williams, 26–27). Here the work was earth-bound and *chthonic*, going deep into mud, far down the spine, seeking help supine and blind. But in either instance, the instinct is the same: the body is the bible of the beast. The work is to work up one form into another, to become many skins, multiple kin, to traverse the cosmos by attuning the consciousness, and vice versa, to move between layers of matter, to pile up molecules like sheaths, to travel "morphically."

Even medieval Europe understood the modality: mystics as early as Origin the Egyptian and as late as Teresa of Spain entrained the mind by way of matter (Eliade, 399, 489). *Spirit* emerged from *soul* constrained by *body* in direct synchronicity with a text read as *inner meaning* mediated by *metaphor* derived from *literal surface* that itself opened up the cosmos of *creation* as harboring both *perdition* and *paradise* (Chadwick, 53). The three-fold interior was summoned by way of three-fold text to correctly embrace the three-fold context. Dante organized the triple play into a comedic Christian classic that structured the dilemma of shaman-travel into a drama of going down in order to get up (Zaleski, 4, 57–58). He literally and literarily had to cloth himself with hell before clothing himself with heaven, to crawl the body of Satan and climb the mountain of purgation before cloning himself as light and then returning to the flesh of this world.

But no matter the precise architectonics, it is apposite to note the worldwide means. Where Origin worked fasting into a synchronizing of inner spirit with outer *archon* by way of corporeal sensing, Voudou mobilizes muscle into a meaning of Ezulie or Damballah or Gede by way of drum (Desmangles, 93, 119, 125, 131; Walker, 1972, 104–115). Candomblé coats the cranium with spots of delirium, painted with the blood of goat, glues the feathers of rooster onto the face, effaces the human distaste for intimacy with any save *this* body alone (Drewal, 222; Wafer, 150). San sandwich their bodies in painted rock shelters to "become" swallows to flow with the sky (Clottes, 33–36). Nootka dive to the bottom of the sea to return, bloody-nosed and kelp-covered, with healed soul in hand (Clottes, 27). Lakota hook twig under a nipple to pull skin up from bone and enter the sun (Walker, 1991, 67, 99). The Yaqui ingest peyote to become coyote (Castaneda, 1974, 241, 249). The Hopi descends to the *kiva*-navel of the world to seek rebirth (Mooney, 811–814). The Siberian Samoyed goes into a literal cave to be saved by reindeer women (Clottes and Lewis-Williams, 27). And so on. The diversity, here, is a university all by itself.

But note that *out*-of-body experience is by way of being *in* another body. Spirit transcending matter is by way of alternative matters. The world is not left behind but morphed to reveal its multiplicity. And this is the singular insistence of this argument. The gateways to the spirit world are numerous: drum rhythm, breathing precision, plant eating, blood drinking, vision-seeking in isolation, dream-deciphering in communion with the clan, whirling in dance, chanting in trance, mantric hum, tantric cum, wrapping oneself round with the reindeer-skin-of-a-shaman, wedging oneself into a wall of rock. The work is that of donning matter in a new way, or perhaps otherwise said, perceiving and experiencing the permeability of bodies one to another. The result is certainly that of alternative consciousness, but seemingly always enveloped in other forms of sensuousness, other skins, other rims of other worlds, fins of fish, feathers of flying eagle, head of bison, writhing side of snake, the quake of mandrake on the lake at midnight. It is one body, giving rise to another body.

It is interesting in this light to recognize that whereas for agricultural intensive communities the shamanic decision is felt as spirit-*possession*, hunter-gatherer renditions of the same are embraced as soul *loss* (Clottes and Lewis-Williams, 26). That is, where the community is settled and confined in space, the body gives rise to its alternatives in the form of too much presence inside of too little place, the many inside the one. Where the community roams, on the other hand, the experience is complete displacement and the need for retrieval of the one from among the many. In either case, however, the modality of the means means a new modality of the body. The heart of the matter of trance would seem to be the experience of matter as hybrid.

Returning now to our cave-bodies, the reflection waxes wily. At one point, Clottes paraphrases Lewis-Williams to the effect that, for the San, apparently "the rock was like a veil suspended between this world and the spirit world . . . the potency-filled paint created some sort of bond between the person, the rock veil, and the spirit world that seethed behind it" (Clottes and Lewis-Williams, 33). Shaman-artists would perhaps then have taken as their task the coaxing of "creatures and spirits of the underworld through the rock . . . making palpable what they experienced and saw on their subterranean out-of-body journeys" (Clottes and Lewis-Williams, 33). Judging from the smudges and handprints, touching the wall appears to have been as important as painting it (Clottes and Lewis-Williams, 33–34, 35). The animated wall-face may have acted as a reservoir of spirit-grace; when potency was needed, tracing an outline or touching an etching may have occasioned something like the conductivity of an electric charge, catapulting the shaman into trance as a spirit-animal. The fauna here then are not mere replicas of those outside. Careful attention to minute detail reveals them rather as shaman-bodies ballooned out across the three-tiered spirit world, morphing through the vortex of enlivened matter, spinning into the space of hybridity, looking back upon their humanity as simultaneously also feral and mineral. The wall is not picture, but panel, hiding its transcript of an altered state like a mysterious gate, waiting, like a stage set for the shaman-initiate to plunge a hand or eye through the molecule and free the animation behind.

# The Mack[1]

And having set our own stage now, we can track a new moment of such artistry. It seems clear that part of the trance-task had to do with plumbing the depths, going down, braving dark and stark "surround," using cave as a grave-like stimulus to spring elsewhere, free energy, face gravity, growl in the bowels of the ground like a serpentine augur, auguring for spleen-gold. To what degree can we map topography on top of anatomy and psychology? It seems no mistake that cave art works especially with the proclivity of the snake, winding its way down to rest and up to feast (Clottes and Lewis-Williams, 28, 34). Kundalini is at least as old as Egypt, as Edward Bynum makes us aware, imaged as a halo of cobra over the head of pharaoh, revered for healing in the caduceus (Bynum, 82, 107). Caves seem clearly to contain refrains of "underworld" work, the shamanic mnemonic of battling for insight and healing in the nether regions of sickness and death.

The idea of a liberation from below shows up in quite varied traditions of critical release around the world—seemingly surging from the earth itself in testaments like that of cures connected with the phonolite stone at the shrine of St. Foy of Conques, France, leaping from river mud in renewing the metal of an exhausted mother in Toni Morrison's account of escaped slave Sethe struggling for her life on the banks of the Ohio, striking, unbidden, like lightning up the leg from concrete itself in the recent report of a Lakota woman turned Muslim in Atlanta, Georgia (Green, 153–154, 257, 263–266; Hopkins, 71; Stands-Ali, 7). What *Voudou* practices as corn-meal drawings, summoning *lwa*-spirits up the central axis of the peristyle from the midnight realm below, Hindu yoga imagines as a snake-awakening, trained to traverse the seven-station *chakras* along the spine, before cresting in an Enlightenment outbreak from the crown of the head, and falling, like a sudden rain of bliss (Desmangles, 101–107; Bynum, 38, 74, 96–97). Is it the psyche we are mapping here? The skeletal track of neuromelanin coatings? (Bynum, 100, 141–142). The spirit world behind the physical world, hidden like an undetected Heisenbergian cosmos? In a shamanic encompassment of the matter, it wouldn't matter; it would all be the matter of spirit and the spirit of matter.

A recent comment by an East Indian musician, adept at sitar sounds and synthesizer surrounds, opens the final concern. Hip-hop rhyme, he opined at a recent conference, is fundamentally *mantric*, syncopating the rhythmic universe with a sonic probe whose effect, in the Sanskrit lexicon of such things, is that of the *subda-brahmanic* word (Paul, 1, 4–5). In contemporary rap, it represents a vector of percussive intervention aimed at the release of the second *chakra*, vibrating sexual energy into electric currents of hard-edged liberation. In the Vedic tradition, such a focus on a complex harmonic of clipped and chopped consonantal effects was understood as intensely manic, aggressively dynamic, and quintessentially male. Saying such, of course, I realize I am instantly out on the thin ice of patriarchy, skating wildly off the edge of the ethical world of left politics, touting a taut that is largely untaught— whether old school or new—and patently dangerous to women and men alike. But the remedy is not in its repression. I am not concerned here primarily for rap's lyrics or its all too often misogynist politics or purile erotics, but rather for the hypnotics of its public effect. How do we read such? What is the heart of the matter of the worldwide chatter of *griot*-rhyme and sublime head-spinning–leg-windmilling spines and the spray-can splatter of loud-shouting letter in the clutter of urban demise we demonize as the postindustrial gutter?

Hip-hop culture, I would suggest, is a stiletto to the wall of the ghetto, letting the spirits out. Which kind of spirit-animals you see depends in part on which side of the divide you occupy. Du Bois described his early experience of the racializing gaze—of a grade-school girl refusing his greeting card gift with a peremptory glance— as a veil dropping, splitting his world in two, walling him in and resources out (Du Bois, 1961, 16). Not merely parental inflection and educational convention intervened between the two worlds, but in later century, concrete street and the beat of police baton, skin sheath and leaf of lawbook, history and church consistory and mysteries large and small. Color has been made the container of all manner of mythic projection. Shaman-work inside such an epidermal wall of domination has ever looked "black" on the outside. But within the veil, the skin is invested with all manner of rocking spirits of resistance and rhyme, like a time bomb. "Blackness" is hammered into a living shaman-robe hosting a continuous spirit-battle against the threatened loss of soul . . . or life.

The cave of the hour, in our time, I would argue, is this minefield of the walled-in city, walled out of mind, surrounded by sirens, surveilled in the satellite eye, secured by the white lie serving the suburbs more than their fair share of the pie. And here the augury gets interesting, in comparison with past cave work. The world over, the wall is growing—gated domains of the dollar, fated domains of the hollowed out fodder-field of the poor, each the product of the other, bistro and boutique of the elite "eating" the *barrio*-body of the defeated. The underworld today is an overworld production, North Atlantic neoliberal consumption of Southern substance creating demographic "caves," hosting waves of migrating maize farmers and rice growers and spice dealers from Afghanistan to Yucatan.

In the last twenty years, a graphic has begun to grow on the underworld wall that divines the rind chewed in the halls of power. But it also augurs an alternative power of pleasure. Its grapheme is primarily rhythmic, even when it writes its mind on the façade of brick, in thick stick syllables oscillating "color" as the new form of contagion. From the dank of ghetto dirt, from under the dark skin, from the cave of raging waves of denied dreams, a defiance has emerged that returns the signature to the signing hand of treaty. GATT and NAFTA, CAFTA and the Euro-Alliance, and all their supporting institutions, such as the WTO, IMF, the Trans-Atlantic Business Dialogue (TABD), and the World Bank, are all the creations of fathers who have sons and daughters. The wall that walls in and out has not been able to stop the shout up the spine of a sampled rhyme. White youth in the suburbs, elite youth of enclosed enclaves the world over, have been penetrated by a sonic intention of animation that defies the public transcription of compliance with subservience (George, 201–207; Spencer, 166, 169–171).

The hidden transcript of the matter that we all "are" is a vibration of erotic inscription that loves conniption, confection, excitation, and interpenetration, *writ large*. Just ask Bullworth.[2] More to the point, ask your local evolutionary biologist about the percentage of plumage devoted to arousing the image of desirability. We may think we are presenting the paper to advance the career, but underneath that endeavor, there is a whole "other palaver" that is constantly tickling that more serene surface. At the deepest level, we are all Macks. Humans are indeed possessed, all the time. Matter is itself *mantrically* erotic, vibrating with the pulsars of attraction and repulsion that the laboratory tracks as gravity; sexuality is simply gravity gone humanoid. At the primal level, beneath all our civilizing veneers of vanity, the grin is from the groin, the place where delirium is death-in-drag and vice versa, where the one drives to the many and the many show up inside the one. It has ever been the burden of the shaman to divine the devil inside the god, the soul inside the sickness, the beast in the rock, the spirit in the matter, the variation inside the vibration.

What the wall reveals in the cave of old, the rhyme congeals in the rhythm of this new age. Matter is not primarily a commodity; it is the

polymorphic possibility of ribaldry in the tightest of places, the most
solid-seeming space, the most lithic face. This is the triumph over terror
Charles Long elaborates in raiding Rudolph the Lutheran's notion
of *tremendum* and swinging it to the time of a people on the rise
against their demise inside a shackle (Long, 1986, 9, 162–165).[3] Or
inside their own skin. And this is where the matter gets most maverick.
The epidermal wall is the new shamanic stall—the place of writing
wild motion against the granite grain. Melanin is the postmodern surface of the healing spell, but the modality is primarily musicality, not
paint. "Paint" has been the control tactic of the colonizing tyranny,
making skin yield a curse,[4] making the eyeball king, raising the screen
as the ultimate technology of racial supremacy. Today, the necessary
counter erupts as time, the off-beat repeat of the bass line, fracturing
the design of white melody.[5] The return of the repressed may look
messy, pants all baggy, lip leering contumely, gesture fuming. But the
meaning is reciprocity. What goes round *has* come round. Walls leak.
Matter mediates spirit in multiple form on either side of the Mall wall.
It is white youth who are dropping the dime, big time, in this country,
to buy a sublime fantasy of a surrogated fate inside an outlaw body of
party and crime.[6] If we don't like the vision, perhaps we need to
change the action. Blaming the shaman is just more of the same.

   I, for one, choose to look in the mirror of rhythmic reflection. What
I see there is a white man's body being morphed into defection, into a
multicolored surprise.[7] But it is also a demise.[8] The meaning of the rap
*mantra* in the overworld is indeed

> locked up in the Mack,
> stacked in the store at the top of the rack,
> parleyed into a Puff Daddy pleasure-attack,
> packaged in a pimp-label,
> made to outsell Public Enemy's more militant fable.

But like Tupac, Chuck D had the Machiavelli-line right on time.[9] It *is*
a Black Planet rising.[10] The move of this *mantra* is not into, but *out of*,
the second *chakra*. The next skeletal stop is the sublime navel center of
Power. This cave-rhyme is indeed the design of a "Thug" mind,[11]
defined otherwise as a Warrior Coming, not to commit crime and do
time—but for recompense!

   September 11, I'm afraid, was only the beginning. The ultimate
meaning of the towers that fell is a death knell: Babylon brought to its
knees by the soldier-bees it has trained. The 500-year old fascination

with the ratiocination of a short-sighted whiteness that is modernity's mythological self-colonization is merely a slight blight in the unfolding fate of the late great planet earth. The final date is with the heavyweight sight of a light that is primarily dark. This is matter's true mate. Everything else is mere fronting.

# IV

# Market Liturgy, Indigenous Pedagogy, and the White Body

The final section offers two essays that embrace the counter-shamanistic critique of the overt/covert supremacies embedded in American institutional practices and cultural norms and works with such in creatively constructing alternative idioms of spiritual identity and "white" struggle. The issue is framed as one demanding a break with domination and its conventions, not only or primarily at the level of expressed content, but even more importantly at the level of rhythmic code and physical mode of occupying space. If some eighty percent of what human beings communicate in any given interaction takes place (as those who study such tell us) below the level of consciousness in the "dark" realm of cultural *habitus* and somatic rhythm, then confession and consciousness are not the primary modalities of either Christian conversion or white enculturation. Encounter has more to do with a mutually negotiated dance of the body; embrace of critique and alteration of behavior has to do with something like a liturgical reinscription of motor memory. Whether posed in connection with "market liturgy" in commodity culture at large or material pedagogy in inhabiting urban space, the stakes of such a "break" remain elusively high. Mainstream Christianity and middle-class sobriety face implicit interrogation and explicit confrontation about their self-promulgation as "superior" and their self-adulation as "enlightened." The demand is for radical reinterpretation of the popular rhetoric and reformulation of social practice from the very heart of indigenous imagination of "other worlds" and "other time(ing)s."

The first essay of this last section (chapter 7) grew out of an invitation to present a talk on popular culture and liturgy for the Sacred Music

Colloquium at Yale Divinity School in November of 2001. Originally entitled, "Monstrous Polyphony/Tricky Antiphony: On Breaking Liturgy Out of the Market," the piece addresses the profound shaping of sensibility and value our postmodern venue represents. Here the pedagogy under critique is commodity culture itself, especially in its form of advertising, which is constructed as *the* soteriology of the age in America, *the* process of spiritual formation par excellence, that is reshaping human consciousness and enculturation worldwide today. Once again, indigenous ritual is invoked as a counterpoint, this time in terms of rites of initiation, which had the effect of reprogramming and re-encoding the body itself in an alternative knowledge of its cosmological "surround," its enveloping universe of other bodies and other meanings. I argue that the result of such indigenous rites was a knowledge and indeed a wisdom, inculcated at the level of muscle and bone, not just the mind, that one's "universe of origin" was arbitrary and always in question before implicit alternative possible universes. The challenge to supremacy here is one that queries the entire drive "to civilize, develop and reengineer" that animated European conquest of the globe, as itself a mistake loaded in at the front end of modernity's encounter with its others. It has resulted in a violence that cannot be remedied merely by verbal fiat or hand-wringing acknowledgment. The demand is rather for serious rethinking of the meaning of living and reprioritizating of what Christianity is willing to live and die for.

The last essay (chapter 8) circles round to the beginning to explicitly examine the ethico-political formation of whiteness itself. Originally written for an anthology produced by Indiana University Press on modes of male embodiment, "The Body of White Space" outlines a phenomenology of the dominant physical presence organizing American social space. The emphasis here is on a certain kind of genealogy—tracing the gendered psychophysical "artifact" of a 500-year-old project of projecting pale skin and Euro-kin as the evident winners of an evolutionary struggle to attain dominance over the species. The focus is on the way space codifies race, technology teases or trains bearing, habitat inculcates a *habitus* of expectation and ratiocination that is finally rooted in routines of the body. The chapter argues that supremacy as a project is much more than skin deep and that its "outing" and "exorcism" require attention to what might be called the "micrologics" of introjection and internalization. Whiteness is finally "viral" in its effects in insinuating its presumptions and presuppositions of superiority at deep levels of cultural codification and expression that usually become conscious only in the moment of confrontation with other ways of being a body in public. The final word is that the choices, which begin to appear in the wake of such encounters—constrained and convoluted as they may seem to be—are moral in import and (today) global in consequence.

# 7

# Monstrous Polyphony/Tricky Antiphony

*When the great lord passes the wise peasant bows deeply and silently farts.*

—*James Scott* (Domination and the Arts of Resistance, *v*)

Friedrich Nietzsche, Walter Benjamin, and Theodor Adorno could perhaps be said to have erected the epigraph into a new mode of argument, trying to condense the whole of their Germanic gravity afresh in each succeeding sentence of their work. If it is possible to convene an entire topic in a single terse line—how much more three such, bumping up against each other in "non-sequitur-ial tension" that forms the matrix of thought? Such will be the *entre* offered here.

## Epigraphic *Encore*

Yale's eminent sociologist/anthropologist, James C. Scott, opened his remarkable 1990 treatment of power relations called *Domination and the Arts of Resistance: Hidden Transcripts* with the ancient Ethiopian proverb quoted above. For the subject-under-oppression, flatulence can be the very essence of liturgy. Dissimulation—bowing low and at the same time silently using the body to signal an entirely different posture—may be the height of resistance, the only doable dignity possible, when resources are few and power commands from the height of a horse. If so, it is worth doing with relish!

In a different mode of struggle-against-constraint, jazz virtuoso Sun Ra devoted his talents to crafting an aesthetic exit from the insanity of the "saneness" of his time (post–Black Power America), by creating the poor man's version of space travel. He said simply of those who would seek alternative universes in a bit of wind blown through a bend of metal,

> The instrument—That's you! (Berendt, 125)

And from much further back along the Western timeline, under a boot distinctively Roman, the Apostle Paul once wrote with less pith and more misleading,

> For the same reason you also pay taxes, for [the authorities] are liturgists [literally, *leitourgoi*] of God, attending to this very thing. Pay all of them their dues, taxes to whom taxes are due, revenue to whom revenue is due, respect to whom respect is due, honor to whom honor is due. (Rom. 13.6–7)

That Paul may well have been speaking in ironic double-speak—at once seeming to conform to imperial demands for compliance and yet signaling defiance in a subtext only the insider-community could decode—is only recently beginning to be understood in biblical scholarship (as we shall see below).

The burden these three unseemly "acts of sacramentality" seek to dis-burden finds its focus in a question about the political formation of the human body as a structure of obligation. In what follows, I seek to "out" the material indebtedness of our postmodern identities to market exigencies and to offer the rudiments of a reorientation toward a more human and humane "liturgy" of existence.

## Advertising Ubiquity

It is perhaps the great question of our time—or at least one of the questions that human beings everywhere must ever and again test themselves on—to whom do we owe what? In modernity, we inhabit societies that are structured in a fundamental contradiction: we are taught on all sides of the modern project that the primal unit of human being is the individual; yet, this very idea is not itself the product of an individual, but of a social pedagogy (Bellah, 84; Esteva and Prakash, 11). We are thoroughly liturgized into the notion that liturgy is utterly irrelevant. The individual is all; we choose our respective destinies and dispositions; we are the great masters of our own fates! If none of us any longer wears paisley shirts or pastel blouses, that is just because all of us happened to mature our individual notions of "good taste" at the same rate, at the same moment, fortunate and clairvoyant folk that we are. All the while, we are literally bombarded—to the tune of

3,000 commercials per day on "individual" average in this society—with the great salvific discourse of our time that is Advertising, which is precisely about the business of conforming us to the latest commodified embodiment of good taste (Kilbourne, 3; McGrane, 4).

Advertising is one of the world's largest industries today, employing the best brains money can mold to fashion human beings in the mold of money. What is a human being but a vastly complex "desiring machine"? (Deleuze and Guattari, 1–50). What is advertising but the most ubiquitous discourse of our everyday lives, continuously updated by the cleverest of the clever to get inside our desire and intensify it in the direction of a given product? And anymore, the ruse is so patently successful, the rhetoric can go blatantly public. Ford saves! Nike is righteous! Hilfiger is the deafer dandifier, the jaminest jingo on the slaminest silk an erect nipple can elevate! Advertising is without argument the most powerful spiritual force on the planet, *the* "soteriological dissertation" of irresistible declamation par excellence!

What is its basic structure but that of any good effort to reengineer humanity in the direction of divinity? It is designed to accomplish two primordial interventions (McGrane, 4). Its first task is to get inside every errant psyche and inculcate a single profound sentiment—that "you," whoever you think you may be to the contrary, are *not* OK as you are. The first moment of every commercial is the crux: we must be subtly or blatantly sold the idea that we "lack," that we should be disconcerted with what we currently are, that we are not yet the freshest phat fly on the pudding. Its first moment is the irreducible mission to raise up discontent somewhere in the body (but inevitably connected sooner or later with the pelvis). Never will we see a commercial the burden of whose message is, "Turn this off and sit down and breathe and delight in what you are right now without a single other thing added to your situation, person, habitation, mode of transportation, workstation, email delineation, vacation, or preferred form of recreation: You are great!—as is!" Never!

And having accomplished that first, not exactly impossible mission with respect to most of us, the second moment of Advertising is entirely, dazzlingly, unpredictable. "It just so happens, that right here, purchasable for a mere pittance of the world's plundered resources, is the little package of wholeness that will fill up your incompleteness. Here is a little quantum of salvation, nicely nestled in a shapely set of signifiers, colored to candify your eye, perfumed to pull at your sleeping reptile memory, soft as your fingers' most salacious sample of the world of matter." And we laugh, confident that we see through such huckstered hullabaloo, absolutely certain we can resist any given psychic onslaught. And we are right. And we are thereby led astray. Because the issue is not a matter of the individual moment, the single product, the commodity that cries before my eye right now.

The issue is the discourse that we live in, the sea of imagery that waxes our eyeballs every moment, that colors our sky, that *is* our world. The issue is not any given commercial, but the utterly commercialized ecology we now inhabit as our newly minted, postmodern *niche*, that plays back into our every heart beat, our fixations of fantasy, our menagerie of possibility for what life means and who we are in it and how we are to live. Make no mistake, human beings are profoundly permeable and social creatures, the quintessential political animal says Aristotle, constituted in ritual, designed in the Sign, shaped in signals traded at every crossroads of encounter, molded in a mere millisecond of hard-directed gaze. We are chameleon-like, and in our world, the great reigning "Principality," if we want to use the Apostle Paul's language (Eph. 610–17), the great shaping ideology of identity and destiny seeping into every pore and climbing every hair follicle with war and roses on its breath, is the commodity offered as soteriology. The preeminent liturgy of the time, coding all of reality in a price tag, reifying the body, regulating activity, rehearsing monopoly, incarnating deity is the market. As Thomas Frank says, today we are "one market under God" (Frank, *One Market Under God*).

## Imperial Liturgy

In such a contemporary situation, Paul's word regarding Roman imperial liturgy noted above (as an epigraph) is "good to think with." Recent exegetical work on the passage in Romans, chapter 13 proposes reading the rhetoric as a savvy piece of riposte inside of the well-policed policies of empire. Baptist biblical exegete Will Herzog invokes Yale's James Scott to open an angle on evasion.[1] According to Herzog, Paul is offering neither general ethical treatise on good citizenship nor theological analysis of taxation. He is *dissembling*—floating innocuous admonition in the ear of power while speaking coded resistance to those with "ears to hear." He is writing on the run, in context, to a community under surveillance, caught on the razor's edge of impossible loyalties. Rome styles itself divinely mandated and Olympically crowned. Caesar is son of deity; the imperial mother is the *diva* of Pax Romana. The coin of the realm is integral to the apparatus of control. The empire is a tribute-collecting machine, the *denarius* is its dominating sign. It is no accident that the major collection is called a head tax (*tributum capitis*). Rome regulates its subject populations by focusing taxation on the fact of having a body. Merely to exist in the flesh—inside the precincts of Caesar—is to be indebted. Taxation is a ritual of regulation, the very life-blood of the empire. The primary *leitourgoi* of Paul's day are the bureaucrats who, in his own words in Romans 13.6, "constantly occupy themselves" with the ever-renewed demand to extract from their subject-populations everything but the barest subsistence.

Paul counsels seeming compliance. But read under the rubrics of Scott's delineation of public and hidden transcripts, the text of chapter 13 belies mere cooperation. The characterization of ruthless imperial rule as "ministry for your good" represents a masterful shift of semantic fields, according to Herzog. Paul deadpans Rome as a Camelot-like realm of royal restraint, where authority is cast in the image of "table-waiting humility," intending only well-being for those it "serves." The bite of sarcasm is scarcely concealed; the allusion is ironic in the extreme and could not but occasion a grunt of laughter. Yeah sure—Rome as "table servant"—Rome the ruthless conqueror and colonizer, Rome the chainer of a thousand thousand slaves, beheader of wrongly blinking house-servants, crucifier of suspected resisters, drinker of the blood of gladiators and lion-mauled women and children, launcher of living Jewish bodies as bombs against the barricades of Masada! Yeah—Rome as "humble table waiter" working for "your good"!

In Herzog's view, what we actually have here is a momentary uncloaking of contrast in an otherwise innocuous rhetoric of compliance—a stiletto-sharp stab of rebuke emerging for a flickering second from the carefully concealed councils of the oppressed community, a brief public airing of hidden transcript, just as quickly again dissimulated in the remainder of Paul's message. After all, in this empire, spies are everywhere; the letter could easily be intercepted by the imperial police and bring severe retribution. But the take-home meaning for those in the know is patent: outward rebellion in an ancient imperial context is utterly futile and foolish. It knows only one outcome—total destruction. But *interior* rebellion is not only possible, but it is also imperative for alternative identity and loyalty. Pay the tax—but do so *not* in submission, but (as it literally says in the Greek) as a "pay back," a return and refusal expressing *defiant agency*, indeed an act of conscience, giving Caesar the only thing he can really claim—his own coin of oppression—but not an iota more! Do not give fear, do not give resignation, do not give timorous obsequy. "Pay back" what the empire is, in fact, *forcing* from your hand anyway. But "give" only to those who are "due."

## Capitalist Economy

And thus the question for us, in our time: what is due the market? Or framed more carefully, what are the constraints that operate on our forms of embodiment that force our hands to "pay tribute"? And what gestural habits and attitudinal affects, indeed, might serve as rituals of "righteous rebellion" inside our own liturgies of public conformity? (Eagleton, 149). The emphasis on "embodiment" in the imperial head tax example above points to the necessary place of inquiry. The body is the elemental material in human existential experience (Stallybrass and White, ix, 2–5). It is the prime symbol (Leonard, 30–34, 38, 77). It comes already coded—an artifactual production of social institutions—long before any of us can claim it as our "own" (Foucault, 1977, 30, 1980, 103–108). Anthropological work on ritual activity and postcolonial work on discourse analysis alike help excavate the archaeology.

Anthropology makes us aware that we are, in fact, living social hieroglyphs, walking signifiers of political positions and cultural predilections before we are consciously "ourselves." The "self" we imagine we choose to become is in some large measure predetermined by the social history and pedagogical program we have already undergone by the time we begin to conceive we have "choice." Indeed, in our society, the idea itself of "choice" is probably the great ideological triumph of the time (Bellah, 84). We emerge at the outset of adolescence, poised at the brink of a vast panorama of privilege, a heretofore-in-history almost unimaginable landscape of options, waving fictions of power, shouting seductions of selfhood, bearing bar codes, blaring through the ozone box, aura-ed in pixel. And of course already here, the immediate question that should caution the eye that reads is which "we"? Of whom am I speaking? My argument is on the point of begging before I have even marshaled it. Do I speak of males or females? The middle class or the underclass? Latina-identifying, blue-collar lesbians or African American buppie jocks wearing dreads and Phat Farm labels or sallow-shaded, pink-when-bathed, red-when-embarrassed, blue-when-cold, yellow-when-scared, "white" people? And the question is appropriate. But so is the generalization—as my argument shall argue.

When we look away from our "modern" selves and study so-called aboriginal culture, we are perhaps more clearly certain and more comfortable. Of course, the data then is about "them"—whoever the analysis may entail. Anthropology can easily identify the ritual passages when the culture is "other" and the codification "exotic." It is harder to see when we turn the analysis toward home. But it is also the case that today "home" threatens to wax global. Western cultural prerogatives and priorities are gathering global adherence and reorganizing indigenous identity in localized versions of the Same seemingly everywhere today (Esteva and Prakash, 19–20). It is a patently kaleidoscopic Same, an image and identity, organized in the commercial, that proliferates through an endless prodigality of change and shape-shifting search for differentiation and desirability. But it does bear a common testament and tag. It is a possibility marshaled in the market, mobilized on the screen, screaming salvation now!

Exactly how human creative capacity to enculturate difference, to encode desire with variety, is holding up in the process is an open question. Ecologists descry the environmental damage of the day in terms of the rampant disappearance of biological diversity (Rasmussen, 114). Ethnographers echo a similar refrain in reference to language and human culture (Rasmussen, 140–141). Capitalist hegemony in our hour has learned how to grab every latest and least gesture of difference, every grunt of protest or groan of resistance, and package it for purchase within a day or two of its first offering. What is lost in the package, however, is the reflex effect of the effort to conceive and organize the idea in the first place. Or said another way, "initiation" in our social process no longer exorcises and incises the body, but only exercises and inscribes it (Goodman, 219–221).

## Indigenous Plurality

Older cultures, on the other hand, had clear points of passage, bush schools run by elders that carefully created the social conditions for identities to be "killed" and raised from the ground in new forms. They understood the depths of difference making in a way we perhaps do not (Goodman, 219–221; Murphy, 1994, 6–7). We want difference to be a matter of the mind, a change of ideas, an entertainment of new imagery. We want newness without opaqueness—a nonthreatening novelty that does not displace the all-surveilling eye incarnate in modern modes of being. Real alteration at the level of the body is probably a different difference, however. Native cultures attended to this kind of difference in careful choreographies of re-enculturation and paradox (Babcock-Abrahams, 157, 185–186; Brandon, 142; Walker, 1972,

104–115). A friend of mine, during grad school at the University of Chicago, who had undergone such an initiation rite while a young adult told me about the uncanny-ness of the experience one day.

Tulani (we'll call him for the sake of anonymity) was a United Church of Christ pastor and youth leader in the Black Consciousness Movement in the late 1980s in South Africa. He was summoned by his village chief to return from Durban to his "homeland" to undergo bush school with the village teenagers. The chief figured Tulani for the leader he was indeed showing evidence of becoming, and determined that initiation was an experience he needed to have "under his belt" (so to speak) no matter what his actual arena of activism might be in the future. The process was weeks long—even in truncated form due to apartheid pressures—and involved complete isolation from society other than elders and fellow initiates. Much time was spent supine, lying in a hut in the dark. Village dances and rituals and tribal myths were taught and memorized. Speaking was very limited, and when permitted, the Xhosa mother tongue of the young men had to be used in direct inverse of its use in everyday life. "Light" now meant "dark" and vice versa, "up" meant "down," "in" implied "out," "old"–"young," "male"–"female," and so on. After a few days, Tulani said, the effect was surreal—he felt as if he was walking around "on tilt," as if gravity itself had shifted its axis and his body was now moving at a 45-degree angle to the Earth.

My own response to his story was, and is, wonder. I suspect that a deep part of such a pedagogy is a matter of profound wisdom: the knowledge—not just at the level of abstract awareness, but in all the concrete-ness of one's own bodily schema—that the world is plural (Albrecht, 155). A recodification of skin and muscles, nerves and bones alike that acts like a new template of memory (Brandon, 148; Goodman, 218–219). Never again could one insist that one's own map of meaning was the only, or even preeminent, one. I agree with the voices that tell us "time" and "space" are a function of bodily orientation (Levi-Strauss, 200–203). Reconfigure the body and the cosmos itself is remade.

But the insight is not that of traditional cultures and initiation processes alone. Marginalized peoples all over the modern world have been made to know a similar meaning. Feminist writers speak again and again of the experience of many women, under the violent stric-tures of patriarchy, "watching ourself [in our bodies] being the self that we know is not our self" (Albrecht, 65). Native peoples on this conti-nent, forced off of their traditional lands and out of their ancestral habits in the late nineteenth century, plunged into a parallel universe of ritual activity that the U.S. military subsequently ridiculed, but also feared, as "Ghost Dancing" (Mooney, 653). Pacific Islanders reconfigured their takeover by the West in so-called Cargo Cults (Worsley, 239–242). In Atlanta, at the turn of the century, W. E. B. Du Bois famously figured the post-slavery dilemma in terms of double-consciousness, simultaneously "gift" and "affliction": the "peculiar sensation" of ever "looking at one's self through the eyes of others," ever feeling "one's twoness . . . two souls, two thoughts, two unreconciled strivings; two warring ideals in one dark body, whose dogged strength alone keeps it from being torn asunder" (Du Bois, 1961, 17).

Du Bois's formula has become significant for many postcolonial theorists. It is also no accident that Du Bois spoke of such a prototypical (post)colonial experience in terms of a hint of shamanistic equipping—being "born with a veil or *caul*," endowed with "second-sight," being unable *not* to see into the violent underside of things (Bambara, 310). And indeed, three-quarters of a century later, Historian of Religions Charles Long will take up Du Bois's travail of twoness and transpose it into the key of "initiation rite"—as broad as modern history itself, commonly endured by conquered indigenous peoples the world over, who reworked their alienating conscription in Western scientific discourses (of anthropology, sociology, political economy, and philosophy) into new forms of ritual practice that gave them an intimate home underneath or inside of Western surveillance (Coleman, 52; Long, 1986, 9, 110, 181, 193). In the process, according to Long, they became people of parallel universes, capable of opening out hidden secondary spaces of freedom and hope inside the project of domination itself (as we have examined in previous chapters; Long, 165, 167).

In indigenous communities, life after contact must be engaged under the tutelage of "Absolute Being" understood not as a Fascinating and Sustaining Mystery, but as a "Tremendousness" (Rudolph Otto's *Tremendum*) that is Terrible. Compared to such unsoundable depths of indigenous experience, Western religious practice and ritual engagement roll along quite prosaically. Its myth of origins has never been similarly broken, its terror never made so palpable, its re-creative capacity never so challenged (Long, 1986, 123). And it is not surprising, then, says Long, that we find the West turning to indigenous spirituality for "new age" solace when the going gets tough in late modernity (Long, 1986, 137–139). Mainstream Christianity can succor middle-class sleights and sufferings, but it can't handle the terror of real contingency, or insanity, or violent death.

It is "God" as *Tremendum* that is the real conundrum of religious practice in history, and only those people "know it" who have been initiated into the nethermost depths of the human struggle to embody meaning in the face of annihilation. If the body is the prime symbol, its primal liturgical "labor," I would argue, is that of incarnating alternative possibilities of vitality and identity inside the vaunted transparencies and absoluteness of this world's pretension to totality. The basic potency of the symbol is its insistence that inchoate darkness is the primary place of birth and that that founding "blackness" can never be entirely eclipsed by the white light of domination (Ricoeur, 15).

## Postcolonial Monstrosity

But however we wish to arrange our theoretical apparatuses to probe some of these historical possibilities, the question remains one of the body. In postindustrial capitalist society, commodity fetishism has invaded the consumer body. We live inside a label, hang thread, dye hair, pierce skin, posture bone, reiki muscle, rap vocal, riff whatever latest image we think will lend credibility or substance to our naked individuality shivering alone before the mirror in the midnight of our own uncertainty. And we lose our potential "thickness" inside the commercial. We try to buy, rather than make, identity. Listen, for a moment to Karl Marx, writing late in his game, on the phenomenal effect of the factory:

> While simple cooperation leaves the mode of working by the individual for the most part unchanged, manufacture thoroughly revolutionizes it, and seizes labor-power by its very roots. It converts the laborer into a *crippled monstrosity*, by forcing his detail dexterity at the expense of a world of productive capabilities and instincts; just as in the States of La Plata they butcher a whole beast for the sake of his hide or tallow. Not only is the detail work distributed to the different individuals, but the individual himself is made the automatic motor of a fractional operation, and the absurd fable of Menius Agrippa, which makes man a mere fragment of his own body, becomes realized. (Marx, 360; emphasis added)

Here, I would suggest, is the real "possession cult" of modernity, the place of incarnation of Adam Smith's Invisible Hand.[2] Far from triumphing over "animism," modernity has simply narrowed its register (Taussig, 129). Blue-collar labor was incarcerated, in capitalism's industrial phase, inside a function of the machine, reduced to a small muscle of the body, a cramped detail of personality. In late modernity, in postindustrial paraphrasing, we have shifted into submission to a sign—more mobile, more tantalizing, focused now not on production, but consumption, but in certain ways even more truncated. The monstrosity remains—complex desire reduced to the range of Calvin Klein anorexia—and it is not even good monstrousness.

Mikhail Bakhtin had it right, I think, in musing with great perspicacity on the peasant bodies of the Feast of Fools in the late Middle Ages (Bakhtin, 5–8). There, something wonderfully grotesque loosed its moorings for the time of a broadly communal festival. The serf body defied its locus and definition and recovered its orifices. Life and death, meat and shit, genital protuberance and ribald exuberance, anal flatulence and oral flippancy were all asserted and celebrated (Bakhtin, 29, 33). Whether on the whole the ritual bought off rebellion or stoked its fires in memory just waiting for the right political ignition is beside the point (Stallybrass and White, 13, 26). It did offer a stage for exploration of the body understood as "relation" rather than mere station—and in so doing did what a good ritual should do. It encoded the possibility that things could be other than they are. It syncopated time with "difference."

Human beings are embodied beings, and the body, not the mind, is the final locus of change. Colonial regimes understood this—even though they probably did not understand that they understood it. "Converting" native culture was a matter of square architecture and bells and clocks, not just new discourses (Comaroff and Comaroff, 12, 64, 191–192). It was also a matter of outlawing the drums and dances of memory (Spencer, xv).

But memory is also finally genetic. Under the evolving skin, the majority argument in biology now goes, we are all African. But the spiritual ramifications remain as yet unheralded (Bynum, 3, 21, 54, 74, 79–102). Five hundred years of white supremacy is not enough to erase millennia upon millennia of living before the sun with melanin—no matter how ruthless the regimentation and denial (or how ubiquitous the colonial use of "blackness" as the trope of journey into interiors and the unexplored, Mills, 47). Robert Farris Thompson captures something deep in his work on African stylistics when he notes that one of the most unanticipated results of the slave trade is that "the entire Western world now rocks to an African beat" (Robert Farris Thompson, in a talk given at the African American Museum of Detroit, November 8, 1997). The drive for percussion, the metronome sense, the propensity for multiple-meter and off-beat phrasing, the polyrhythmic proclivity of music and textile alike in diasporic communities does not just reflect a waning wishfulness on the part of post-slave populations

(Thompson, 1983, xiii–xiv). Under the surface of the colonial body, the beat was insurgent. Who really conquered who may not become ultimately clear until the great fat drum in the sky sounds.

But whatever that ultimate assessment, earthly drums are clearly driving an increasingly delirious bargain with Western designs to dominate (Rose, 61). That youth today throughout this land of the free and home of the brave—and indeed, across the globe—increasingly turn to hip-hop rhythms and rap riffs to articulate their tensions and contemplate their possibilities serves serious notice (George, 201–207). Yes, the market immediately intrudes and buys off, repackages the ribaldry away from real political realization and offers toughness as tame entertainment. Nonetheless, the resource remains extant. As with the Feast of Fools, bodies are given moments of alternative disposition, desire is given another economy to explore itself in. Syncopated rhyme and sampled history are not simply "efflorescence of city," a bottled perfume of "attitude." They tattoo memory with the experience of a body in defiant motion. They constitute liturgy. The only question is whether they can be made to serve the need for ongoing exorcism of our possession by the commodity or are simply recuperated back into the devilish reign of capital.

## Intimate Polyphony

If we turn here to where we began these reflections, to the Apostle Paul, we find language that may once again be intriguing "to think with." The Pauline employment of neo-Platonic schemes of metaphysics has been recovered in our day by the likes of theologians William Stringfellow, Walter Wink, and Bill Wylie Kellermann. "Principalities and Powers" language points up something that is often elided and denied in modern discourse. Speaking is a species of possession. Language is an environment we inhabit, inflected with subjection, organized in institutions, anchored in *pathos*. It is bigger than its speakers and bends us to its directions. We are not masters of our mouths, but boasters of much more and less than we know (Derrida, 279). In older theological terms, we participate in angelic and demonic forces in each crack of the tongue. The utterance that ceaselessly tries to make its meaning palpable through all of our lips is vast and finally ineffable. Our words and wiles are just so much approximation of the great huge "Something" that haunts humans like an irrepressible haint. Those who would claim a Bible or Qur'an or Veda as somehow "basic" do well to take stock.

The tradition *Christians* claim, for instance, is actually a memorialization rooted in a moan, incubated in a groan, crying prophecy, sighing for destiny, descrying the status quo (Perkinson, 105–106, 112–113). It is much more about inchoate urgency than doctrinal orthodoxy. It began with the mutterings of slaves in Exodus (Ex. 2.23–25), enshrined its reciprocity in protections for moaning widows, orphans, and the poor at Sinai (Ex. 22.22–27), constantly listened for the stranger's whispered protest in Canaan (Ex. 22.21), raged in the wide-ranging jeremiads of Isaiah and Ezekiel (Jer. 8.18–21, 20.7–9; Ez. 2.8–3.27), rallied in the preachments of the Baptist (Mk. 1.2–4), finally incarnated itself on the cross in a cry rending earth and sky alike without redress (Mk. 15.33–39). It is not so much a tradition of solution as of question (Gn. 3.9; Hb. 1.2; Mk. 15.34), the eternal licensing of muttered dissent (Dt. 15.9; Ez. 9.4; Lk. 18.1–7, 35–43), the vision, says Paul (Rom. 8.22–23), of a whole creation groaning in labor pains. Read with attention to the priority of the moan, it reveals itself as privileging the messiness of hard-labored, insurgent expressions of vitality. It is hardly bourgeois in its decorum. It began against the grain of its time, recognized the bombast necessary to clear silenced spaces in official places (like a synagogue or temple) of their orthodox strictures of propriety so peasants could dare risk their own moans of anguish and joy (Mk. 1.21–28, 3.1–6; Lk. 13.10–17; Mt. 21.12–17), and culminated in a scream of torture in the execution ritual of empire (Mk. 15.33–39). That *Logos* theology (based on the Logos-hymn of Jn. 1.1–18) came to dominate such a tradition would be the height of irony were it not for the fact that the tradition itself anticipates its own eventual imperial colonization in concepts and control, and counsels constant vigilance against such (Mk. 13.1–37; Jn. 16.1–2).[3]

In our day, I am arguing that vigilance is patently not to be found in seminary soliloquy but in black whooping and latina lyricism and rap rancor and the sheer "'gettin' down ugly' ugliness" of gospel and funk and jazz inventiveness . . . or perhaps native chant or Afghani hum. But then "what we gonna do up here in the hallowed halls of academe?" The work that needs doing is labor at the level of the spleen. There is a tremendous anger abroad in the world that defies definition or simple therapy. It requires not only a mind capable of organizing the energies into causes with reasons, but also perhaps even more, a body capable of working the anguish into doable forms of redress over the course of a lifetime.

In a word, global capital is a huge structure of idolatry, enshrining infinite accumulation and unrestricted expansion as an untouchable birthright for 20 percent of the planet's population—no matter the consequences to the other 80 percent and the rest of the biosphere's life forms (Rasmussen, 149–154). The consequences, in fact, are lives of increasing disruption and dislocation, the desertification of Africa, the despoliation of Amazonia, the wild redistribution of resources up and away from indigenous populations who are then forced into urban slums of almost unimaginable sprawl, the prostitution of their young, figuratively and literally, for the sake of survival, the nonsurvival of all the diverse languages and different cultures and dissimilar strategies evolving sustainable relations in varied ecological niches that humanity has elaborated with great cost and patience over eons.

And that reorganization of the body of *Gaia*, if you want, of the ever-intensifying web of interdependence and interconnection, under the sign of absolute growth, is the intransigent "possession" of our age. What can dislodge such a demon? Inside the human body, the cell that locks itself into the imperative of absolute growth and begins careening around the bloodstream like a wanton teenager, sure the whole rest of the body is simply "there" for it alone, like a ripe plum for the ravaging, converting the surrounding tissue into its own prerogative of limitless expansion, ingesting and expanding, eating its way into organ and bone, organizing all else into its own adolescent logic and lunacy—that cell we call "cancer." Global capital probably looks like nothing so much as the social form of that dreaded disease to the rest of sentient life on the skin of the planet today. And we who are "religious" and oriented to a modicum of concern for something other than more "stuff" to stick in the attic are faced with a profound question of liturgical re-formation and ritual re-creation.

The only remedy I know, the only source of hope I see, is not of the same scale as the problem. Indeed, the bigger part of the problem's problematic is its ability to enervate efforts of scale (Esteva and Prakash, 21). Human beings, in globalization's pretensions, are not allowed to be local and limited (Esteva and Prakash, 31). Sustainable rootage in relation to a community of flora and fauna peculiar to place is nowhere part of the transnational picture (Esteva and Prakash, 22). The vision is rather a gated community inside a gated country, elevating its own policed gardens to the significance of Babel while relegating the rest of the globe to life in a parking lot. Curiously, tellingly—in the face of such a characterization—any urgency then expressed about relearning our liturgy seems utterly fatuous and hopeless. But it is not. It is precisely the turn to memory that bears the only likely remedy (Esteva and Prakash, 32, 53, 72, 95, 166, 200).

# Tricky Antiphony

What if what our various religious "classics"—whether written texts of scripture or living scriptings of dance—actually encode is an old struggle, anciently engaged, never resolved, definitive of human being and becoming since first we gurgled a significance in sound? What if that old conflict is precisely the conflict between infinite desire and finite body, organized socially as a conflict between empire and ecology: on the one hand, the human community imaged as ever-expanding, conquering space, homogenizing time, walling itself bionically inside silicon and steel and encasing all other life in an ever-thickening skin of concrete; and on the other hand, that community lived lightly on the surface of space, in concert with all other life forms understood as communion and kin, resolute in its commitment to locality, reserving pride of place not to economy, but liturgy, evolving complex forms of interiority and relationality, understanding spirit as primarily an inten-sification of meaning worked out "up against" an accepted limit?

So many of our traditions articulate a primitive struggle against *hubris*, against humanity halo-ing it efforts as a climb toward the heavens in block and cinder, cylinder and stone, towering scheme and aggrandizing ego. So many of our stories encode the primary revela-tion as coming through an animated cosmos—a burning plant on Sinai (Ex. 3.2–3), a dove on the shoulder in the Jordan (Lk. 3.22), a midnight visitation of titanic being in a cave on Mt. Hira outside Mecca (Armstrong, 137–138), a crow over the canyon in Sioux-land, a cow in Calcutta, a Dahomean snake full of craft and wisdom in West Africa or on the Caribbean coast (Thompson, 177–179, 191). Anthropologists tell us many aboriginal communities had their eco-nomic function down to 3–5 hours/day and spent the rest of their time in Dream-Work, elaborating vision, thickening meaning, intensifying the communal bond with mystery and time (Gowdy, xxi; Sahlins, 18).

I do not intend here to offer a simplistic admonition to "go native," or even just a Luddite repudiation of modernity. But I do want to raise issue with whether economic aggression toward the earth or ritual re-creation of life is to be primary in human colloquy and destiny (Goodman, 222–223). I do want to say that what happens when I birth a poem—giving up my own place in the world, giving space to something that is happening through me, saying "yes" to a possession that does not entirely submit to my intentionality, risking my embodi-ment in service of a significance that I neither simply actively "author" nor just passively "receive"—is that somehow I touch close to the core of my DNA. By extension, when I listen to a John Coltrane fighting a slight membrane of air in a bent piece of brass into an eloquence of despair and a wildness of desire and an ultimate incandescence of hope against the night he faced—I am ready to fight for what I find alive there.

And that I take to be the final delineation. I am not willing to die for more caviar or a new K-Mart in the neighborhood. I am not willing to die for the fatuous and demonic hope of, one day, *not having to* die. I *am* willing to struggle for certain momentary realizations of Beauty or gestures of Goodness that—like everything else in the physical and metaphysical world alike—cannot ever be secured against their fleetingness and disappearance. I want to live a life that refuses to kill other human beings for what I can put in my mouth, but does not finally refuse to share the destiny of all other bodies at becoming "food" for future generations of beings, if necessary, for what could come out of it. Such a lifestyle, I believe, can only be elaborated as a possible vision in a practice of relationships that honor reciprocity—not riches—as their ultimate resource (Berendt, 84–85, 119, 161–165; Leonard, xii, 6, 20, 38, 63). And here is the simple aphorism of the hour for me.

After the "turn to the subject" in the Enlightenment and the "turn to language" of late, I want to ask if what is now before us is not a kind of life and death "turn" back to a rhythm of reciprocity:

—to respect for cadence and caterwauling calliopes;
—for soft slides of sound and syncopated squawks of insane love affairs;
—to time understood as seasonal and cyclic in swellings and recessions of significance;
—to growth outward complimented by an even more important growth back inward;
—to diminishing the amount of space we require and matter we consume, for the sake of an interior efflorescence of that wisdom that appears only in the eyes of old people and old animals, etched in gnarled trunks and lichened rocks, and the wonder of a billion billion galaxies stretching back and forth in space as the very meaning of time itself.

I take my hope from all of the hurting and howling hordes of night, those people who have created and re-created themselves in spite of the odds, again and again, and do so even now:

—the *chutzpah* of the Jewish tailor in Buchenwald who, forced to shred the sacred text and make his guard a Torah-scroll jacket, chose only those portions of the script that bore curses so that his captor walked around, unknowingly advertising the hidden transcript of the harried in full view of the uncomprehending eye of their torturers;

—the political genius of a Gandhi, recreating jail cell as bully pulpit, inspiring peasant and pundit alike to resist British dominance, insisting homespun saris were the dignified counter to British textile mills and dyes;

—the religious resilience of slaves complexly encoding spirituals as public service announcements in the very ears of their masters, broadcasting news of Harriet Tubman's nearness and the need to make a decision about the life-risk of an "underground" trek north to freedom, in a simple-sounding song like "steal away to Jesus";

—the courage of Caribbean *rastas* and Haitian *voudouistas* and even Cuban communists—fallible as they all have been—in making island paradises harbor *fiestas* and *collectivas* that gesture toward a different economy of human desire;

—the panache of Palestinian Muslim mothers raising sons and daughters for whom a better world for others is worth great risk and the possible sacrifice of oneself, regularly liturgized in a communal ritual of kneeling together;

—the work and witness of traditional cultures around the globe today—*zapatista*-led and otherwise—who are learning to refuse the siren song of the dollar sign, and all the crushing consumer culture it brings in its wake, and insisting instead on the primacy of local community and ancestral memory and ritual vitality over market rights and upward mobility.

The litany could go on and on, and will undoubtedly go on and on, at great cost, over the unrequited cry of spilled blood and lost childhoods and raped womanhood and deformed manhood and dying woods and disappearing fisheries and polluted waters, all of it asking "why?" Why this great rush to sell and buy everything, until meaning itself is marketed for dime, a crime, and a famous fifteen seconds on prime time? Why? Toward what are we developing? Perhaps it is high time we learn all over again to listen to those who have gone before.

# 8

# The Body of White Space

*The reality is that one can pretend the body does not matter only because a particular body (the white male body) is being presupposed as the somatic norm.*

—*Charles Mills* (The Racial Contract, 53)

"So, we have had more than thirty contact hours of discussion about race, class and gender, in this course. Now I want to know what *you* think. Do you guys think we still have a problem with racism today?" The mocha-skinned woman's challenge was as much a matter of eyes punctuating the bob of her head as of her tongue forming syllables. The two other African American women in class sat eager to the question, eyes on alert, "reading" through every pore. Every one of the four white males addressed by their fellow student's "throw down" squirmed his response. Not one could speak to it; all four spoke away from it, discharging their nervousness in long dissembling rambles about not-quite-related subjects. As subjects of speech, their speaking exceeded their own subjectivity. The dis-ease was almost literal, an affliction of a dis-articulate body, unable to find voice, performing its awkwardness with all the eloquence of an infection. The classroom suddenly became clinic for a virus[1] that is ubiquitous in this country. More than mere surface appearance gestured here like a symptom. White male embodiment spoke its speechless code like a fever.

The structure and meaning of that restlessness is the subject of this writing in a multiple sense. The classroom scene hinted at above is emblematic of something as broad as the society that gives rise to its gendered, black question and as intimate as the hand that is trying to write toward its answer. I argue in what follows that there is such a thing as "the white male body"—as surely as Rodney King's on the concrete was made to be "black and bestial"[2]—that is simultaneously (only) social construct and (yet also) lived experience. I will not speak about male embodiment in general, nor middle-class male embodiment everywhere all the time, but only white middle-class male embodiment in its partial constitution and practice as normatively "white." And in elaborating plausible textures and technologies of that particular form of *habitus*,[3] I will not escape my own inquiry. For I also remain the subject of this subject, however much I, too, "speak away from it" in focusing on other white males as my surrogates, my substitutes, my saviors-in-drag.

What follows is an attempt to think through something that does not readily appear in mainstream American society because it is the ground from which that social space is typically envisioned and practiced. The white middle-class male body remains the presupposition of gaze, the norm of ontology, the artifact of institutional discipline, the criteria of ethical interrogation, despite its increasing displacement from the presumption of control. I will not seek exhaustively to investigate its reservoir of phenomenality or its law of constitution. The work here is more a matter of heurism, of occasioning a moment of recognition, displaying a possible genealogy, underwriting the projection of an ethical correction. Its method will be resolutely "double," seeking to gain purchase on "whiteness" by continual reference to "blackness," seeking to bring into examined contradiction what more normally is simply presumed contradictory, and raising in the space of that contradiction the possibility of agency. In sum, and by way of anticipation, I will seek to demystify white male embodiment as a privilege of given-ness and rework its ethical "placement" as a lifelong practical demand.

## White Middle-Class Maleness as Invisible Norm

The hypothesis already limned in the above story is that white middle-class male forms of embodiment in this country are largely unconscious and inarticulate. They tend to encode technologies of normativity that normally do not require the work of conscious performance. They constitute an unproblematic physicality in the body politic. They navigate social space—both public and private—unobstructed, un(re)marked. The policing of such a body is an accomplished fact of middle-class pedagogy that rarely requires external reinforcement. It is this body that stands as the hegemonic body par excellence. Its particular constellation of meanings—its whiteness, maleness, middle class-ness, and heterosexuality—are produced and reproduced in discourses that are not simply verbal. Indeed, a large part of this body's social inscription is accomplished in and by its production and occupation of certain spaces in a normative[4] "realization" of quite particular protocols. That such is the case only begins to come to consciousness for most white males in the challenge of other forms of embodiment that have enough power in a given confrontation to resist those protocols and either explicitly or implicitly interrogate their "normativity." Paramount among such moments of challenge, as prototypical of the particular history of this country from its very inception, is the encounter with black male performances of the body.

African American innovations of public "blackness"—as embodied forms of social commentary and contestation—realize the quintessential counter-hegemonic possibility of what it means to be a human being in America. They do so in various modes of gender inscription and sexual orientation. And they do so in no small measure because blackness historically has been made to appear (in the discourses of white supremacy and white racism) as the mutually exclusive opposite of whiteness, as a quality of humanity that was essentially fixed and irreducibly different from the whiteness it licensed as its "other" pole of meaning. Whatever the actual negotiation of white normativity overall, whether the individuals in question otherwise challenge the social order of domination or largely reinforce its requirements, it is black cultural elaborations of the body that give sharpest relief to the arbitrariness of social norms of embodiment. Black occupations of public space regularly and continuously challenge the limits of allowable deviance in gestural style, sartorial statement, physical posture, and verbal volatility.[5]

In such everyday public improvisations of black embodiment as a cultural semantics of domination and resistance, "whiteness" is forced onto the surface of the social body and into question. In the actual moment of such a conjuration, black urban male forms of embodiment most profoundly unmask "invisible whiteness" as itself a gendered, heterosexual class formation. That this writing began with an instance of black female confrontation of white males does not gainsay that claim, but only points to the complexity of the way race engenders body language and vice versa. It is also important to note here that white middle-class females, as indeed white working-class females and males, and white participants in gay and lesbian lifestyles also stand as partial "challenges" to the taken-for-grantedness of the dominant forms of white male embodiment. Just as importantly, other ethnic identities and cultural heritages likewise pose implicit critiques of the way whiteness, maleness, and normative power tend to be conflated in the dominant culture of this country. How such a conflation is made to cohere and what the theoretical stakes are in recognizing it requires a layered analysis.

## Framing the Question of the White Male Body

Again, the basic presupposition here is that the white male body is not innocent of social history or ethical content. Whiteness and maleness and middle class-ness intersect in a form of embodiment that populates certain social spaces with a living norm of ontological power. In a sense, what I am attempting to reveal here is a male body that is not so much a "person" or "subject," as an "archetype" or "hieroglyph," an embodied enactment that is prescripted so well, it could be said to stand as the quintessential postmodern form of possession.[6]

The analogue here would be possession-cult enactments like those found worldwide in the ritual practices of indigenous religions[7] in which initiates regularly give their somatic powers over to energies or scripts that manifest one or another coherent personage for their local communities. In the practices of Haitian Vodun or Cuban Santeria for instance (both of which gain increasing relevance here as they are finding more widespread expression in the urban centers of America in recent years[8]), "possession" is understood to be a normal and central part of communal life. Indeed, in these particular West African-derived rituals, the moments of possession dramatically realize embodied archetypes in the presence of the gathered community. Each of these archetypal *personae* (known in their own traditions as *loa* or *santos*, respectively) is recognizable in the theatricality of the ritual performances by virtue of a thickly textured set of bodily enactments, articulated in terms of a highly specific drumbeat, preferred food and drink, select clothing style, manifest set of behaviors, characteristic dispositions, likely discourse, well-known likes and dislikes, and so on. Although prescribed in some measure, these "spirit-*personae*" actually serve as the basis for a highly improvisational time of interaction between the possessed person (or "medium") being "ridden" by a particular spirit-*persona* and the rest of the "spectating" community, around real issues of power and meaning that are current in the community's life outside of the ritual time and space. These alternative identities, unconsciously embodied by otherwise "normal-behaving" community members for the space of the ritual, are recognized and embraced as the immediate manifestations of mythologized forces and figures (Shango, Yemaya, Eshu-Elegba, Erzulie, Guede, etc.) whose presence has gained practical valence in the community as dramatically enacted models of different ways of being human. Here, the multiplicity of the figures embodied in any given ritual celebration gives dramatic currency to the value and experience of plurality. And while specific to each of their historical communities (i.e., indigenous or immigrant Haitian or Cuban groups), these encoded bodily performances are to some degree recognizable across differences of national origin and language throughout the West African diaspora in terms of their rhythmic stylistics and gestural economies.

In some ways, the white middle-class male body enacts a similar "possession," likewise recognizable across national boundaries in the dominant North Atlantic cultures (nuanced, obviously, by certain cultural differences of comportment and gesture).[9] But as part of the hegemonic formation of these cultures, this embodiment serves to underwrite notions of homogeneity more than plurality. And while the white middle-class male body certainly differs from the possession figures outlined above in its ambient consciousness, at another level (as already hypothesized in the introductory remarks), it could be thought of as not yet having awakened from its possession. Only under pressure from experiences of sustained encounter with other forms of embodiment does a rudimentary awakening even become possible.

The classroom scenario described in opening this work depicts one such moment. The discomfort of the white males was not just "mental," but it was a moment of physical dis-ease, of becoming aware of an ignorance in the body, of embodying an uncertainty, an inarticulate-ness, a supplementarity that was (apparently) evident and "speaking" to others without license or intentionality, but had not yet been wrestled into speech and knowledge in and for itself. On the other hand, an asymmetry of knowing also seemed to become apparent: the black women knew something corporeally that was more than just skin color. Their "blackness" in that moment of confrontation was an embodied knowledge, a challenge that was "thicker" than the face value of either their words or their body surface. It spoke in their eyes, their posture, their silent movements, their command of the floor in that moment. It represented what Michel Foucault would call "subjugated knowledge" in a moment of insurrectionary display, a "local knowledge" rupturing a dominant discourse (Foucault, 1980, 81–84). In part, this writing represents an attempt to become articulate about the precise nature of that moment of confrontation, of what the black women knew in and as a form of embodiment that the white men did not know in and as their own form of embodiment.

### Challenges to the White Male Body

Having said as much in relationship to the opening scenario, I want to repeat that I think black male forms of embodiment represent the deepest moment of challenge to the white middle-class male body. While the black male body emerges in the imagination of the dominant culture under different stereotypic figures of speech in different moments of history (e.g., in the nineteenth century, as "Uncle" if older and "mellowed" or "Zip Coon" if younger and "dandified"; in the 1960s, as "militant" if defiant and black leather-jacketed; in the 1990s, as "gangbanger" if young, verbal, and demonstrative, etc.) and (only) as relatively more or less "frightening" depending upon its relative darkness of skin, size, build, age, hair-length, and so on, that body remains a regularly revisited "touchstone of terror" in the culture at large. Its attributed terror is constructed out of the gendered significance of its racialization.

The racialization of the black male body is part of a long history of conceptualization structured (in part) by the almost two-thousand-year-old notion of the "Great Chain of Being," inherited by Europe from ancient Greece, elaborated and intensified by Christian theological convictions during the Middle Ages, that became part of the modern articulation of "race" after 1492. In early modernity, the Great Chain schema organized observable reality into a hierarchy that positioned Africans underneath other human types (ascending from that "African" baseline in a developmental order moving through "Native Americans" and "Asians" to the "European" top of the line), immediately next to or even still within the category of animality. While constantly revised under "scientific" input, the schema has remained residually operative in the dominant cultural imaginary of modernity such that even in today's multicultural *melange* of "different forms of difference" in America, "blackness" continues to mark the greatest distance from a dominant and dominating whiteness (which congeals its own normativity and conceals its power, "unmarked").[10]

In the contemporary effects of such a schema, the social field of vision is regularly (forcibly) opened to historically shifting perceptions of ethnic and cultural difference that are presumed to attach to various types and colors of bodies (e.g., the meanings that attend categories like "Latino," "Pacific Islander," "Asian American," etc.). But in most places in the United States blackness remains a virtually inassimilable otherness that establishes a kind of "absolute" difference from whiteness, in proportion to the degree it is made to bear public meanings of vital potency, virulent hostility, and uncontrollable sexual desire. And while this eroticized imagination of blackness attaches to both male and female bodies of apparent African heritage, the desire it encodes is heterosexually male in its orientation. The white male domination constellated out of eroticized blackness is most violently disturbed, and made visible, when the body it faces most clearly challenges its own dominating desire. A body "apparently" potent, hypersexed, wild, strong, uncontained (i.e., "black") and *male*, raises immediate issue with the certainty/power of the maleness codified as "white." But clarifying how such a threat is at one and the same moment *constituted* and *coerced* into a public recertification of white middle-class male (pre)dominance requires careful examination of the machinations of public meaning-making.

One such moment that could easily occupy an entire book of analysis was the 1991 beating of Rodney King. The bringing to bear of baton on body in a certain social location that simultaneously established that body as "black," "deviant," "criminal," "bestial," "violent," and "threatening,"[11] also silently reestablished another body, not immediately present on that scene, as not any of those things predicated of King's body. That absent body made its presence felt, and reinforced the particularity of its meanings, through the institution of policing that particular social space. King was the wrong kind of body in the wrong place with the wrong timing. The disciplinary[12] subduing of his body "clarified" that space as already inhabited by this other body.

On the other hand, Damien William's moment of going upside Reginald Denny's head with a brick in South Central after the acquittal of King's assailants represented a kind of return of the repressed, a clarification that some spaces in the urban center are not so easily claimed by the norm of white middle-class maleness. Centrally significant in that South Central theater of contestation was William's dance of glee afterward. The moment was not gratuitous violence; it was ritual theater with profound communal significance. It staged a retaliation, a brief disclosure of the logic of urban space-wars. Just prior to that televised "horror," at the same corner, the police had beaten and arrested another member of the Williams's family and two neighbors (Davis, 1993a, 220–243).

Whatever we might think of the individual morality attending any of these (re)actions, what is apparent is that the meeting of these bodies in space and time was not primarily a matter of individual anything. The encounters were profoundly social, complexly racial, densely gendered, thick with negotiations of desire and fantasy and repulsion. None of the figures was merely him- or herself (one of the officers who initially stopped King was female). Rodney King was made to figure young black maleness in all of its polyvalent terror and fascination for white male authority. Reginald Denny (in spite of his working-class appearance) was made to stand in for white male middle-class privilege that had secured its prerogatives one more time in the Simi Valley courtroom at the expense of black male humanity. Violence was the nexus between the two forms of male embodiment, differentially entering into the constitution of both. But the violence that appeared in those two moments is "normally" expressed in a much denser history involving bodily negotiations of place that are not so apparently directed against each other. How that nexus is more normally mediated in this society is a function of both time and space, both history and geography. Perhaps the best way into analyzing that mediation is through consideration of a little-known piece of the Rodney King beating that may have occasioned much of its virulence.

## The Space of Race

According to the officer who first halted King, California Patrolwoman Melanie Singer, in her testimony against the LAPD officers, King was acting a little silly, laughing and doing a little dance when he got out of his inexpensive Hyundai (Baker, 38–50; Gilmore, 23–37). Stacie Koon's defense attorney offered a slightly thicker description from Koon's deposition for the Simi Valley trial. He repeated Koon's testimony that King was "on something"; "I saw him look through me," and when Singer told King to take his hands away from his butt, "he shook it at her . . . he shook it at her" (Gilmore, 29). In retrospect, then, an unanswerable but unavoidable question emerges. How much of the blackness King was made to bear in his beating issued from a vague experience, on the part of the white males present, of "impotence"—the paradox of armed authority uncertain before an unintelligible performance apparently directed to a white female in their presence? Seemingly, white male identity was face-to-face here with a threatening "something" that it could sense, but neither interpret nor tolerate. In effect, it interpreted its own violent uncertainty onto that body, made it bear white authority's own brutality in a moment of radical displacement and projection.

The tangled density of the signifiers crowding that fraught moment on the pavement between King and the LAPD harbored a long history. Unpacking the overdeterminations would require explorations of the institution and continuing effects of numerous historical practices: slave plantation techniques of producing/managing desire through the controlled breeding of slaves (Spillars, 65–81); the violent preservation of the cult of white female virginity and the violent rape of black women/emasculation of black men by white masters; the eroticizing of white fears of slave revolts like those in Saint Domingue (Haiti) or, closer to home, Nat Turner's in Virginia; nineteenth-century white working-class traditions of a pornographic form of "blacking up" on the minstrelsy stage before going out and beating up, sexually mutilating and/or killing actual black persons;[13] the ritualized lynchings in the Jim Crow South in which castration constituted an essential element of the violence; the way miscegenation fears entered into the real estate, mortgage lending and insurance practices giving rise to northern ghettos; corporate management of the simultaneously titillating and terrifying cross-over power of black musics like blues, jazz, R&B, and gospel, eventually producing an Elvis Presley and the phenomenon of rock and roll; the more recent frenzy of consumption of modern day "gladiator"[14] sports figures like Michael Jordan as fetishized primitive in national rituals of surrogate masculinity, and the like.

Likewise attention would have to be focused on accounting for the broad cultural ideology of scientific racism underwriting the above. This ever-shifting, yet seemingly (given the popularity of books like Richard Herrnstein and Charles Murray's *The Bell Curve*) ever-reproduced ideology absolutizing black difference from whiteness was originally constituted in an eighteenth-century amalgam of Anglo visceral horror for things black (Jordan, 7–8), Calvinist theological evaluation of dark skin as indicative of a heart recalcitrant toward God and (thus) predestination to perdition (Bastide, 270–285), Enlightenment taxonomic classification of persons of color and cultures of contrast (to northern Europe's own) as lower on the scale of human development, and renascent Greek aesthetic ideals denigrating swarthiness, large lips, flared nostrils, prominent chins, protruding buttocks, and the like (West, 1982, 47–65). Tracing the (per)mutations of this Anglo-Calvinist-Greco-Enlightenment social formation, in and through the proliferation of historical practices sampled above, would only begin to adumbrate the density of the interaction on California Highway 210.

Whatever may have been King's actual intention in his little dance (we were never given his own words about the entire event in any of the news coverage), black and white male negotiations of embodiment in that moment could not *but* have been overcharged with meaning and energy. Many historical discourses, many cultural norms, many institutional disciplines, many social presumptions, even many family pedagogies suddenly confronted each other on the California concrete in March 1991 outside their usual venues of mediation. While it is beyond the scope of this writing to do more than simply recognize the overdetermination of that encounter, it is worth giving rough outline of the stereotypical organization of its drama.

Rodney-King-meets-LAPD-on-California-tarmac enacted that urban space in terms of its racialized gender coding. It was street theater minus its producer-director. The space itself supplied much of the apology. Presumably among other unseen actors on the stage that day was the long history of white male fear of the black male body briefly summarized above. A white woman's "integrity" was seemingly violated by innuendo and suggestion, in a space that constituted the domain of white male prerogative. The challenge of King's little dance was arguably perceived as addressed not so much to the police as police, but to white men in general, more specifically to frontline white male protectors of more well-heeled white male organizers and planners "contained" further inside that white space. Two technologies of male embodiment were thus suddenly on display. The black male body was forced to deal with its motions and meanings absent material technology or legal symbolism. It had to perform its tactic in the key of improvisation, against the odds, in the face of terror, with only its own corporeality for a tool. The white male body, on the other hand, was split: its light blue-suited enactor had hands on the implements of coercion and sleeves full of visible license, while its dark blue-suited possessor was cloistered in the towers of transaction and labyrinths of power at the heart of this suddenly compromised white space. The types here are obviously stereotypes. Yet for all that, they continue to code the spaces and encode the bodies. The work of culture critic Stephen Haymes, labor historian Michael Davis, and social historian Thomas Dumm help us further explain the relationship between space and embodiment contributing to this urban "theater of the absurd."

In his book, *Race, Culture, and the City: A Pedagogy for Black Urban Struggle*, Haymes has developed an analysis of the contemporary city as a spatialization of the meaning and values of race. Not only individual persons and collective groupings, but also social spaces themselves are organized on the basis of racialization (Haymes, 4, 21–22). The replacement of black low-income "settlements" with white gentrified neighborhoods, for instance, materially reconstructs the city in terms of an urban mythology in which "white places" are deemed to be civilized, rational, and orderly and "black places" to be uncivilized, irrational, and disorderly. Within this cognitive mapping of public space, blackness represents the dangers and disorder of the *id* and whiteness the civilizing consciousness of the *superego*. The white supremacist thinking undergirding such mythologies mandates "spatial regulation and control." By means of discriminatory housing practices and redlining, the city is made to realize a form of urban apartheid, racial ideology actualized in the material landscape. In relationship to our LA example, it is important to recognize that Highway 210 is a major linkage between what could be called "white spaces." King's black body was interdicted as a foreign substance polluting the purity of place and the LAPD officers constituted an ad hoc assemblage of antibodies, attacking the infection on sight and reasserting the compromised code.

Davis and Dumm deepen our appreciation of the stakes. Davis has written various works on the emergence of postindustrial LA as an example of the racialized city, in which business assets and voter power have fled to surrounding suburbs or "edge cities," leaving behind urban communities of impoverished unemployment, "black market" drug traffic, deteriorating housing (granting tax write-offs to many of its absent owners), and policing practices that border on those of postcolonial "war" situations (like Belfast during The Troubles or the West Bank during the Intifada). In post-uprising LA, however, Davis has witnessed a new wrinkle in the management of urban realities. Recent meetings of geographers, urban planners, traffic engineers, and developers have generated excitement about the imminent advent of geographical information systems (GIS). Under this regime, complex urban systems—traffic flows, zoning, and the like—will be managed via the linkage of LANDSAT satellites to GIS software. Image-resolution capabilities of commercial satellite systems are now already approaching the threshold of distinguishing individual automobiles, and soon may be able to distinguish people and their pets. The ramifications have not been lost on GIS experts: one remarked to Davis that "this will quickly revolutionize the policing of inner-city areas" (Davis, 1993b, 149). Here, we confront the frightening possibility that Michel Foucault's metaphor of the panopticon could become all too material in the urban reality of the near future.

According to Dumm, however, the growing technical possibility of this "all-seeing eye of surveillance" is only half of the picture. The other new technological watchword is "monitoring." Its security task is more modest. Unlike surveillance techniques, monitoring is not concerned with keeping tabs on individuals; it is rather about the control of spaces. Monitoring tracks movement through space by way of cameras and/or security guards concerned not so much with individual identities as with body types in their range of departure from a putative male norm that is white, heterosexual, and middle class. Its analogue is the "enclosed community"—a homogeneous environment constituted through consumption and normalized across a range of behaviors, styles, and appearances. Simi Valley marks its model. In keeping with postmodern notions of a fractured and multiple subjectivity, these sites of monitored sameness do allow for some measure of deviance. The personal fashion statements continuously pushed forward for consumption by corporate America are allowed for, but only within a carefully established range of tolerance. "Outside," more menacing forms of difference are kept at bay through closely monitored points of entry and exit.

Articulating with this new mode of monitoring is a refurbished ideology of law enforcement tending toward the "somatotyping" (or "body-typing") of conservative criminologist James Q. Wilson (respected enough to be named president of the American Political Science Association in 1992). According to Dumm, Wilson's approach to criminality has developed "anatomical correlates of crime," predicting the probability of particular kinds of behavior (Dumm, 183). Physical traits such as broad chest, low waist, relatively large arms, prominent muscle relief, and the like, and of course "color" all point to the possibility of a criminal predisposition. (Under these rubrics, for instance, Rodney King's body "could be said to have informed on him to the police.") (Dumm, 183). While no one trait is definitive, the more such characteristics cohabit any given body, the more likely that body is to commit crime. A slim, light-skinned African American would thus be slightly less predisposed to criminality than a stockier, darker one—or so goes the theory. But whether such nuances of body-morphology-*cum*-skin-color actually translate into less, or less violent, arrests is anybody's guess (I'm guessing not). In any case, as indicating only a statistical "probability," such traits are not held to erase personal responsibility. The individuals so typed paradoxically remain accountable and thus punishable.

In net effect, then, technology and ideology are once again combining to produce new forms of differential geographies. On the one hand, enclosed communities monitor their borders with ever more sophisticated devices (or is it that monitors devise their communities through ever more sophisticated enclosures?). The result is a citadel of sameness laboring under the straight-up normativities of white, suburban, middle-class, heterosexual law-abidingness. The enclosures embrace various "others," but only so long as they do not deviate too far from the acceptable norm. On the other hand, those who are structured out of these enclosed communities are consigned to the "deviance management" of the judicial apparatuses (e.g., according to 1995 Justice Department data, 30 percent of black men between the ages of eighteen and thirty were in prison, paroled, or on probation). Their lot is surveillance on their own turf; monitoring if they attempt to circulate into the new enclosures.

But this tale of two cities also gives rise to a tale of two bodies. If blackness is in some sense corporeally constituted in surveillance, whiteness emerges as the bodily schema corresponding to monitoring. Again, these statements are stereotypic and misleading at one level. But as characterizing a set of experiences typical of certain spaces, as emblematic of normative expectations that inform certain practices, they open up perspective on white and black male forms of embodiment.

### Black and White Negotiations of Embodiment

While once again space limitations on this writing do not permit in-depth exploration, it is important to emphasize that W. E. B. Du Bois, at the turn of the century, had already formulated a thematics of black embodiment that underscored its constitution under an invasive gaze or surveillance. In his first published writing, Du Bois underscored the power of the eye to constrain the body. His first paradigmatic experience of the meaning of racial difference took place when a grade school classmate interrupted the classroom exchange of greeting cards by refusing his offering "peremptorily, with a glance." That glance, by itself, contained the entire meaning of race for Du Bois. It dropped a veil, shattered a paradise, cleaved his cosmos into two unbridgeable worlds. It is not surprising that Du Bois's later theorizing of race continued to privilege the disciplines of sight. In his most famous paraphrase of black distinctiveness in *The Souls of Black Folk*, black identity emerges as a peculiar "consciousness of one's twoness" in which one is ever "looking at oneself through the eyes of the other" (Du Bois, 1986, 17). It is a gaze with physical effect. It results in the sensation of "two souls" or "ideals" warring with one another in "one dark body whose dogged strength alone keeps it from being torn asunder" (Du Bois, 1986, 17). Said another way, for Du Bois, black self-consciousness has ever been the discovery that one's own time and space is already populated with other bodies, other powers, other eyes with peremptory intentions *that cannot be kept entirely outside of one's own flesh*. Blackness (in the United States, at least) *is* the body under surveillance.

More formally, I would argue that Du Bois's double-consciousness is a statement not only about black consciousness within the individual black body, but also about the spatiality of blackness in general in this country. It foregrounds the fact that black "room-to-be" has constantly been under the threat of invasion, a threat based not only in black imagination of white intention, but also in the historical reality of white violence. Black preoccupation with "the gaze of the other" is rooted in the concrete memory of *having actually been* invaded and *made* to deal with the other on the inside—not only the inside of one's head, but also inside one's body (in the form of the whip or penis or baton), inside one's house (whether in Africa or on the plantation or in the ghetto), inside one's community (in the form of the overseer or social worker or police officer), inside one's culture (in the form of religious doctrine, musical instrumentation, pedagogical instruction, artisanal tools, domestic artifacts, clothes), and the like. That, today, surveillance should be technologized to the point where an entire urban environment can be made to function like an outdoor prison, invaded by a constant supervisory gaze, is, at one level, not anything new or different for black experience in America.

In the face of such an invaded circumstance, black survival could then be understood, in part, to have been a constant struggle to combat the effects of such an intrusion, to develop tactics for living under and around such a surveillance. Whatever forms it took, the antidote for such would obviously have to be capable of countermanding that invasive force "in kind." Against the hard eye of a watching white culture, black response for over three hundred years now could be said to have taken collective shape (in part) as a harder eye[15] of communal support and surreptition. Anthropologist Thomas Kochman is helpful in grasping, from a comparative white point of view, some of the distinctiveness of that response.[16] As a counterforce to oppressive white voyeurism, black culture developed a performative counter-competency (Kochman, 110, 131).[17] In the forums of barber shops and beauty parlors, in street rituals of "capping" and porch rituals of "spec-ifying," in call and response from the pew and "you can't touch this" antiphonies on the dance floor, in a hundred different tiny gestures of everyday life, black cultural protocols demanded and reinforced an oppositional facility (Kochman, 18–19, 24, 127).[18] They inculcated dramatic expressivity and elaborated a contrastive sensibility capable of deflecting the power of a controlling gaze by communally pro-liferating the gazes before which the body-on-display negotiated its meanings. The contradictions of race were relativized in a percussive "multiplication" of the body, elaborating hidden living space in plain view under the surface-significance of the incarcerating category (of "blackness"). Again and again, culture critics and race theorists have remarked on the difference between white and black enculturation in this country in terms of a different set of expectations regarding public expression and physical exhibition. Black culture expects social time and space to be aggressively negotiated and contested in forms of communication that are physically and emotionally demonstrative.[19] Its own pedagogical forms rework the body as what Stuart Hall calls a "canvas of representation" (Hall, 27–29).[20]

But if black forms of embodiment can, indeed, be understood as (in part) the cultural products of ongoing attempts to deal with various kinds of surveillance, white habituation in the body is also partially glossed in the correlative notion of contemporary monitoring. White embodiment in the public spaces of this country, historically, has been more about the meeting of norms, quietly fitting in,[21] not causing a spectacle (Pile, 230). It has been constituted in a gaze that solicits conformity, not subversive stylizations of individuality (Kochman, 114, 155).[22] It has been disciplined not so much in intense forms of local community that act as a confirming chorus[23] and supply a range of innovatory[24] models and improvisational motives, but rather in a more plastic mode of spatiality, governed by more generic ideals. In its genesis as an "empty negation" (Dyer, 44), a largely vacuous assertion "that whatever else I may be, at least I am not black," white-ness has not been generative of a white community per se; there has been no positive white cultural production coming into being in a serious struggle against invasive powers. Where "white" identities have indeed forged profound expressions of culture, it has been under the impress of other necessities, other exigencies of survival. American versions of Irish blarney, German industry, English understatement, Italian humor, Jewish spunk, Dutch Reformed discipline, East Coast sophistication, West Coast trendiness, Midwestern practicality, Bryn Mawr taste, Southern hospitality, and so on—all find their conditions of creation in something other than "white struggle." White desire (as "white") has simply not been that contested or threatened. Whiteness, as such, has had no daunting historical enemy. It has faced no hard eye of opposition (until, perhaps, the emergence of the Black Power Movement of the 1960s).[25] It has more simply been either fascinated or frightened and acted accordingly, usually with impunity. Its only formative condition has been the blackness it projects and punishes. But there, in fact, we can identify the one operation that gives whiteness a certain common character.

## Black and White Embodiment in Formation

If blackness is invasive for blacks, an imposition of meanings that has produced a range of somatic modalities of resistance, whiteness is evasive for whites, a cloak of presumed attributes that grants an invisible "surround," requiring only the maintenance of distance (from blackness). In political economy terms, whiteness is perhaps the ultimate mystification; it is the (cultural) surplus value realized from subjugating a people inside the category of blackness.[26] Unlike the effect blackness has in the body that is made to bear its meanings, whiteness makes no demands of its bearer other than assent to belonging. Whereas surviving black skin in America requires constant active response to one's own bodily schema—a constant exorcism of invading powers, a continuous "tricking" of syntagmatic meaning by way of creating meaning in the paradigmatic register (Gates, 49), deepening the pejorative surface significance of darkness into a polyphonic density of signification, a promulgation of pride, a codification of savvy, a stylization of sophistication—being white is more nearly passive, a gratuitous inheritance. Surveillance makes of the (black) body surface a site of conflict, a point of aggression, soliciting counterforce. It results in an excavation of depths, away from the eye, a violent demand to create a zone of difference inside the body, between the signifying surface and the safer depths. In the struggle with such a gaze, black agency makes the body itself a construct of difference. Monitoring, on the other hand, does not solicit bodily negotiation and self-knowing with the same kind of relentless intrusion. It rather fosters a one-to-one correspondence between a surface that matches its space of movement (and thus moves largely uncontested) and the deeper recesses of one's experience, such that the surface, in effect, disappears.

White embodiment oscillates "plastically" between fantasy and fear. Where white experience of everyday life takes shape as a form of fascination,[27] moving unimpeded through the consumer spaces of the culture, the reflex in the white body is simply naïveté, presumption. (And here something of the class coding implicit in the normative formation of "whiteness" shows up.) White identity in its ideal mode of embodiment is today a creature especially of the suburban enclave (or gentrified neighborhood carved out of urban geography by way of walls and policing and security mechanisms). Middle-class social space (the mall, the suburban street, the office, etc.) is space that appears immediately transparent to the white body (especially if male, as we shall see below). Or said the other way around, the white body is the physical form that most experiences this space as unobstructed, as open to the gaze, vulnerable to the grasp, intelligible to the question (and to the degree even light-skinned bodies do not experience this space as hospitable because of certain differences of class or orientation expressed in clothing or gesture, they are then not fully constituted as normatively white). The body that invests such a space, that absorbs and reproduces its presumptions, that receives its inscription, is what is most nearly constituted, in the "common sense" or "political unconscious" of the dominant culture, as "whiteness." It is a form of embodiment that is not a problem to itself; indeed, it does not appear to itself.

But where white desire perceives a "black" threat, and draws a line of exclusion (e.g., the gate of a gated community, the subtle shrinking of the body on an elevator when a black man enters, etc.) demarcating imagined danger, the reflex effect has been that of an interior distancing. The retreat away from the contestation of contact, the refusal to engage in the negotiation of surface signs effects a fixation of meanings and certainty. The projection of "otherness" outside, on the black-appearing body, condenses a sense of self-sameness on the inside, in the safety of an assumed transparency. The pay-off of this forcible halting of the vulnerability of exchange is an attempted auto-exorcism of the terrifying ambivalence of desire/disgust.[28] The physical body is closed off in its correlation with its imagined spatiality, reduced to an isomorphic surface, uninitiated in the contradictory depths of either the social or the psychic body. The subjectivity so installed is something less than its imagined space of interiority: the historical obsession with purity translates into a profound social investment in "staying in place," cloistered away from the grotesquerie of polluting surfaces.[29]

We could perhaps then generalize that whereas the racialization of black bodies involves an unwanted experience of the body surface as a site of conflict and a dialectical mobilization of the deep structures of the body as (potentially) an agentive resource for knowing and refiguring, the racialization of white bodies constitutes an abandonment of agency to an already decided topography of (presumed) transparency in the relationship between body surface, body depths, and social space. The result is a white illiteracy in reading/writing texts of the body.

## White and Black Male Embodiment

While the above characterization is offered as a partial apology for the ways race insinuates itself in the constitution of bodily schemas by means of subtle transactions of gaze, negotiations of space, displacements of propriety, and the like, gender is not outside the equation. White male middle-class bodies establish the normative modes of power in middle-class space. Taught early to refrain from touching (other males) off the football field or basketball court, schooled in "macho" affective protocols that dictate hiding or not even feeling the more tender emotions, bombarded relentlessly with Madison Avenue imagery of male potency, rewarded incongruously for conformity to the ideals of dress, gesture, cadence of speech, and the like, dictated or managed by the corporate world, white middle-class males, all too often, fall into forms of embodiment that are largely imitative. By internalizing the subtle cues for bodily performance the culture of bourgeois patriarchy puts forward, such a body is offered social space as a gendered receptacle of bodily being. Space is unproblematic and penetrable, ripe for conquest. It is not encountered as resistive force, demanding counter-resistance, risk of violation, performative displacement. It is simply traversed, unthought. The body is not educated as a tactic of negotiation: it has not been forced to deal with itself as dominated from without by disciplines (classroom protocols, police batons, prison bars, troubling glances, etc.) that reduce it to something less than itself or other than its habitual way of being in public. It has thus also not had to do the work of elaborating its own communicative capacities—in concert with other, similarly troubled bodies—into surreptitious codes of counter-meaning. It has never had to wrestle with its own opacity, its lack of "fit" in a given space, communicated by suspicious eyes, backed by procedures of pain. It has more normally experienced its space as (erotically) available, its imagined reflection in other eyes as desirable, its rhythm as on time. The white female body has provided some degree of resistance to white male physicality, but most often been violently constituted in thrall to that body's cathecting gaze as its desired object. The black female body historically has either been dismissed as unattractive or likewise cathected as a sexual object. Only the black male body (and to some extent, the gay body, whatever its color) has regularly offered the kind of contrapuntal coding of time and impenetrable blockage of space that forces the white male body into a confrontation with its own surface, its gendered finitude in time and space, its own peculiar locality and contingency.

Black male otherness again and again has become the target for (white) aggressions that irreducibly owe some of their virulence to socially mediated displacements of emotional conflict in the struggle of male children to come into gendered subjectivity. The genealogical filiation of this violence is profound and polymorphic. The black male adult body emerges before white male awareness as something not only aberrant and fearful—a "darkness" bearing a penis[30]—but also as prolific in its creativity and expressivity. Its threat as sexual competitor does not merely derive from its unintelligibility. It is also a function of its *competence* as a body.

Of course, all of this is tacit; not many white middle-class males would admit to such cognitions at a conscious level. But the dominant culture in our time does. Commodified urban attitude as cipher for male virility—again, the ritualistic core of the national fetishization of sports—clearly finds its icon of choice in the black male body at the peak of its performative powers. As a commodity form, this kind of black maleness is ironically increasingly assimilated in our day as an appendage to white male middle class-ness (Haymes, 50). Very few white middle-class high school basketballers would not affirm a teammate's good play with a high five or make a move on an attractive girl at a school party without a certain kind of rhythmic dance step (ultimately traceable to black innovations through a long line of white imitation going back, obviously, through Elvis to bluesy forms of movement). And to the degree gentrification represents the postindustrial form of a renascent male quest to return to the "pioneer spirit" of this country (Haymes, 106), black male cultural productivity stands before that spirit as the equivalent of "noble savagery." Yuppie enclaves carved out of former working-class or ghetto neighborhoods offer the prospect of appropriating and enjoying urban edginess: the danger of the city is ritually celebrated in dance venues and blues clubs where black creativity can be assimilated minus its downside costs or its context of desperation. At the same time, the prison–industrial complex grows apace as the second armature of white male middle-class embodiment, structuring actual black lower-class males as far away from white male life-worlds and from white women as is conceivable in our increasingly crowded social habitats.

In net effect then, white male middle-class embodiment is in part predicated on black lower-class male embodiment—and vice versa. The (unconscious?) white male fear of raising a daughter (or retaining a wife?) in proximity to a "free" black penis is profoundly part of the social structure of the suburb or edge city, played out in a long history and a dense layer of materiality. The management of that penis in a range of institutional disciplines can be tracked from the slave plantation, through the postbellum convict-lease system, Jim Crow ritualizations of terror in the South, enghettoization and criminalization of blackness in the North, continuing red lining and housing discrimination, resistance to school desegregation, the more recent gutting of affirmative action reparations giving blacks access to historically white schools, the constitution of enclosed communities of affluence around the male norm of white middle-class heterosexuality whose borders are monitored for conformity to the norm (allowing some dark-skinned males the possibility of partial access as long as the other requisite lifestyle signs of "normalcy" like clothes, cars, quality of commodities, etc. are carefully maintained). The effect of those institutional structures of racialized management is to create spaces that regulate their allowable bodies, which in turn reproduce the norms of the space.

Black lower-class maleness, on the other hand, is confined to "other" spaces in a complex operation of ideology, policing, drug-trafficking, shadow-banking, withdrawal of services, flight of meaningful jobs, stereotyping, and bureaucratic social welfare depersonalization. Without question, the hegemony reigning in such spaces conforms its own inhabitants to varying degrees of complicity in the destruction. But simply learning to survive such spaces also creates a profound encounter with the contingency of embodied life that does not cease to reproduce the black body as a cultural artifact of no mean accomplishment. That rap music and hip-hop culture find their greatest market among young males in white suburbs and define one of two operative youth subcultures in a country like contemporary Russia as well as pervasively influencing ethnic musics and youth styles worldwide, suggests that something attractively vital is perceptible in black male work with the body as a site of creative resistance (notwithstanding hip-hop's obvious and justifiably criticized misogyny and sexist violence). In a certain sense, black lower-class maleness is forced to face the underside of modernity as a surrogate of sorts, to undergo its terrors and treachery as a kind of prophylactic for those "on top." It works out, in its stylizations of the body and syncopations of expression, the new meaning of masculinity as a heroic struggle with danger and death,[31] before being forced to yield those creations to the process of commodification, making those reincarnations of male virility available to the broader culture of white maleness (as part of the shamanic "therapy" black culture has been forced to yield for the dominant society as examined in the previous chapters).

On the other hand, the very economic wherewithal that is part of the definition of white middle-class maleness (cf. Cheryl Harris's legal definition of whiteness as "property") exempts the white middle-class social structural from the worst consequences of late-capitalist consumerism, the ongoing and ever-shifting dynamic that de-develops certain spaces (urban cores, ethnic enclaves, Third World countrysides, etc.) for the sake of overdeveloping other spaces (luxury estates, elite neighborhoods, First World metropoles, etc.). But those entropic spaces become important sites for the production of existential symbols of a refetishized wildness that cannot be produced with the same potency in the leisure spaces of security and comfort.[32] As with the innovations of athletic prowess in the gladiator arenas of spectator sports, so with the innovations of existential attitude in the gladiator arenas of everyday life: the inner city here becomes a site of both danger and desire, the young black male body a cipher of both violent bestiality and vigorous masculinity. The 'hood becomes a laboratory for the system whose Viagra-like product is for sale far away from the processing plant.

## The Ethics of White Male Embodiment

To the degree white middle-class maleness is not simply, or even primarily, a matter of an individual coagulation of cells given gestural efficacy and communicative competency by an autonomous rationality sitting in the boardroom of the head, the body marks the site of a necessarily (im)moral assessment. In the products it consumes, in the spaces it assumes, in the postures it incarnates, in the gestures it assimilates, in the powers it learns, and the structures it confirms, the body is a moral substance.[33] It both marks an ethical placement and means an ethical predisposition. It is innocent of neither its history nor its destiny. Quite apart from its own intentionality, it is already the presupposition of a politics, the metabolism of an economics, the status of a social mobility. The body does not just carry these things; in an important sense, it *is* them. The language of ontology is necessary to get at the depths of the consequentiality. But the choice of words is tactical. The metaphysics proposed here is not finally essentialist: it is an ontology that is partially subject to ethical agency in historical struggle. And the question that emerges with a kind of subtle vengeance is this: What would it mean for a white male middle-class body to begin to live its embodiment in a way that challenged those silent inscriptions and rendered them socially articulate and culturally specific?[34] Given that this body is the presupposition/product of "the system," is a de facto norm of a now globalizing culture, how can it be made to signify a different possibility of being human than simply its own reproduction? Even imagining this question as politically relevant is made profoundly difficult by the economic prerogatives today of being able to buy identity in the form of style.

Postindustrial capital has become extremely proficient at mobilizing the least human gesture, the subtlest syncopation of space, the tiniest movement toward innovation, into a new product line. Why bother with a question of the body? To the degree one is successful in partially escaping social inscription and the reproduction of one's position, this very exercise of freedom itself will only be recaptured and made to serve the regnant hegemony. The destiny of freedom as "incorporation" is patent in late capitalism.

And yet, it is equally true that freedom is also always—however epiphanic and fleeting—embodied. Freedom that does not get realized (at least) at the level of everyday living, of bodily gesture and local space, is just more ideology. For those whose subjectivity already encodes dominance and normativity at the level of the body, physical displacement becomes a prerequisite for critical thinking and ethical struggle. bell hooks' challenge to white feminist "colleagues" to meet the oppressed not at the center, but in the margins, on their own turf, is doubly *apropos* of white male "allies" (hooks, 1990, 151–152).

The insinuation of macrostructure at the level of microstructural codes of the body would seem to imply that one of the preconditions for political struggle and ethical judgment is a bodily *habitus* that embodies the contradictions giving rise to struggle and demanding theoretical attention. Putting the white male body "out of its place"[35] by subjecting it in and to other spaces, other protocols, other codes, indeed, other forms of embodiment, is part of the process of "thought." Thought is always a function of a physicality. The testament of the likes of Frantz Fanon, W. E. B. Du Bois, and bell hooks is that critical thought, creative thought, radical vision, motivated struggle, and ethical precision are, in part, a matter of trying to close a gap in one's own experience of embodiment, seeking to give political texture to the social violence felt within one's own bodily schema (Du Bois, 1986, 17;

Fanon, 109–114; hooks, 1991, 148–150). This is not to wish violence on anyone; it is rather to suggest that an ethical approach to the violence that is already structured into a sociality is somehow to comprehend that violence in one's own physicality, to become partially vulnerable to its power to rearrange, in a way that affects one's profoundest sense of deportment and renders consciously agentive attempts to resist such structures. Saying such is not to ask for masochism; it is to ask for conscious embrace of a vulnerability that is already mutual and concrete incarnation of a reciprocal give and take.

Part and parcel of the argument offered here is a belief that relationship is the very core of ethical assertion and indeed the very essence of human being, that interdependence is the presupposition of value, that "individual morality" is, in fact, an (ideologically not innocent) oxymoron.[36] It is the very meaning of such an ethical perception to insist that overt violence in one social geography, rupturing and determining bodily experience there, is necessarily simultaneously disruptive of the geography and physicality it seems to serve, no matter how inchoate or unconscious the effects of that disruption might prove to be. White male forms of "neutral" and "innocent" embodiment would then necessarily be constituted in a deformation of fear at some subtle social level in inverse proportion to black forms of contestatory embodiment. Only if the violence predicated of Rodney King's body is traced back *both* to the hand wielding the baton that produced that violence *and* to the seemingly cleaner hands that underwrite and profit from it, will it be possible to bring whiteness under ethical interrogation. But only if that latter form of white maleness is itself also publicly *revealed* as problematically male in its erotic surveillance, middle class in its "normal" aspiration, pervasive in its discursive predominance, and specifically limited in its enculturation, will something else become possible. That something else will at least involve white males actively renegotiating their meanings and positions and forms of embodiment in relationship to blacks (and "Latinos" and "Asians," and gay and lesbian styles, and women of all ethnic backgrounds, etc.). Anything less will leave the hegemonic body immured in a normative form of ignorance secured by a structural form of virulence. White men can be cured of their dis-ease. But only if they learn to speak—and live— "otherwise."

# Notes

## Introduction

1. One of the originators of techno and a continuing player in the scene of electronica's emergence as a world music that began in the 1980s in Detroit and is now celebrated every year in Motown on the last weekend in May in the largest such gathering on the planet.
2. See my book *White Theology: Outing Supremacy in Modernity*, also published by Palgrave Macmillan, whose original title was *Signified Upon and Sounded Out*.
3. See especially Kristin Hunter Lattany's article on off-timing in the Gerald Early edited anthology, *Lure and Loathing* (Lattany, 165–166).
4. Its insistence that academic argument about such a reversal of the categories of differentiation and domination must itself display some of the troubling of hegemony being traced in its own rhetorical style. Here, theoretical incisiveness must be wedded to poetic elusiveness to display the claim made in the materiality of the language used.
5. Its examination of hip-hop in terms of its sonic effects, arguing that rap lyrics are not the primary source of hip-hop attraction or the primary modality of its work. By juxtaposing hip-hop productivity to shamanistic activity in its various historical modalities (in cave art, in indigenous rites of healing, in colonial situations of oppression, etc.), it is possible to imagine rap rhythm as effecting a certain kind of shamanistic delirium that both capitulates to and struggles against the structures of domination and constraint.
6. The theoretical construction of the ultimate stuff of reality as vibratory "strings" giving rise to different aspects of the universe by means of different frequencies of vibration.

## I  Beyond Occasional Whiteness

This chapter was previously published as "Beyond Occasional Whiteness." *Cross Currents* 47.2 (July 1997): 195–209.

1. Article I of the Constitution reads: "Representatives and direct taxes shall be apportioned among the several States which may be included within this Union, according to their respective numbers, which shall be determined by adding to

the whole number of free persons, including those bound to service for a term of years, and excluding Indians not taxed, three-fifths of all other persons." "Three-fifths of all other persons" referred to those bound in "the peculiar institution." "Slavery" was not mentioned in the Constitution until 1865, when it was abolished.

2. A mystery of the Dutch side of my family is the family name "Banta," traced back to the first generation born on American soil. The genealogy book on this name cannot account for its origins, as it appears nowhere in the Netherlands itself. Curiously, the book does note its affiliation with "Bantu," as a designation applied to "a group of African races and languages, extending over a large part of Eastern, Central and Southern Africa" (Theodore M. Banta, *A Frisian Family: The Banta Genealogy*, New York: 1893). What "forgotten" piece of family history underlies the sudden appearance of the appellation of "Banta" in my ancestral line? Who knows?

3. Cf. Michael Lind, *The Next American Nation: The New Nationalism and the Fourth American Revolution*.

4. For a discussion of the peculiarity of the "American" environment from the point of view of "soul-loss" that corroborates the analysis here, cf. Richard K. Fenn, 17–20.

5. For an analysis of black identity in terms of mimetic transfigurations of terror into sublimity, cf. Paul Gilroy, 1993, 36–40.

6. Leki's article was again suggestive here.

# 2   Modernity's Witchcraft Practice

This chapter was previously published as "Reversing the Gaze: European Race Discourse as Modernity's Witchcraft Practice," in the *Journal of the American Academy of Religions* 72:3 (September 2004), 603–630, and a slightly different version is scheduled to be published under a different title as "Between Unconsciously White and Mythically Black: European Race Discourse as Modern Witchcraft Practice," in an anthology to be entitled *Cultural Amnesia, the Academy, and the Racialized Foundations of Knowledge*, by Illinois University Press, Fall 2005.

# 3   The Gift/Curse of "Second Sight"

This chapter was previously published as "The Gift/Curse of Second Sight: Is 'Blackness' a Shamanic Category in the Myth of America?" *History of Religions* 42.1 (August 2002): 19–58.

# 4   Constructing the Break

This chapter was previously published as "Constructing the Break: 'Syncopated Tricksterism' as Afro-Diaspora *Kairos* Inside Anglo-Capitalist *Chronos*." *Social Identities* 8.4 (2002): 545–569.

1. See, for instance, Johannes Fabian's citation of Northrup's comment on Bergson (Fabian, 181).
2. Note especially the assertion of Babcock-Abrahams that tricksters simultaneously reveal to humans the connection between creativity and the margins (where rules can be inverted or queried) and their propensity to refuse to live inside "the cage" and the traditional trope of the bluesman securing his beguiling talent at the crossroad, mythic space of agency and choice, presided over by the African trickster figure Eshu-elegba in one or another of his manifestations, where order and power finds its genesis in disorder and dilatory desire.
3. It is worth noting that Marx already theorized in the nineteenth century a reduction of industrial wage-laborers to "crippled monstrosities," becoming in the repetitive processes of mass production, mere fragments of their own bodies (Marx, 360). Foucault takes the reflection a stage further in emphasizing the shift from exercises of sovereignty on the subjected body to that of "micrologies of surveillance," in which an internalized "supervisory eye" becomes the subjective correlate of his generalized "panopticon" (Foucault, 1980, 92–100).
4. I am indebted, for this particular phrase, to performance poet and national slam champion, Regie Gibson, whose "praise-song homage" to the creative geometrics of African American hair styles underscores the uses of such to negotiate power in various public spheres and to articulate uniqueness, drama, humor, etc., in the presentation of one's *persona* (Gibson, 70).
5. See the similar point made by Stallybrass and White in relationship to the ambiguously subversive potential of carnival (Stallybrass and White, 14).
6. Mills identifies the white male body as normatively presumed, and thus unmarked, in the global white supremacy he theorizes as "The Racial Contract" (Mills, 53).
7. Thompson traces what he calls this "great migration style" through New World realizations of the influences of Yoruban reflections of *ashe* in statuary, Kongo cosmograms of *veve* chalk drawings, Dahomean *drapeau de vodun* mediation flags, Mande cone-on-cylinder architecture and rhythmized textiles, and Ejagham *nsibidi* writing (Thompson, xiv–xvii).
8. Thematized in song titles like "Get Right Church and Let's Go Home," "He'll Let Me Come Home," "There's a Dark Cloud Rising, Let's Go Home."
9. Berendt notes that the range of the ear is ten times that of the eye (Berendt, 17).

# 5   Rap Rapture and Manic Mortality

This chapter was previously published as "Rap as Wrap and Rapture: North American Popular Culture and the Denial of Death." *Noise and Spirit: Religious and Spiritual Sensibilities of Rap Music*. Ed. Anthony Pinn. New York: New York University Press, 2003.

1. For more instances of the former, we have the harder yet still aversive forms such as "kicked the bucket," "bought the farm," "passed," or "passed away." And we experience no visceral cramp or sweaty palm in citing "dead batteries" or "dead letters," "deadlines" or "dead beats." I bring it fully into the first person when I am "dead on my feet," "dead broke," "dead drunk," "dead to the

world," "scared to death," or "could just die." I quite unrepentantly "kill time," "kill the lights," "die of laughter," "slay an audience," "kill the bottle," and throw out a "dead soldier." And you may well be "dead wrong," "deadly dull," a "deadhead," a "killjoy," someone who "flogs a dead horse" and who will be "the death of me, yet." Good marksmen hit the target "dead center," basketball players may have a "dead eye" or be "dead shots."

2. Cited in a talk given by Joe Feagin, entitled "Racism and the Coming White Minority," on April 20, 2000 at Wayne State University, Detroit, MI.

3. Race does not entirely determine who is included in the Great American Dream and who is not—but it is hardly a secondary factor either. Racial perception and racist effort have continuing (and very often today, redoubled) effects in every major institutional domain—from influencing relative residential mobility to dollars spent per pupil in the classroom, from educational access and support to likelihood of incarceration, from availability of jobs to availability of credit, from relative pay received for a certain kind of work to relative size of mortgage granted for a certain level of income. Simply growing up in this society is already to have been profoundly shaped by its entrenched mechanisms of disparately arranged life opportunities and obstacles on the basis of skin color. In short, all good intentions to the contrary, race continues to police the gate.

4. I am especially indebted here to the work of anthropologist Nahum Chandler both in *Callaloo* and in personal discussion (Chandler, 88).

5. Nelson George characterizes hip-hop as a "society-altering collision" over the last two decades "between black youth culture and the mass media" (George, ix). Underneath the crossover is conflict, below the level of the video is a "loud, scratchy, in-your-face aesthetic that, to this day, still informs the culture" (George, xi). At one point, George notes its effect as that of "a deadly virus" (George, xi).

6. "It is essential to understand that the values that underpin so much hip-hop—materialism, brand consciousness, gun iconography, anti-intellectualism—are very much by-products of the larger American culture. Despite the 'dangerous' edge of so much hip-hop culture, all of its most disturbing themes are rooted in this country's dysfunctional values. Anti-Semitism, racism, violence, and sexism are hardly unique to rap stars but are the most sinister aspects of the national character" (George, xiii).

7. George speaks of DJs in Jamaica giving "back-a-yard" parties where "the bass and drum pounded like jackhammers" in a dub style that "stripped away melody to give reggae's deep, dark grooves throbbing prominence" (George, 6). In rap, the "massive rumbling" of this "subterranean assault" is combined with disco's "magic art of mixing" and DJ "toasting" to form the unique synergy of hip-hop. Later, hip-hop was reinvented in the image of the video, transliterating the underground vitality of beats and rhymes into the visual culture of TV and cinema.

8. The phrasing in these last three sentences is beholden to bell hooks's aphorism for the systemic reality defining the context of struggle as "white supremacist capitalist patriarchy" (hooks, 153).

# 6   From Mega-Lith to Mack Daddy

This chapter was published as "From Mega-Lith to Mack Daddy: Hip Hop Mantra and the Hidden Transcript of Matter." *Journal of Religion* 16.2 (2003): 51–70.

1. A "Mack" or "Mack Daddy" is an African American street term for one who is able to "sweet talk" women, who operates smoothly in the domain of seduction, who is adept at hustling, who is a "player" (Smitherman, 157).
2. Reference here is to the late 1990s movie "Bullworth," starring Warren Beatty as a white politician who eventually attempts to go "black" in his sympathies and tastes for language and love, who at the end of the story offers that perhaps what the world needs is for everyone to sleep with everyone and stop pretending to be able to maintain absolute boundaries between persons, cultures, nations, etc.
3. Reference here is to Long's work in taking up Rudolph Otto's phrase *mysterium tremendum et fascinosum* as a category for religious comparison across cultures and breaking it into two on colonial experience, claiming that where Europe seemed merely to be confirmed in its sense of superiority and of God as (merely) "fascinating" in the colonial encounter, indigenous groups around the globe were forced to know the Absolute as an inscrutable and overwhelming power of "Tremendousness" and "Fear," and themselves as contingent and "creaturely."
4. As in the so-called curse of Ham, theologically deployed by colonial Europe to "explain" the inferiority it projected and imposed on the dark-skinned populations it conquered and pacified. "Race" emerged as the European shorthand by which visual appearance was encoded with epidermal significance and eternal consequence. Racialization is above all a manipulation of perception by way of a preconception of derogation.
5. Afro-diaspora populations have regularly used "time" and "timing" as a resource to displace their oppression through white control of space (of land, of residential mobility, of institutional life, etc.). Making innovative use of West and Central African modalities of "off-timing" and polyphony has been a primary tactic in bending dominant codes (of language, of culture, of gesture, of dress, of music, etc.) to an alternative meaning (controlled by communities of color) (Thompson, xiii–xvii).
6. As of the late 1990s, white youth comprise roughly 70% of the market for rap music in the United States.
7. That is, my own attempt to defect politically from "whiteness" and work vocationally against the power and privilege it assembles and concentrates as a form of supremacy and global mastery.
8. "Whiteness" as a meaningful category will someday, by force of resistance by people of color or by sheer evolutionary dilution, disappear.
9. The references here are to rapper Tupac Shakur's release entitled "Makaveli" and Public Enemy's vocalist Chuck D.
10. From a Public Enemy album.

11. Shakur's "Thug Life" theology used the term as a kind of historical acronym for an "original sin" of white making: "the hate u (you) gave little infants f . . . s everyone."

# 7 Monstrous Polyphony/Tricky Antiphony

1. The discussion above owes much to the comments of William Herzog in a talk given on September 28, 2001 at the Ecumenical Theological Seminary in Detroit.
2. For instance: "As every individual, therefore, endeavors as much as he can . . . to direct that industry that its produce may be of the greatest value; every individual necessarily labors to render the annual revenue of the society as great as he can. He generally, indeed, neither intends to promote the public interests, nor knows how much he is promoting it . . . by directing that industry in such a manner as its produce may be of the greatest value, he intends only his own gain, and he is in this, as in many other cases, led by an invisible hand to promote an end which was no part of his intention. Nor it always the worse for the society that it was no part of it. By pursuing his own interest he frequently promotes that of the society more effectually than when he really intends to promote it" (Smith, 1937, book IV, ch. 11, 423).
3. Both Islam and Hinduism already anchor their intuitions in a carefully guarded tradition about the priority of sound. Islam recounts its earliest stories of conversion in terms of the haunting beauty and compelling sonority of spoken Arabic—and has refused ever since to countenance any other poetics as adequate to the particular echo of revelation found in resonant arabesques of muezzin eloquence (Armstrong, 139–140, 144–146). Hinduism has elaborated an entire theology of vibration rooted in the antiquity of the *rishis* who first heard the Vedas before writing them down and whose primary mode of transmission has been guru-granted mantra, whispered in the ear, pulsing ever-after in the *guha*-cave of the heart.

# 8 The Body of White Space

This chapter was previously published as "The Body of White Space: Beyond Stiff Voices, Flaccid Feelings, and Silent Cells." *Revealing Male Bodies.* Ed. Nancy Tuana et al. Bloomington: Indiana University Press, 2002. 228–261.

1. For such a characterization of race on an "infection" model, see Michelle Fine, Linda C. Powell, Lois Weis, and L. Mun Wong, "Preface." *Off White: Readings on Race, Power, and Society.* x.
2. For the idea that King's body was already comprehended as "animal and dangerous," see Patricia J. Williams, "The Rules of the Game." *Reading Rodney King, Reading Urban Uprising* (51–55).
3. As constructed by Pierre Bourdieu, "habitus" designates the taken-for-granted patterns of perception and calculations of response to one's cultural environment

and social others. These patterns normally operate almost outside of consciousness, but can be brought to the forefront of intentionality if put under pressure by sudden change (Bourdieu, 17).

4. For a discussion of the normativity of whiteness, see film critic Richard Dyer's article, "White" (Dyer, 44–64).

5. For a generalization of black cultural practice under the rubrics of "kinetic orality," "passionate physicality," and "combative spirituality," see Cornel West, "Black Culture and Postmodernism," *Remaking History* (West, 1989, 93).

6. Arthur Kroker underscores the degree to which postmodern subjectivity is a mode of being constituted in "possession" (via computer and television imagery and language) in his work, *The Possessed Individual: Technology and the French Postmodern.*

7. Many cultures have one or another form of possession cults; while distinctive and constantly undergoing change in their historical contexts, they resemble each other in some ways. See Sheila Walker's, *Ceremonial Spirit Possession in Africa and Afro-America: Forms, Meanings, and Functional Significance for Individuals and Social Groups.*

8. This is due both to growing numbers of immigrants from Haiti and Cuba and to increasing interest and adherence among already "naturalized" Americans of various cultural and ethnic backgrounds, including those thought of as "white." See Karen McCarthy Brown, *Mama Lola: A Vodou Priestess in Brooklyn.*

9. Though what to call the possessing spirit is up for grabs. Elsewhere (in chapter 6 of my book *White Theology: Outing Supremacy in Modernity*, Palgrave Press), I have somewhat facetiously called it the *Fascinans* incarnate (see also the second paragraph of the section entitled "Black and White Embodiment in Formation," and footnote 27, below), or as a mode of lived speech, the "Order of Monotony" (literally a monotone of control and propriety), Stuart Hall's the "endlessly speaking empire." In the Pauline language of the "principalities and powers" (Eph. 6.10–15), we could perhaps venture something like the "Principality of Unconscious Arrogance." African American authors have variously named it "Blue-eyed Devil," "The Man," "Massa" (in the slavery era), "Babylon" (if speaking the Rastafri lingo of "Dread"), "The System" (in the 1960s), or "The Thing" (if one of Toni Morrison's women of funk). Perhaps its real character is best left unnamed as stealth and unconsciousness are its primary manifestation in its host body.

10. For instance, recent statistics indicate a marked increase in "interracial" dating in the United States, except for the coupling of "whites" and "blacks." Statistics regarding residential mobility continue to indicate African Americans as the least mobile segment of the population.

11. For a careful unpacking of the racial seeing of King's body as already violent and the ramification of that perception in the subsequent beating, see Judith Butler's, "Endangered/Endangering: Schematic Racism and White Paranoia." *Reading Rodney King, Reading Urban Uprising* (Butler, 15–22).

12. The reference here invokes Michel Foucault's ideas of the modern "disciplinary body" explored in his *Discipline and Punish: The Birth of the Prison.*

13. David Roediger notes that this phenomenon occurred immediately after city leaders outlawed white participation in black-led public celebrations like

Independence Day in the 1830s. The implication is that it may reflect, among other things, a kind of warped nostalgia for what had been a vitalizing form of control (Roediger, 106).

14. I am indebted for the term to Robert D. Kaplan (Kaplan, 55–80).

15. See Robert Ferris Thompson's description of West African traditions of *ashe*-eyed elders, communicating potency and power through the quality of their gaze (Thompson, 5–9). It is not hard to imagine the quality of this gaze, reinforced in the experience of slavery and racism, as ramifying that form of communication as a survival tactic.

16. Kochman argues, for instance, that both oppressive social conditions and the need for status among peers, on the one hand, and a distinctive aesthetic sensibility, on the other, contribute to the "spectacular exhibitionism," "intensity," and "aggressivity," and "vital expressivity" of black cultural protocols (Kochman, 110). "Doing your thing" is a matter of asserting oneself *within* the group, "playing off against others—competitively and cooperatively at the same time"—so that all benefit from the power demonstrated.

17. This counter-competency is encoded even into everyday behaviors, such as the rhythmic style of walking called "bopping" or the hand-to-hand exchange called "giving skin" that ignite a sense of spiritual connection and invite and even demand reciprocity. Kochman notes that black performative style has been particularly admired by the larger society in the performing arts (such as music, dance, theater, and sports), while generating mixed responses at the everyday level of attire, or of ways of walking, standing, talking, greeting, etc. and encountering out-and-out rejection in the schoolroom and workplace.

18. For instance, Kochman differentiates the classroom style of blacks from that of whites by emphasizing that because the former "consider debate to be as much a contest between individuals as a test of opposing ideas . . . attention is also paid to performance" (24). Winning, here, "requires that one outperform one's opponents: outthink, outtalk, and outstyle them. It means being concerned with art as well as argument" (24). "Individuals develop and demonstrate their degree of togetherness by respectively developing and demonstrating their ability to contend. Black performers do so when they heat up the environment while . . . proclaiming their own cool" (127).

Kochman analyzes the interlocking and synergistic "revitalization of energy through emotional and spiritual release" characteristic of black cultural activities under a three-fold *call and response* pattern: "(1.) a sufficiently powerful agent-stimulus to activate the emotional (spiritual) forces that the body has imprisoned, (2.) a structure like song, dance, or drum that allows for the unrestricted expression of those forces that the agent-stimulus has aroused, and (3.) a manner of participation that gives full value to the power of the agent-stimulus and to the individual's ability to receive and manipulate it" (108). The latter "manner of participation . . . entails a mind/body involvement of considerable depth, what blacks call *getting down into* the mode through which emotional release and spiritual rejuvenation are effected" (108). What then appears to whites as a loss of emotional control is actually a ritualized expression of greater control in which blacks "transferred a measure of control from themselves to the feeling mode (sorrow, exultation, spirit possession) and to the cultural form (song, dance, greeting exchange, call and response) through which the emotions are released and within which they are also contained" (115).

19. Indeed, Kochman asserts, "The requirement to behave calmly, rationally, unemotionally, and logically when negotiating is looked upon by blacks as a political requirement—and to accede to it in advance is considered as a political defeat" (40).

20. Hall has remarked that the distinctiveness of black diasporic traditions is reflected especially in the uses these cultures have made of the body, along with a focus on style as the primary subject, rather than merely accidental accretion, of cultural production, and on music, rather than writing (or its deconstruction). As the depth-structure of cultural life, bodily performance pinpoints one of the major places of contrast between diasporic and dominant cultures. Hall offers that black cultures worked on the body as a "canvas of representation" because it was often "the only cultural capital [they] had available" (Hall, 27). In arguing such, Hall asserts that the repertoires of black popular culture "were overdetermined from at least two directions" (28): by their inheritances and by the diasporic conditions in which those connections with heritage were forged. "Selective appropriation, incorporation, and rearticulation of European ideologies, cultures, and institutions, alongside an African heritage," Hall says (while citing Cornell West), "led to linguistic innovations in rhetorical stylizations of the body, forms of occupying an alien social space, heightened expressions, hairstyles, ways of walking, standing, and talking, and a means of constituting and sustaining camaraderie and community" (28).

    The importance of such a recognition, according to Hall, is that black diasporic cultures exhibit "no pure forms at all" (28). Rather, these forms are always "the product of partial synchronization, of engagement across cultural boundaries, of the confluence of more than one cultural tradition, of the negotiations of dominant and subordinate positions, of the subterranean strategies of recoding and transcoding, of critical signification, of signifying" (28). Black popular culture produces vernacular forms that are marked by hybridity on the *inside*, which thus appear as contradictory by definition. The signifier "black" carries the weight not of an essential differentiation of diasporic from dominant culture—a self-sufficient "their tradition versus ours"—but rather of a dialogic strategy of adaptation, "molded to the mixed, contradictory, hybrid spaces of popular culture" (28). It is an aesthetic strategy of difference that rewrites the binary opposition black–white in terms of an "and" in the place of the usual "or" (e.g., black *and* British rather than black or British) (29). But Hall is also insistent that such a claim not be read as simply another form of binarism. As with his colleague Paul Gilroy's way of thinking about "double-consciousness," Hall argues that such a strategy is rather a way of dislocating or moving outside of the oppositionality altogether. Identity is not exhausted in the "and" any more than it was clarified in the "or." Hybridity, here, simply encodes one particular historical struggle in which identity is sometimes caught and out of which it is forged. There are other struggles that give rise to other forms of identification in the same life.

21. Kochman, *Black and White Styles*, 30. In describing white self-assertion, for instance, Kochman says it "occurs as a social entitlement" that, even

when granted, must be "low-keyed . . . showing detachment, modesty, understatement."

22. Kochman cites a communications study in which the observed performances of "white and well-to-do black first graders reflected the cultural norms of the dominant society" in being literal, obedient, modest, and uniform, with "little to distinguish one child's performance from that of another" (Kochman, 154). On the other hand, "the poor black children" who were part of the experiment "were literally performing, emphasizing both individuality and vitality . . . greater verbal creativity and more dynamic oral presentation" (155) for which they would have received failing marks had the experiment been an actual test in school. Kochman says, "White culture values the ability of individuals to rein in their impulses. White cultural events do not allow for individually initiated self-assertion or the spontaneous expression of feeling" (Kochman, 30). "[C]lothes should be drab and inconspicuous, colors of low intensity, sounds quiet, smells nonexistent, words emotionless."

23. In noting the group quality of black performance, its emphasis upon call and response, Kochman says "the black performer's role is not just to demonstrate but also to instigate," to vitalize the energies and images "from which the performer and the audience together draw spiritual sustenance" (Kochman, 134, also 107). In comparison, the undemonstrative behavior more typical of whites is pejoratively labeled "gray" by blacks and failure by a black person to come up with sufficient intensity of response in a black-on-black interaction may be criticized as "acting white."

24. Kochman notes "the emphasis on developing one's own style also helps to explain why one does not see in the black community the kind of public imitation of star performers that one finds in the white community . . . To do so would signify to other blacks a lack of individual resourcefulness, imagination, and pride" (135).

25. For a discussion of the historical distinctiveness of white positionality since the Black Power Movement, see Howard Winant, "Behind Blue Eyes: Whiteness and Contemporary U.S. Racial Politics." *Off White: Readings on Race, Power, and Society* (Winant, 41–53).

26. Cheryl Harris, for instance, glosses whiteness as "property" in her article, "Whiteness as Property" (Harris, 1709).

27. Here again, Charles Long's discussion of colonial contact in terms of experiences of numinosity that for colonizers are primarily in the mode of the *mysterium fascinans* has relevance (Long, 1986, 137).

28. See Steven Pile's discussion of this ambivalence with regard to urban space in his book, *The Body and the City: Psychoanalysis, Space and Subjectivity* (Pile, 207).

29. Again, see Pile for a similar discussion (Pile, 250–256).

30. Playing off of Freud's problematic epigram of adult woman's sexuality as a "dark continent" (Freud, 91–170).

31. George Hegel's discussion of the recognition economy resulting in the struggle that ends up in the master–slave relationship resonates interestingly here (Hegel, 117–119).

32. For a discussion of a related phenomenon in the late Middle Ages, see P. Stallybrass and A. White, *The Politics and Poetics of Transgression* (Stallybrass and White, 5).

33. The discussion here, though not the claim, is informed by Robert Bellah's discussion in *Habits of the Heart* (Bellah, 71–81).
34. I am indebted to Gloria Albrecht's discussion of the role of embodiment in contesting domination (Albrecht, 98).
35. In the sense in which Michel de Certeau has differentiated "place" and "space." Place is the provenance of strategies of domination; in its operation, dominating forms of power constellate, secure, and attempt to valorize a particular location. On the other hand, the tactics of resistance are more opportunistic; subordinate powers seize spaces in momentary takeovers that usually must be quickly abandoned (de Certeau, xiv, xix, 35–39).
36. Bellah, *Habits*, 76–78, 84.

# Bibliography

Albrecht, Gloria. *The Character of Our Communities: Toward an Ethic of Liberation for the Church*. Nashville: Abingdon Press, 1995.

Anderson, Victor. *Beyond Ontological Blackness: An Essay on African American Religious and Cultural Criticism*. New York: Continuum, 1995.

Aries, Philippe. *Western Attitudes Toward Death: From the Middle Ages to the Present*. Trans. P. M. Ranum. Baltimore: Johns Hopkins UP, 1974.

———. *The Hour of Our Death*. Trans. H. Weaver. New York: Knopf, 1981.

Armstrong, Karen. *A History of God: The 4,000-Year Quest of Judaism, Christianity and Islam*. New York: Ballantine, 1993.

Babcock-Abrahams, Barbara. " 'A Tolerated Margin of Mess': The Trickster and His Tales Reconsidered." *Journal of Folklore Institute* 11.3 (Mar. 1975): 147–186.

Baker, Houston. "Scene . . . Not Heard." *Reading Rodney King, Reading Urban Uprising*. Ed. R. Gooding-Williams. New York: Routledge, 1993. 38–50.

Bakhtin, Mikhail. *Rabelais and His World*. Trans. H. Iswolsky. Bloomington: Indiana UP, 1984.

Baldwin, James. *The Fire Next Time*. New York: Dial Press, 1963.

———. *The Price of the Ticket: Collected Nonfiction, 1948–1985*. New York: St. Martin's Press, 1985.

Bambara, Toni Cade. "Deep Sight and Rescue Missions." *Lure and Loathing: Essays on Race, Identity, and the Ambivalence of Assimilation*. 1993. Ed. Gerald Early. New York: Penguin Books, 1994. 163–174.

Barfield, Owen. *Poetic Diction*. Middleton: Wesleyan UP, 1928.

Bastide, Roger. "Color, Racism, and Christianity." *White Racism: Its History, Pathology and Practice*. Ed. B. N. Schwartz and R. Disch. New York: Dell Publishing Co., 1970. 270–285.

Baudrillard, Jean. *For a Critique of the Political Economy of the Sign*. St. Louis, MO: Telos Press, 1981.

Beby, Francis. *African Music: A People's Art*. 1969. Westport, CT: Greenwood Press, 1975.

Becker, Ernst. *The Denial of Death*. New York: Free Press, 1973.

Bellah, Robert. *Habits of the Heart*. Berkeley: University of California, 1985.

Berendt, Joachim-Ernst. *The Third Ear: On Listening to the World*. 1985. New York: An Owl Book, Henry Holt and Co., 1992.

Bongmba, Elias Kifon. *African Witchcraft and Otherness: A Philosophical and Theological Critique of Intersubjective Relations.* New York: State U of New York P, 2001.

Bourdieu, Piere. *Outline of a Theory of Practice.* Trans. R. Nice. Cambridge and New York: Cambridge UP, 1977.

Braga, Joseph and Braga, Laurie. "Introduction." *Death the Final Stage.* Ed. Elizabeth Kubler-Ross. Englewood Cliffs, NJ: Prentice-Hall, Inc., 1975.

Brandon, George. *Santeria from Africa to the New World: The Dead Sell Memories.* Bloomington: Indiana UP, 1993.

Breton, Andre. *Surrealism and Painting.* Trans. Simon Watson Taylor. New York: Harper and Row, 1972.

Brown, Karen McCarthy. *Mama Lola: A Vodou Priestess in Brooklyn.* Berkeley: U of California P, 1991.

Burke, Kenneth. *The Philosophy of Literary Form: Studies in Symbolic Action.* New York: Vintage, 1957.

Butler, Judith. "Endangered/Endangering: Schematic Racism and White Paranoia." *Reading Rodney King, Reading Urban Uprising.* Ed. R. Gooding-Williams. New York: Routledge, 1993. 15–22.

Bynum, Edward Bruce. *The African Unconscious: Roots of Ancient Mysticism and Modern Psychology.* New York: Teachers College Press, 1999.

Carter, Stephen L. "The Black Table, the Empty Seat, and the Tie." *Lure and Loathing: Essays on Race, Identity, and the Ambivalence of Assimilation.* 1993. Ed. Gerald Early. New York: Penguin, 1994. 79.

Castaneda, Carlos. *Journey to Ixtlan.* New York: Simon & Schuster, Inc., 1972.

———. *The Teachings of Don Juan: A Yaqui Way of Knowledge.* 1968. New York: Simon & Schuster, Inc., 1974.

Chadwick, Henry. "The Early Christian Community." *The Oxford Illustrated History of Christianity.* Ed. John McManners. Oxford and New York: Oxford UP, 1990. 21–61.

Chandler, Nahum. "The Economy of Desedimentation: W. E. B. Du Bois and the Discourses of the Negro." *Callaloo* 19.1 (1996): 78–93.

Chidester, David. *Patterns of Transcendence: Religion, Death, and Dying.* Belmont, CA: Wadsworth Publishing Co., 1990.

Chomsky, Noam. "Containing the Crisis at Home and Abroad." Transcript of Talk Given at Loyola University, Chicago, October 18, 1994, Made Available Through Alternative Radio, Boulder, CO, 1994.

Clottes, Jean and David Lewis-Williams. *The Shamans of Prehistory: Trance and Magic in the Painted Caves.* Text by Jean Clottes, trans. Sophie Hawkes. New York: Harry N. Abrams, Inc., Publishers, 1996.

Coleman, Wanda. "Primal Orb Density." *Lure and Loathing: Essays on Race, Identity, and the Ambivalence of Assimilation.* Ed. Gerald Early. New York: Penguin Books, 1993. 207–226.

Coleman, Will. *Tribal Talk: Black Theology, Hermeneutics, and African/American Ways of "Telling the Story."* University Park, PA: The Pennsylvania State UP, 2000.

Comaroff, Jean and Comaroff, John. *Of Revelation and Revolution: Christianity, Colonialism, and Consciousness in South Africa.* Chicago: U of Chicago P, 1991.

Cone, James. *Martin and Malcolm and America: A Dream or A Nightmare.* Maryknoll: Orbis Books, 1991.

Coomaraswamy, A. K. "Symplegades." *Studies and Essays in the History of Science and Learning Offered in Homage to George Sarton on the Occasion of His Sixtieth Birthday, 31 August 1944.* Ed. Ashley M. F. Montague. New York: Schuman, 1946. 463–488.

Corr, Charles A., Clyde M. Nabe, and Donna M. Corr. *Death & Dying, Life & Living.* 2nd ed. Pacific Grove, CA: Brooks/Cole Publishing Co., 1997.

Cress Welsing, Frances. *The Isis Papers: The Keys to the Colors.* Chicago: Third World Press, 1991.

Davis, Michael. "Los Angeles Was Just the Beginning." *Open Fire.* Ed. G. Ruggiero and S. Sahulka. Los Angeles: The Open Pamphlet Series, 1993a. 220–243.

———. "Uprising and Repression in L.A.: An Interview with Mike Davis by the *Covert Action Information Bulletin.*" *Reading Rodney King, Reading Urban Uprising.* Ed. R. Gooding-Williams. New York: Routledge, 1993b. 142–156.

de Certeau, Michel. *The Practice of Everyday Life.* Trans. S. F. Rendall. Berkeley: U of California P, 1984.

Deleuze, Gilles and Felix, Guattari. *Anti-Oedipus: Capitalism and Schizophrenia.* London: The Athalone Press, 1983.

Derrida, Jacques. *Writing and Difference.* Trans. A. Bass. Chicago: U of Chicago P, 1978.

Desmangles, Leslie. *The Faces of the Gods: Vodou and Roman Catholicism in Haiti.* Chapel Hill and London: North Carolina UP, 1992.

Drewal, Margaret Thompson. "Dancing for Ogun in Yorubaland and Brazil." *Africa's Ogun: Old World and New.* Ed. Sandra T. Barnes. Bloomington: Indiana UP, 1997. 234.

Du Bois, W. E. B. *The Souls of Black Folk.* 1903. Greenwich, CN: Fawcett Publications, 1961.

———. *Dusk of Dawn: An Essay Toward an Autobiography of a Race Concept.* 1940. Reprint, New York: Schoken Books, 1968.

———. *Black Reconstruction in America, 1860–1880.* 1935. New York: The Free Press, 1998.

Dumm, Thomas. "The New Enclosures: Racism in the Normalized Community." *Reading Rodney King, Reading Urban Uprising.* Ed. R. Gooding-Williams. New York: Routledge, 1993. 178–195.

Dussel, Enrique. *The Invention of the Americas: Eclipse of "the Other" and the Myth of Modernity.* New York: Continuum, 1995.

Dyer, Richard. "White." *Screen* 29.4 (1988): 44–64.

Eagleton, Terry. *Walter Benjamin: Towards a Revolutionary Criticism.* London: Verso, 1981.

Earl, Riggins R. Jr. *Dark Symbols, Obscure Signs: God, Self and Community in the Slave Mind.* Maryknoll: Orbis Books, 1993.

Eliade, Mircea. *Shamanism: Archaic Techniques of Ecstasy.* Trans. Willard R. Trask. Princeton: Princeton UP, 1964.

Esteva, Gustavo and Madhu Suri, Prakash. *Grassroots Postmodernism: Remaking the Soil of Cultures.* London and New York: Zed Books, 1998.

Eze, Emmanuel Chukwudi. ed. *Race and the Enlightenment: A Reader.* Cambridge, MA: Blackwell Publishers, 1997a.

———. *Postcolonial African Philosophy: A Critical Reader.* London: Blackwell Publishers, 1997b.

Fabian, Johannes. *Time and the Other: How Anthropology Makes Its Object.* New York: Columbia UP, 1983.

Fanon, Frantz. *The Wretched of the Earth.* Trans. Constance Farrington. New York: Grove Press, 1963.

———. *Black Skins, White Masks.* 1967. Trans. C. L. Markmann. New York: Grove Press. Reprint, New York: Grove Weidenfeld, 1991.

Fenn, Richard K. "Why the Soul?" *On Losing the Soul: Essays in the Social Psychology of Religion.* Ed. R. K. Fenn and D. C. Capps. New York: State U of New York P, 1995. 17–20.

Fields, Karen. *Revival and Rebellion in Colonial Central Africa.* Princeton, NJ: Princeton UP, 1985.

Fine, Michelle, Linda C. Powell, Lois Weis, and L. Mun Wong. eds. "Preface." *Off White: Readings on Race, Power, and Society.* New York: Routledge, 1997. x.

Foucault, Michel. *Discipline and Punish: The Birth of the Prison.* Trans. A. Sheridan. New York: Vintage, 1979.

———. *Power/Knowledge: Selected Interviews and Other Writings, 1972–1977.* Ed. and trans. C. Gordon, et al. Brighton, Sussex: Pantheon Books, 1980.

Frank, Thomas. *One Market Under God: Extreme Capitalism, Market Populism, and the End of Economic Democracy.* New York: Doubleday, 2000.

Frankenberg, Ruth. *The Social Construction of Whiteness: White Women, Race Matters.* Minneapolis: U of Minnesota P, 1993.

Freud, Sigmund. "The Question of Lay-Analysis: Conversations with an Impartial Person." *Two Short Accounts of Psycho-Analysis.* Ed. S. Freud. Hammondsworth: Pelican, 1962.

Gates, Henry Louis, Jr. *The Signifying Monkey: A Theory of Afro-American Literary Criticism.* New York: Oxford UP, 1988.

Geiger, H. Jack. "Race and Health Care—An American Dilemma?" *The New England Journal of Medicine* 335.11 (1996): 815–830.

George, Nelson. *Hip-Hop America.* 1998. New York: Penguin Books, 1999.

Gibson, Regie. *Storms Beneath the Skin.* Joliet, IL: EM Press, LLC, 2001.

Gilmore, Ruth. "Terror Austerity Race Gender Excess Theater." *Reading Rodney King, Reading Urban Uprising.* Ed. R. Gooding-Williams. New York: Routledge, 1993. 23–37.

Gilroy, Paul. *There Ain't No Black in the Union Jack: The Cultural Politics of Race and Nation.* London and Melbourne: Hutchinson. Reprint, Chicago: U of Chicago P, 1987.

———. *The Black Atlantic: Modernity and Double Consciousness.* Cambridge: Harvard UP, 1993.

Goodman, Felicitas D. *Where the Spirits Ride the Wind: Trance Journeys and Other Ecstatic Experiences.* Bloomington and Indianapolis: Indiana UP, 1990.

Gowdy, John. "Introduction: Back to the Future and Forward to the Past." *Limited Wants, Unlimited Means: A Reader on Hunter-Gatherer Economics and the Environment.* Ed. John Gowdy. Washington, DC: Island Press, 1998. xv–xxxi.

Gramsci, Antonio. *Prison Notebooks*. New York: Columbia UP, 1992.

Green, Hannah. *Little Saint*. New York: Modern Library, 2000.

Halifax, Joan. *Shaman: The Wounded Healer*. New York: Thames and Hudson, 1982.

———. *Shamanic Voices: A Survey of Visionary Narratives*. New York: Arkana Books, 1991.

Hall, Stuart. "What Is This 'Black' in Black Popular Culture?" *Black Popular Culture*. Ed. G. Dent. Seattle: Bay Press, 1992. 21–33.

Haraway, Donna. "The Promises of Monsters." *Cultural Studies*. Ed. C. Nelson and P. A. Treichler. New York: Routledge, 1992. 295–337.

Harris, Cheryl. "Whiteness as Property." *Harvard Law Review* 108.6 (1993).

Haymes, Stephen N. *Race, Culture, and the City: A Pedagogy for Black Urban Struggle*. Albany: State U of New York P, 1995.

Hegel, G. W. F. *Phenomenology of Spirit*. Trans. A. V. Miller, analysis and foreword by J. N. Findley. Oxford: Clarendon Press, 1977.

Hernstein, Richard and Charles Murray. *The Bell Curve: Intelligence and Class Structure in American Life*. Northampton, MA: Free Press, 1994.

Herrera, Hayden. *Frida: A Biography of Frida Kahlo*. New York: Harper and Row, 1983.

Herskovits, Melville J. *The Myth of the Negro Past*. 1958. Boston: Beacon Press, 1990.

hooks, bell. *Yearning: Race, Gender and Cultural Politics*. Boston: South End Press, 1990.

———. *Black Looks: Race and Representation*. Boston: South End Press, 1992.

hooks, bell and Cornel West. *Breaking Bread: Insurgent Black Intellectual Life*. Boston: South End Press, 1991.

Hopkins, Dwight. *Shoes That Fit Our Feet: Sources for a Constructive Black Theology*. Maryknoll: Orbis Books, 1993.

Hudson, Michael. *Merchants of Misery: How Corporate America Profits from Poverty*. Monroe, Maine: Common Courage Press, 1996.

Ignatiev, Noel. *How the Irish Became White*. New York: Routledge, 1995.

Johnson, Clifton H., ed. *God Struck Me Dead: Voices of Ex-Slaves*. Cleveland, OH: Pilgrim Press, 1969.

Jordan, Winthrop. *White Over Black: American Attitudes Toward the Negro, 1550–1812*. New York: W. W. Norton & Co., 1968.

Jumanne, Monifa A. *Affirming a Future With Hope: HIV & Substance Abuse Prevention for African American Communities of Faith*. Atlanta: The International Theological Center, 2001. 2.38–2.40.

Kaplan, Robert D. "Was Democracy Just a Moment?" *Atlantic Monthly* (Dec. 1997): 55–80.

Kaufman, Bob. *Solitudes Crowded With Loneliness*. 1959. New York: New Directions, 1965.

Kellermann, Bill Wylie. *Seasons of Faith and Conscience*. Maryknoll: Orbis Books, 1991.

Kilbourne, Jeane. *Quoted in* The Ad and the Ego: Curriculum Guide. San Francisco: California Newsreel, 1996.

Kochman, Thomas. *Black and White Styles in Conflict*. Chicago: U of Chicago P, 1981.

Kolié, Cécé. "Jesus as Healer?" *Faces of Jesus in Africa*. Ed. Robert J. Schreiter. Maryknoll: Orbis Books, 1991. 128–150.

Kot, Greg. "Yoko Ono Meets Torment Head on in Powerful Show." *The Chicago Tribune* (Tuesday, Mar. 12, 1996): section 5.

Kroker, Arthur. *The Possessed Individual: Technology and the French Postmodern*. New York: St. Martin's Press, 1992.

Kubler-Ross, Elizabeth. *Death and Dying*. New York: Macmillan, 1969.

———. *Death The Final Stage*. Englewood Cliffs, NJ: Prentice-Hall, Inc., 1975.

Larsen, Stephen. *The Shaman's Doorway: Opening Imagination to Power and Myth*. 1976. New York: Station Hill Press, 1988.

Lattany, Kristin Hunter. " 'Off-timing': Stepping to the Different Drummer." *Lure and Loathing: Essays on Race, Identity, and the Ambivalence of Assimilation*. 1993. Ed. Gerald Early. New York: Penguin Books, 1994. 163–174.

Leki, Peter. "Why Be White?" *Chicago Reader* (June 28, 1996): section 1, 12–17.

Leonard, George. *The Silent Pulse: A Search for the Perfect Rhythm That Exists in Each of Us*. New York: E. P. Hutton, 1978.

Levi-Strauss, Claude. "The Effectiveness of Symbols." *Structural Anthropology*. Garden City, New York: Doubleday, 1967. 181–201.

Levy, Mark. *Technicians of Ecstasy: Shamanism and the Modern Artist*. Norfolk, CN: Bramble Books, 1993.

Lhermitte, Jean. *L'Image de notre corps*. Paris: Nouvelle Revue critique, 1939.

Lind, Michael. *The Next American Nation: The New Nationalism and the Fourth American Revolution*. New York: The Free Press, 1995.

Long, Charles. "A Look at the Chicago Tradition in the History of Religions: Retrospect and Future." *The History of Religions: Retrospect and Prospect*. Ed. Joseph M. Kitigawa, Macmillan Publishing Co., 1983. 87–104.

———. *Significations: Signs, Symbols, and Images in the Interpretation of Religion*. Philadelphia: Fortress Press, 1986.

———. "Towards a Post-Colonial Method in the Study of Religion." *Religious Studies News* 10.2 (May 1995): 4–5.

Manning, Kenneth R. "Race, Science, and Identity." *Lure and Loathing: Essays on Race, Identity, and the Ambivalence of Assimilation*. 1993. Ed. Gerald Early. New York: Penguin, 1994. 319.

Marks, Morton. "Uncovering Ritual Structures in Afro-American Music." *Religious Movements in Contemporary America*. Ed. Irving I. Zaretsky and Mark P. Leone. Princeton, NJ: Princeton UP, 1974. 60–134.

Marx, Karl. *The Eighteenth Brumaire of Louis Napoleon*. 1852. New York: International Publishers, 1963.

———. *Capital: A Critique of Political Economy*. Vol. 1, Ed. F. Engels, trans. S. Moore and E. Aveling. New York: International Publishers, 1967.

Mbiti, John S. *African Religions and Philosophy*. New York: Anchor, 1970.

McGrane, Bernard. *Quoted in* The Ad and the Ego: Curriculum Guide. San Francisco: California Newsreel, 1996.

Mills, Charles. *The Racial Contract*. Ithaca and London: Cornell UP, 1997.

Mooney, James. *The Ghost-Dance Religion and Wounded Knee*. 1973. New York: Dover Publications, Inc., 1986.

Morrison, Toni. "Unspeakable Things Unspoken." *Michigan Quarterly Review* 28.1 (1989): 1–34.

Mudimbe, V. Y. *The Invention of Africa: Gnosis, Philosophy, and the Order of Knowledge*. Bloomington: Indiana UP, 1988.

Murphy, Joseph. *Santeria: African Spirits in America*. 1988. Boston: Beacon Press, 1993.

———. *Working the Spirit: Ceremonies of the African Diaspora*. Boston: Beacon Press, 1994.

Nietzsche, Friedrich. *Twilight of the Idols*. New York: Penguin Books, 1990.

Nuland, Sherwin. *How We Die: Reflections on Life's Final Chapter*. New York: Vintage Books, 1993.

Omi, Michael and Howard, Winant. *Racial Formation in the United States from the 1960s to the 1990s*. 2nd ed. New York: Routledge, 1994.

Orenstein, Gloria. "Toward an Ecofeminist Ethic of Shamanism and the Sacred." *Ecofeminism and the Sacred*. Ed. Carol J. Adams. New York: Continuum, 1993. 172–190.

Otto, Rudolph. *The Idea of the Holy*. Trans. John W. Harvey. London: Oxford UP, 1950.

Pagden, Anthony. *Lords of All the World: Ideologies of Empire in Spain, Britain, and France, c. 1500–c. 1800*. New Haven: Yale UP, 1995.

Parker, Sherry. "Making a Case for Personal Social Security Accounts." *Self-Employed America* (Nov.–Dec. 1999): 15.

Patterson, Orlando. *Slavery and Social Death: A Comparative Study*. Cambridge, Mass: Harvard UP, 1982.

Paul, Russill. "About the Yoga of Sound." 2002. www.russillpaul.com.

Perkinson, James W. "Rage With a Purpose, Weep Without Regret: A White Theology of Solidarity." *Soundings* 82.3–4 (Fall/Winter 1999): 437–463.

———. "Theology and the City: Learning to Cry, Struggling to See." *Cross Currents* 51.1 (Spring 2001): 95–114.

———. *White Theology: Outing Supremacy in Modernity* New York: Palgrave Macmillan, 2004.

Pietz, William. "The Problem of the Fetish, I." *Res* 9 (1985): 5–17.

———. "The Problem of the Fetish, II." *Res* 13 (1987): 23–45.

———. "The Problem of the Fetish, III." *Res* 16 (1988): 105–123.

Pile, Steven. *The Body and the City: Psychoanalysis, Space and Subjectivity*. New York: Routledge, 1996.

Porterfield, Amanda. "Shamanism: A Psychosocial Definition." *Journal of the American Academy of Religion* 55 (1987): 728–729.

Postone, Moishe. *Time, Labor, and Social Domination: A Reinterpretation of Marx's Critical Theory*. Cambridge: Cambridge UP, 1993.

Raboteau, Albert. *Slave Religion: The "Invisible Institution" in the Antebellum South*. New York: Oxford UP, 1978.

Rasmussen, Larry. *Earth Community, Earth Ethics*. Maryknoll: Orbis Books, 1996.

Reed, Ishmael. "Foreword." Zora Neal Hurston's *Tell My Horse: Voodoo and Life in Haiti and Jamaica*. Berkeley: Turtle Island, 1983. xi–xv.

Ricketts, Mac Linscott. "The North American Trickster." *History of Religions* 5.1 (Summer 1965): 327–350.

Ricoeur, Paul. *The Symbolism of Evil*. Trans. Emerson Buchanan. Boston: Beacon Press, 1967.

Roediger, David. *The Wages of Whiteness: Race and the Making of the American Working Class*. London, New York: Verso, 1991.

Rorty, Richard. *Philosophy and the Mirror of Nature*. Princeton, NJ: Princeton UP, 1979.

Rose, Tricia. *Black Noise: Rap Music and Black Culture in Contemporary America*. Hanover, NH: Wesleyan UP. Published by UP of New England, 1994.

Rowan, Carl. *The Coming Race War in America: A Wake-up Call*. Boston: Little, Brown and Co., 1996.

Sahlins, Marshall. "The Original Affluent Society." *Limited Wants, Unlimited Means: A Reader on Hunter-Gatherer Economics and the Environment*. Ed. John Gowdy. Washington, DC: Island Press, 1998. 5–41.

Schlosser, Eric. "The Prison Industrial Complex." *The Atlantic Monthly* (Dec. 1998): 51–79.

Scott, James. *Domination and the Arts of Resistance: Hidden Transcripts*. New Haven: Yale UP, 1990.

Siems, Bennett. "Brer Robert: The Bluesman and the African American Trickster Tale Tradition." *Southern Folklore* 48 (1991): 141–157.

Smith, Adam, *The Wealth of Nations*. New York, 1937.

Smith, Theophus. "The Spirituality of African American Traditions." *Christian Spirituality: Post-Reformation and Modern*. Ed. Louis Dupre and Don E. Saliers. New York: Crossroad, 1989. 372–414.

———. *Conjuring Culture: Biblical Formations of Black America*. New York: Oxford UP, 1994.

Smitherman, Geneva. *Black Talk: Words and Phrases from the Hood to the Amen Corner*. Boston: Houghton Mifflin Co., 1994.

Spencer, Jon Michael. *The Rhythms of Black Folk: Race, Religion and Pan-Africanism*. Trenton, NJ: Africa World Press, Inc., 1995.

Spillars, Hortense. "Mama's Baby, Papa's Maybe: An American Grammar Book." *Diacritics* (Summer 1987): 65–81.

Stallybrass, Peter. "Marx's Coat." *Border Fetishisms: Material Objects in Unstable Spaces*. Ed. Patricia Spayer. New York: Routledge, 1998. 183–207.

Stallybrass, Peter and White Allon. *The Politics and Poetics of Transgression*. Ithaca, NY: Cornell UP, 1986.

Stands-Ali, Lois. "A Native American Muslim's Story." *The American Muslim*. July–Sept. (Summer 1992): 6–7.

Stringfellow, William. *An Ethic for Christians and Other Aliens in a Strange Land*. Waco, TX: Word Books, 1973.

Taussig, Michael. *Shamanism, Colonialism, and the Wild Man: A Study in Terror and Healing*. Chicago and London: U of Chicago P, 1987.

Thompson, Robert Farris. *Flash of the Spirit: African and Afro-American Art and Philosophy*. New York: Vintage Books, 1983.

Wafer, Jim. *The Taste of Blood: Spirit Possession in Brazilian Candomble*. Philadelphia: U of Pennsylvania P, 1991.

Walker, James R. *Lakota Belief and Ritual*. 1980. Ed. Raymond J. DeMallie and Elaine A. Jahner. Lincoln and London: U of Nebraska P, 1991.

Walker, Sheila. *Ceremonial Spirit Possession in Africa and Afro-America: Forms, Meanings, and Functional Significance for Individuals and Social Groups*. Leiden: E.J. Brill, 1972.

Wessels, Anton. *Images of Jesus: How Jesus Is Perceived and Portrayed in Non-European Cultures*. 1986. Grand Rapids: Eerdmanns Publishing Co., 1990.

West, Cornel. *Prophesy Deliverance: An African-American Revolutionary Christianity*. Philadelphia: Westminster Press, 1982.

————. "Black Culture and Postmodernism." *Remaking History*. Ed. B. Kruger and P. Mariani. Seattle: Bay Press, 1989. 93.

West, Cornel and bell, hooks. *Breaking Bread: Insurgent Black Intellectual Life*. Boston: South End Press, 1991.

White, Hayden. *Tropics of Discourse: Essays in Cultural Criticism*. Baltimore: Johns Hopkins UP, 1978.

Williams, Patricia J. "The Rules of the Game." *Reading Rodney King, Reading Urban Uprising*. Ed. R. Gooding-Williams. New York: Routledge, 1993. 51–55.

Willis, Susan B. *Specifying: Black Women Writing the American Experience*. Madison, WI: U of Wisconsin P, 1987.

Winant, Howard. "Behind Blue Eyes: Whiteness and Contemporary U.S. Racial Politics." *Off White: Readings on Race, Power, and Society*. Ed. Michelle Fine, Linda C. Powell, Lois Weis, and L. Mun Wong. New York: Routledge, 1997. 41–53.

Wink Walter. *Naming the Powers: The Language of Power in the New Testament*. Minneapolis: Fortress Press, 1984.

————. *Unmasking the Powers: the Invisible Forces that Determine Human Existence*. Minneapolis: Fortress Press, 1986.

————. *Engaging the Powers: Discernment and Resistance in a World of Domination*. Minneapolis: Fortress Press, 1992.

Worsley, Peter. *The Trumpet Shall Sound: A Study of "Cargo" Cults in Melanesia*. New York: Schocken Books, 1968.

Wright, Richard. *White Man Listen!* Garden City, NY: Doubleday, 1957.

————. *Native Sen*, 1940. New York: Harper and Row, 1966.

Zaleski, Carol. *Otherworld Journeys: Accounts of Near-Death Experience in Medieval and Modern Times*. New York: Oxford UP, 1987.

Zepezauer, Mark and Arthur, Naiman. *Take the Rich Off Welfare*. Tucson: Odonian Press, 1996.

# Index